THE VOICE OF DESIGN

SHOW

In the 1970s, French literature and art theorist Gerard Genette proposed the concept of "subtext," which refers to some auxiliary texts around the text of the work, including the cover, preface, advertisement, illustration, plate, font, waist cover, etc., which can be included in the category of subtext. When we read, these "secondary texts" sometimes play a greater role than the real text. How to make these "subtext" play a role beyond their own is the goal of many designers.

Ideas are never created out of thin air, so we need to grab them from the air as they flow around us. As Michelangelo said," sculpture is imprisoned in a block of marble, and only a great sculptor can set it free." What we need to do is to grasp the idea, including how it is generated and how it is used.

What do designers do? Some of them use ingenious packaging forms to conceal books in layers of envelopes. Some hide the information they want to express behind various symbols and images. Designers use a variety of creative techniques to give shape to books, combining unique ingenuity with the art practice of book design.

WRAP

Weave the pages from outside to inside

The external form of packaging determines the reader's first impression of the book. Book packaging not only has the function of protecting books, but also has the function of art decoration. The packaging design of books reflects not only the appearance of the image, but also the personality of the books, and the culture it carries is vividly displayed. In the case that the reader cannot see the internal information of the book, the picture, text and other elements of the external packaging of the book can make the reader intuitively understand the function and characteristics of the book, leave a good visual impression, and play the function of information transmission. The reader's unwrapping and leafing are the personal interpretation of the book.

● Designer: Ye Pang, Ling Peng, Bingzi Xiang, Guojian Liang   Language: Chinese, English

12 Minutes

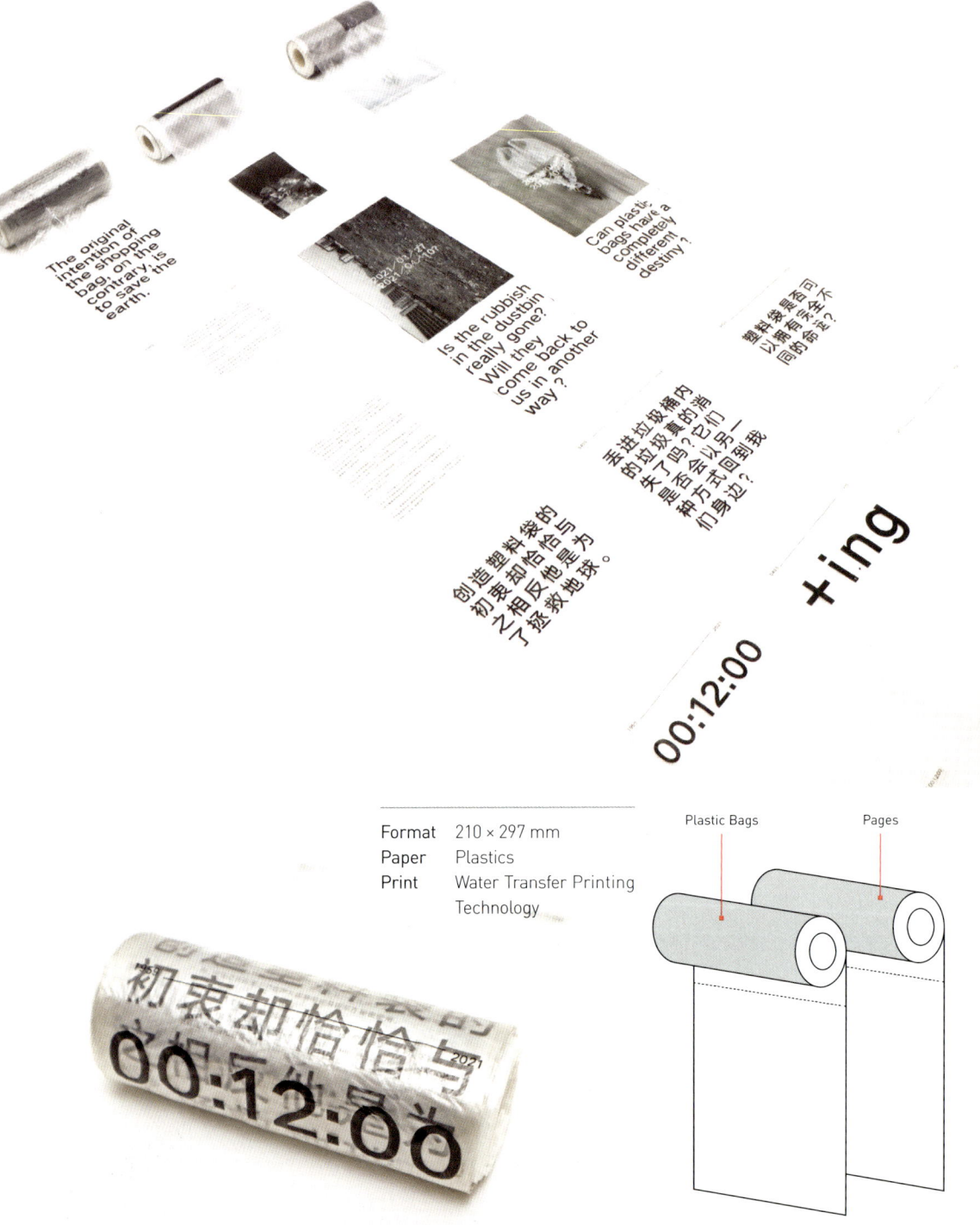

Format	210 × 297 mm
Paper	Plastics
Print	Water Transfer Printing Technology

The work centers on the social topic of plastic bag pollution and environmental protection, taking "the average time people spend using plastic bags is 12 minutes" as the starting point, focusing on the wrong use of plastic bags by human beings and the ensuing environmental problems. The work is presented in the form of a collection of photographs that divides the *Book of Plastic Bags* into three parts: production and use, disposal, pollution and primary utilization, allowing readers to experience the whole process of plastic bags waste.

○ The graphic arrangement of this work is realized by water transfer printing technology, and the reading method is wall-hanging and scrolling down. The most common plastic bag in daily life is chosen as the design materials for its coherence and pull-down nature. In the process of scrolling down, the reader becomes anticipatory of what is unknown on the next page. After determining the plastic material as the carrier of the design, the most difficult issue is the choice of printing method. In the process of experimentation, the author tried self-adhesive, spray painting and screen printing, but ultimately gave up due to the display effects and financial problems. In the end, the tattoo stickers that came with the bubble gum he bought as a child gave him inspiration.

○ According to the author, "Every time I start to design a new project, it is a new challenge, especially in some fields that I have never been involved in before, but when I find the right answer for the moment through the process of continuous experimentation, the sense of achievement is the motivation that drives me to continue designing."

● Designer: United Design Lab. Language: Chinese Client: REX Page: 145

TEXT

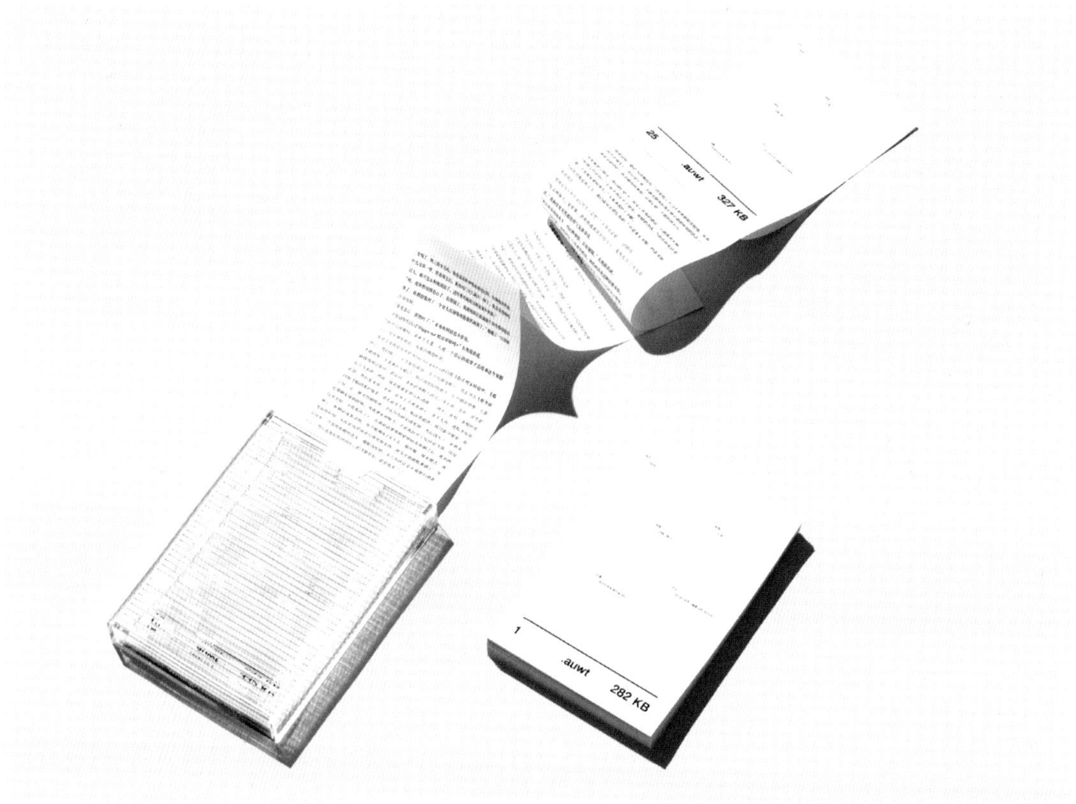

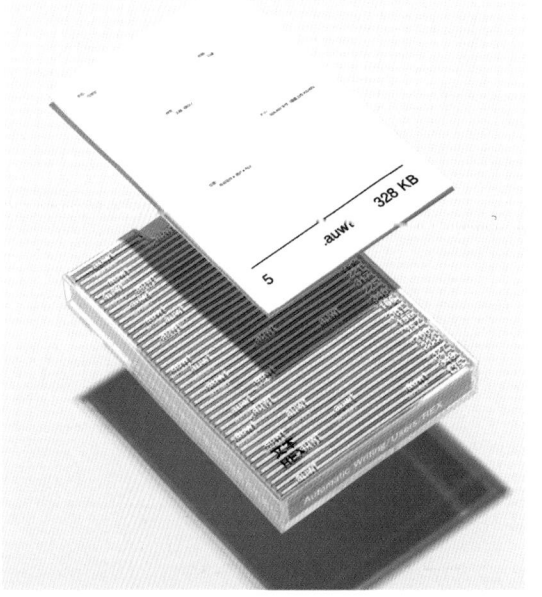

TEXT is a novel about a future world. The designers designed this novel as a reader from some unknown future, with a screen covered with document information and file formats they don't recognize. The content is designed as documents marked with some common file information. The content is fragmented, non-coherent, and you can pull out any piece of the book and enter that world, then read it like scrolling a Microsoft Word file from top to bottom.

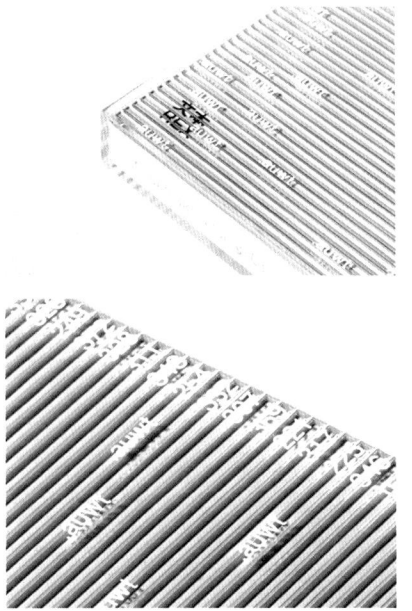
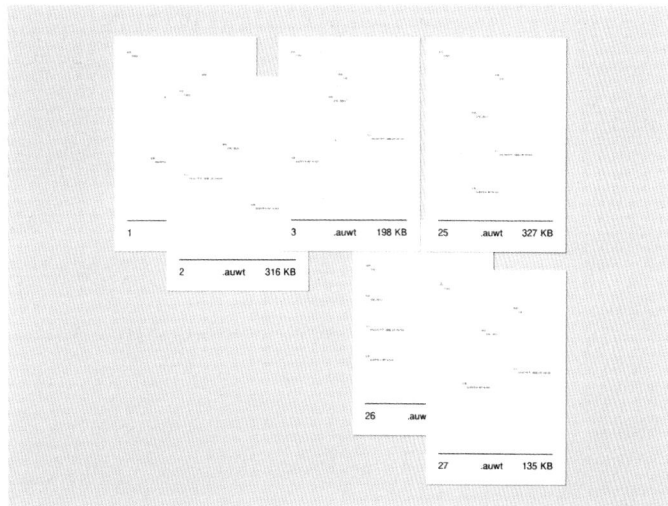

Format   130 × 190 mm
Print   Offset Print
Font   Song, Kai, Minion Pro
Binding Accordion Fold and Slipcase

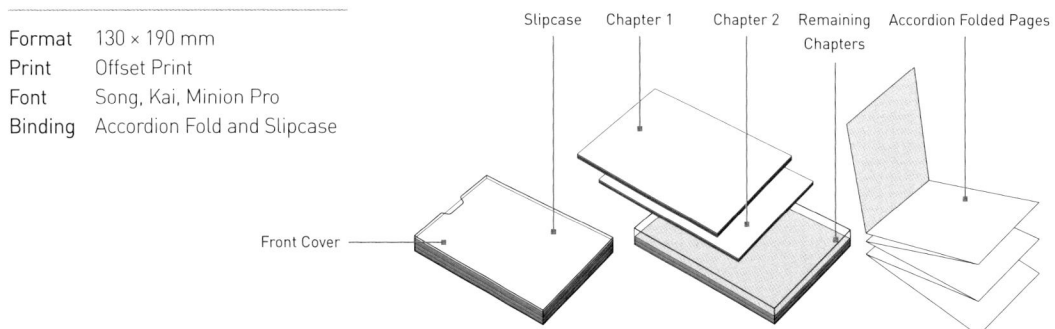

Each Chapter Is Made as a Separate Accordion Folded Page

Designer: Aniko Mezo   Language: English   Page: 368

The Bell Jar: Type & Book Design

Format   168 × 220 mm
Font   Esther
Binding Paperback

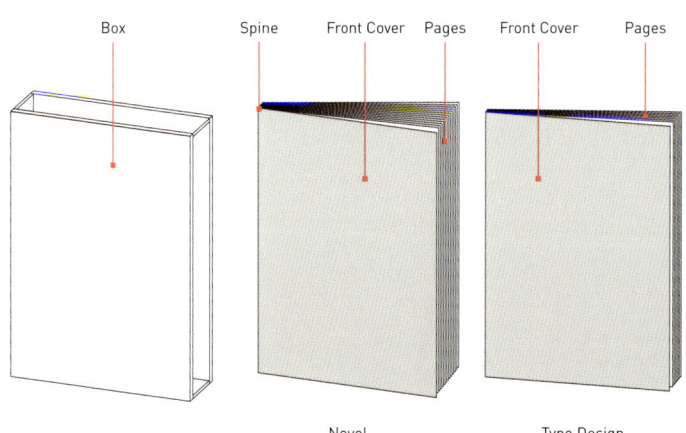

Box   Spine   Front Cover   Pages   Front Cover   Pages

Novel   Type Design

The project contains 2 books, the novel *The Bell Jar*, and another book showcasing the details of the font and the distortion process. These books are stored in a transparent container, and tightly fit in the plexiglass box, also referring to the feelings of the protagonist, the cover's material is a reflective "mirror-like" paper, referring to the topic: the glass material of a bell jar, and the distortive nature of the cover paper emphasizes the distorted characters of the text.

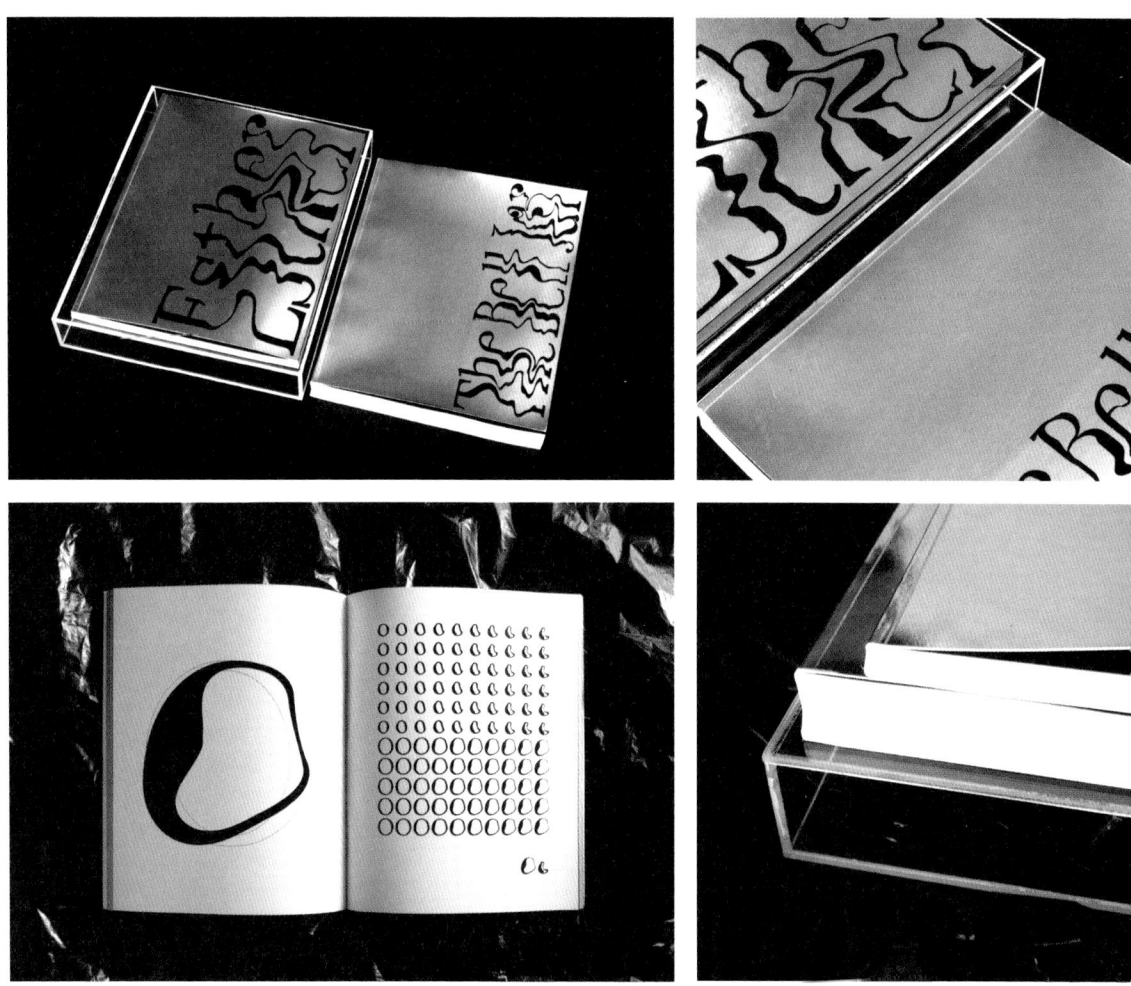

○ The designer's project is a typographic book illustration of *The Bell Jar*, an autobiographical novel by Sylvia Plath which describes the protagonist's descent into mental illness. She designed a variable font based on an existing typeface (Lora). The letters were created as a result of several distortion experiments.

○ The purpose of the project was to illustrate the decay of the protagonist's life and mental state with the constant distortion of the letters, following the story. The characters were distorted the way see things deformed behind a glass, or a bell jar, so at the end of the book the letters are sign-like visual marks — hard to read or almost unreadable — symbolizing the inexpressible feelings that those people experience, who suffer from different mental diseases.

● Desginer: Yeh Chung-yi　Language: Traditional Chinese　Client: Shakespeare's Wild Sisters Company　Page: 408

Wang's Bento: Cooking Shakespeare

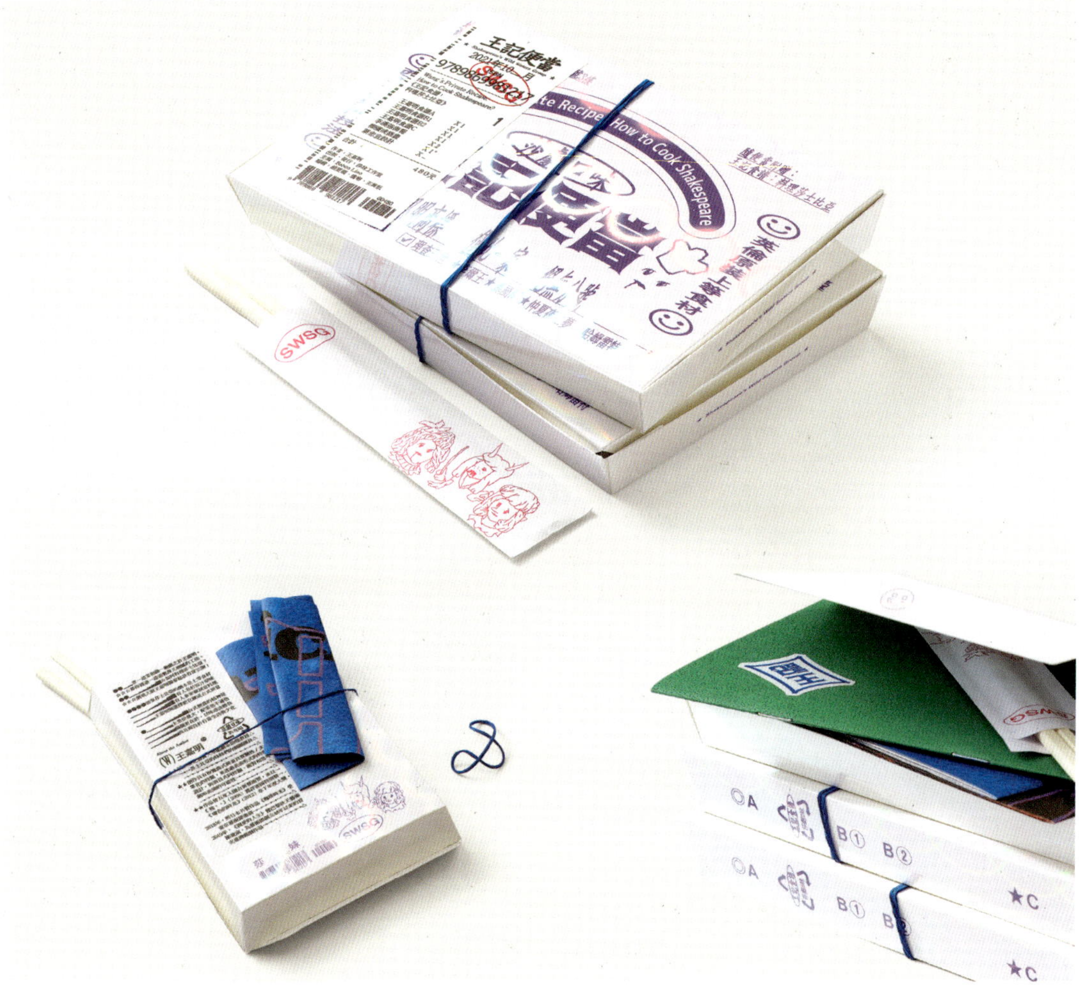

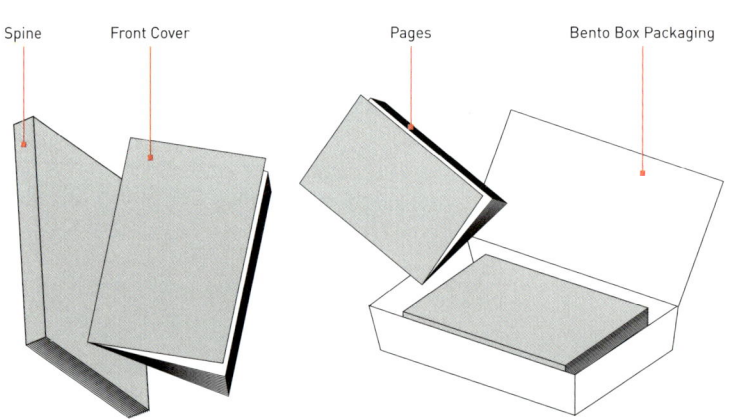

Format　170 × 120 mm
Binding　Taiwanese Bento Box Packaging

Spine　　Front Cover　　Pages　　Bento Box Packaging

Inspired by the connection between cooking and theater, *Wang's Bento: Cooking Shakespeare* is presented in the form of Taiwanese Bento. There are three series in the book. Series 1 features theater chef Wang Chia-Ming's analysis of Shakespearean "cooking" skills, and invites gourmets to write about the chef's daily life related to his cooking. Series 2 and 3 respectively include two recipe books/plays of Shakespeare's, preparation of ingredients, cutting and cooking techniques, and serving, allowing readers to enter Wang's kitchen/theater and have a glimpse of the cooking/creative process. It is accompanied by the director's script structure sheet.

○ Shakespeare's Wild Sisters Company's director Wang Chia-Ming has adapted a collection of Shakespeare's plays *Titus'* and *"Richard III*. There is no food nor drink could be brought to the official performance halls. Since noboby are allowed to bring food or drink to the official performance hall, the designers and the unconventional Shakespeare's Wild Sisters came up with a made-up story. They conceived a scenario whereby, while entering the performance hall with a bento-look script and being stopped and questioned by the guards, the audience can proudly open the bento and let the guards have a hard time, thus allowing the audience to participate in the play even before they watch it.

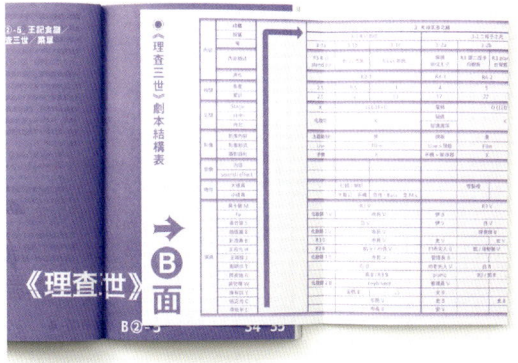

● Designer: Hannah Gebauer & Philipp Stöcklein   Language: German
Client: Academy of Fine Arts Nuremberg   Page: 356

Absolvent: innen2022/2023

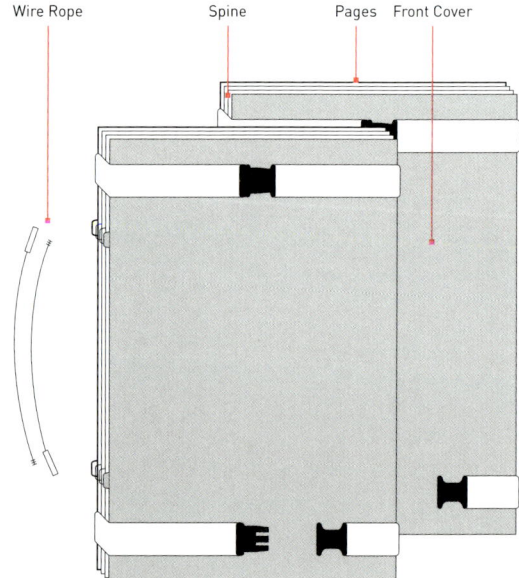

Format	157 × 235 mm
Paper	Cover	Offset Premium White 250 gsm
	Inside	Salzer Touch 120 gsm
Font	Suisse Int'l & Suisse Int'l Mono (by Swiss
	Typefaces), Keroine (by Charlotte Rohde)
Binding	Custom Made Binding, Straps and Wire Rope

Created on the occasion of a group exhibition, the *Absolvent: innen 2022/2023* (*Graduates 2022/23*) catalog contains works from graduates of all classes of the Academy of Fine Arts Nuremberg. Every graduate has their own booklet, containing works, awards, exhibitions and personal information. Bound together by straps and wire rope, these booklets together form the catalogue.

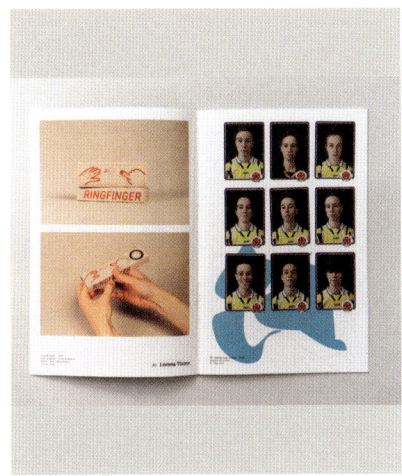

○ The designers' main reason for choosing this rather "lose" book structure came from the nature of it's content: The catalog features a lot of different artists with strong, individual positions. While they wanted (and needed) to create a singular publication for the Academy of Fine Arts, designers also wanted everyone to feel like their positions stand for themself and are represented accurately. That's why they gave everyone their own booklet: It can be taken out and be experienced by itself and also be used as a portfolio to send to clients or as a single booklet to accompany the exhibition of an artist.

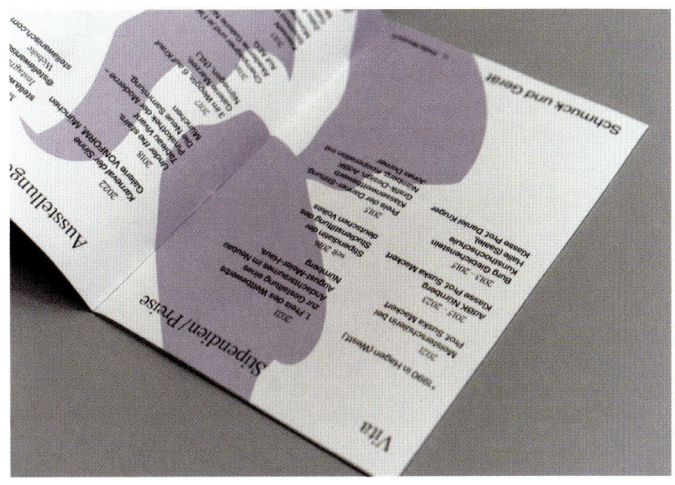

● Designer: CHAN HIU Language: Traditional Chinese Page: 64

Made in Hong Kong vol.1 — The Knock-off Rebuild

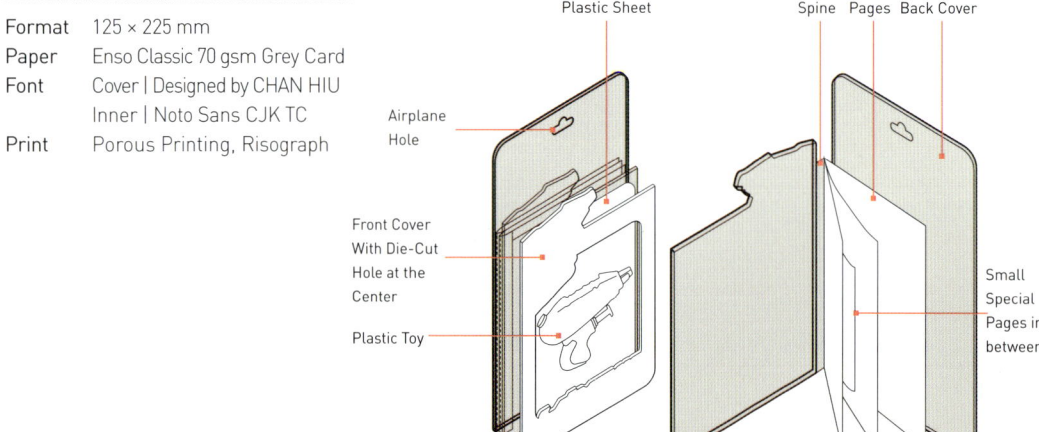

Format	125 × 225 mm
Paper	Enso Classic 70 gsm Grey Card
Font	Cover	Designed by CHAN HIU
	Inner	Noto Sans CJK TC
Print	Porous Printing, Risograph

The Hong Kong knock-off toys seem to be disappearing and be neglected by new generations. The series *Knock-off Toys* reintroduces knock-off toys by documenting their history of knock-off toys in Hong Kong. Among them, *Knock-off Rebuild* is the kick-off of the whole series, which can provide readers with a basic understanding of Hong Kong's knock-off toys, thus deepening their knowledge of the local culture.

○ The cover of this book is made of plastic toy guns held in place by blisters, which evokes collective memories and raises readers' interest. The book is printed with perforated boards, and the strong color contrast echoes the color scheme of the plastic knock-off toys. It is important to note that color loss and inaccurate alignment are often viewed as disadvantages of porous printing, but this book takes advantage of these characteristics. The loss of color when flipping through the pages means that the knock-off toys have disappeared, and the lack of accuracy in the alignment sets off the roughness of the production of the knock-off toys.

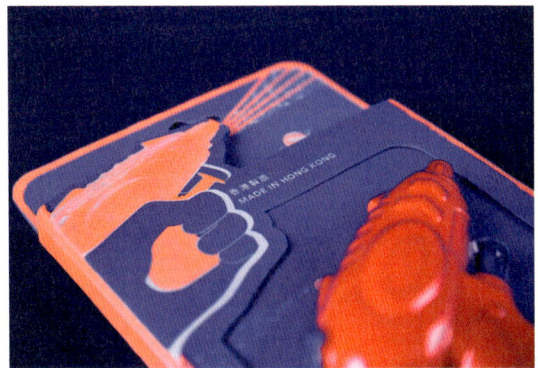

Designer: Yunqi Peng   Language: English   Page: 116

Abyss Staring

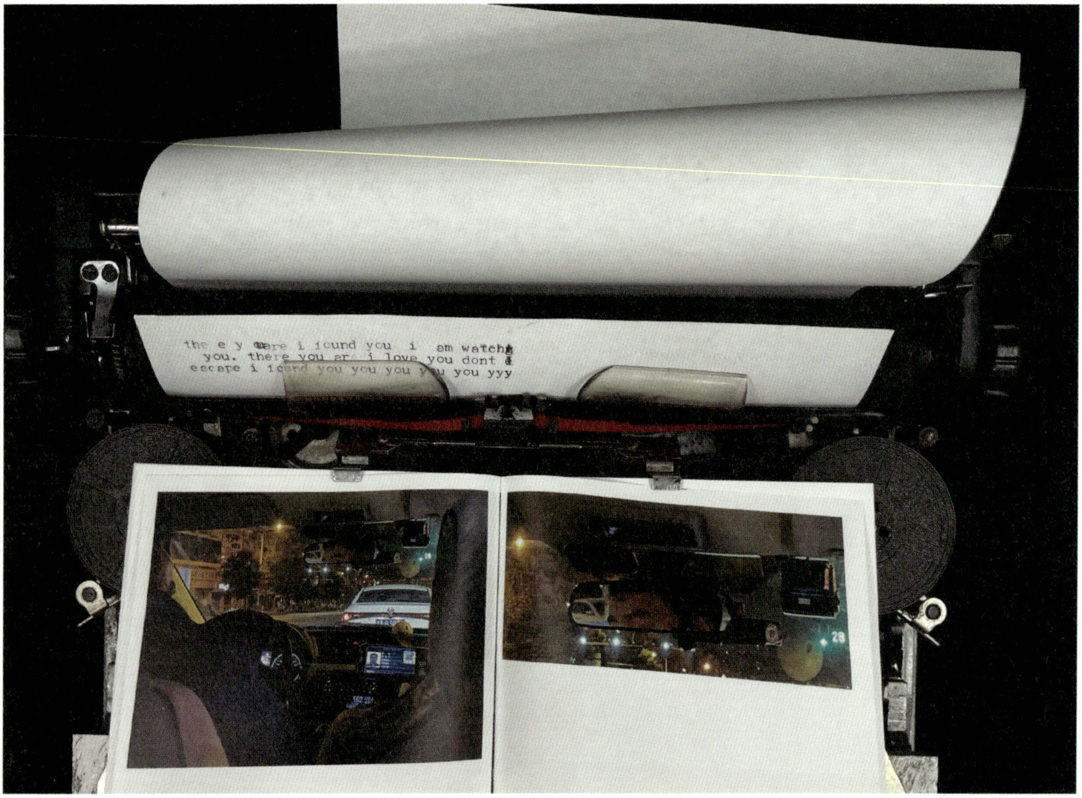

This project is based on the visualization of the techno-ethical issue of the potentially intensified female gaze on social media, and consists of a large brochure, a small brochure, a circular peach-colored PVC sheet, and a long seal that combines them.

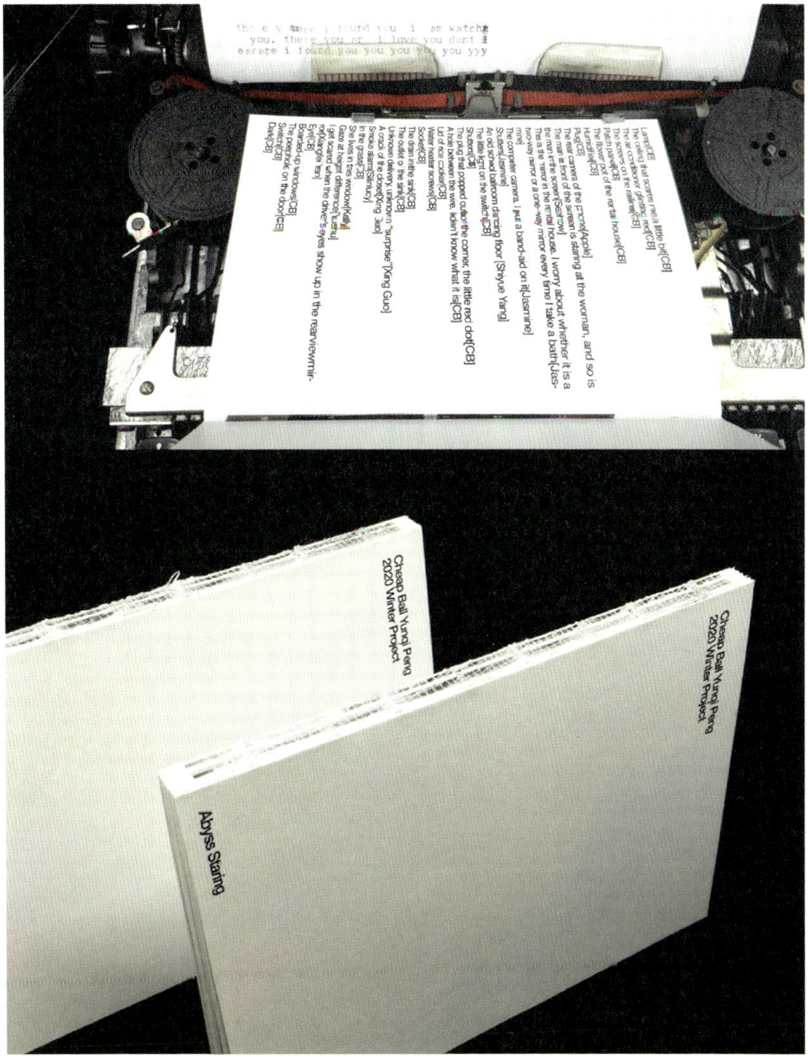

○ The large brochure is an abstract and graphic visual experiment with the keyword "abyssal gaze," creating a messy pattern effect with a certain metaphor for the society; the small brochure, tightly wrapped around the bend of the large one, is a wire-bound and small-format collection of photographs that the designer has collected from women who have been "made to feel like they are being spied on. "The simple, and non-technical images contain many stories to be imagined and feared, and the peach-colored peeping tiles make these horrific images invisible under the shade of color. These stories are fearful facts, often hidden behind the light, and she tried to use this combination to convey this series of metaphorical concepts. The presence of the seals increases the reader's choices when reading: one can choose to remove the seals, making it impossible for the publication to return to its original form after being read, or one can choose to pull the contents out of the seals, read them, and then put them back into their original form, pretending that nothing has happened.

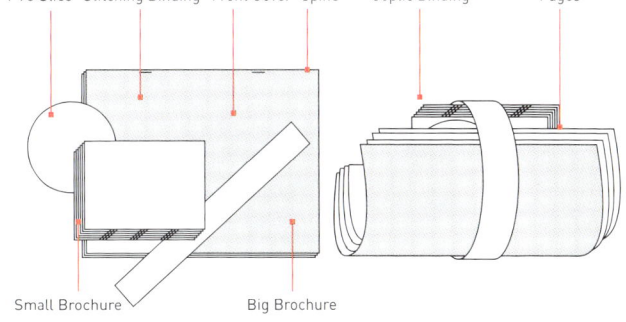

PVC Slice Stitching Binding Front Cover Spine   Coptic Binding   Pages

Small Brochure   Big Brochure

Format	Big Brochure | 210 × 297 mm
	Small Brochure | 105 × 148 mm
	Total | 100 × 297 × 30 mm
Paper	Coated Art Paper 120 gsm/150 gsm
	Pink PVC 120g
Binding	Stitch Binding and Thread Sewing Coptic Binding
PS	Big Brochure | 12 pages
	Small Brochure | 104 pages

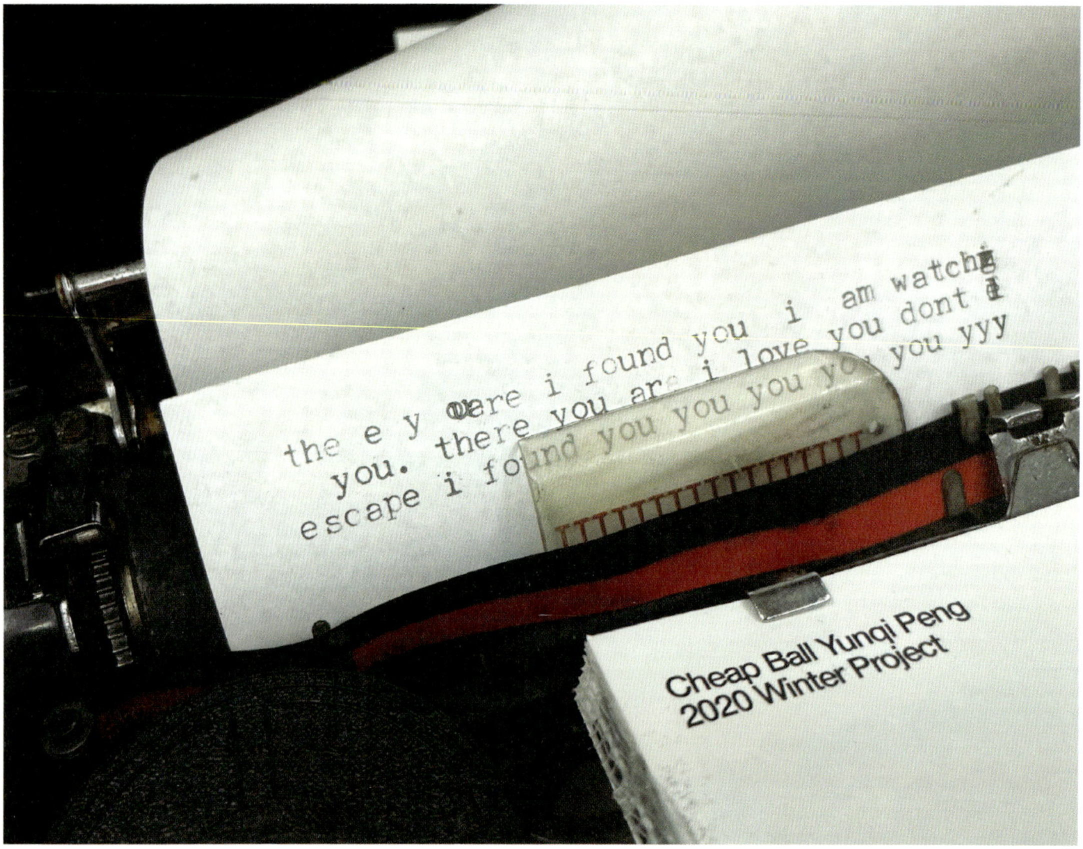

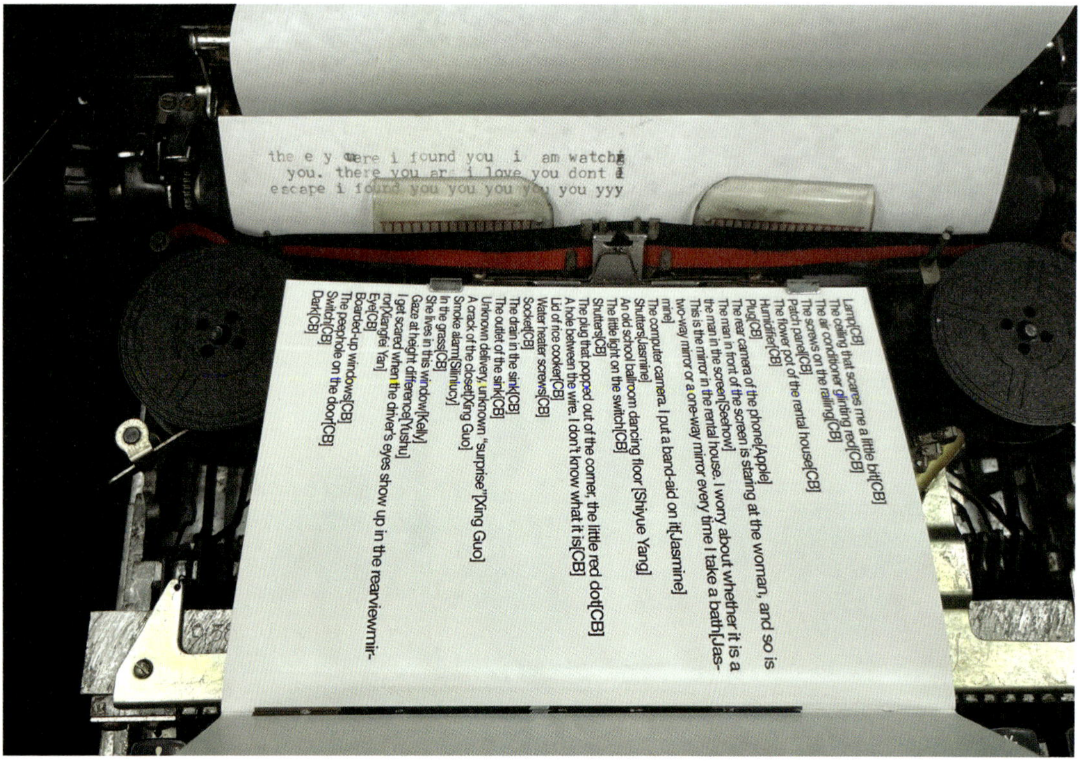

the e y were i found you   i   am watching
you. there you are i love you dont a
escape i found you you you you you yyy

Cheap Ball Yunqi Peng
2020 Winter Project

Lamp[CB]
The ceiling that scares me a little bit[CB]
The air conditioner glinting red[CB]
The screws on the railing[CB]
Patch panel[CB]
The flower pot of the rental house[CB]
Humidifier[CB]
Plug[CB]
The rear camera of the phone[Apple]
The man in front of the screen is staring at the woman, and so is the man in the screen[Seehow]
This is the mirror in the rental house. I worry about whether it is a two-way mirror or a one-way mirror every time I take a bath[Jasmine]
The computer camera. I put a band-aid on it[Jasmine]
Shutters[Jasmine]
An old school ballroom dancing floor [Shiyue Yang]
The little light on the switch[CB]
Shutters[CB]
The plug that popped out of the corner, the little red dot[CB]
A hole between the wire. I don't know what it is[CB]
Lid of rice cooker[CB]
Water heater screws[CB]
Socet[CB]
The drain in the sink[CB]
The outlet of the sink[CB]
Unknown delivery, unknown "surprise"[Xing Guo]
A crack of the closet[Xing Guo]
Smoke alarm[Silinluc]
She lives in this window[Kely]
In the grass[CB]
Gaze at height difference[Yushu]
I get scared when the driver's eyes show up in the rearview mirror[Xiangfei Yan]
Eye[CB]
Boarded-up windows[CB]
The peep-hole on the door[CB]
Switch[CB]
Dark[CB]

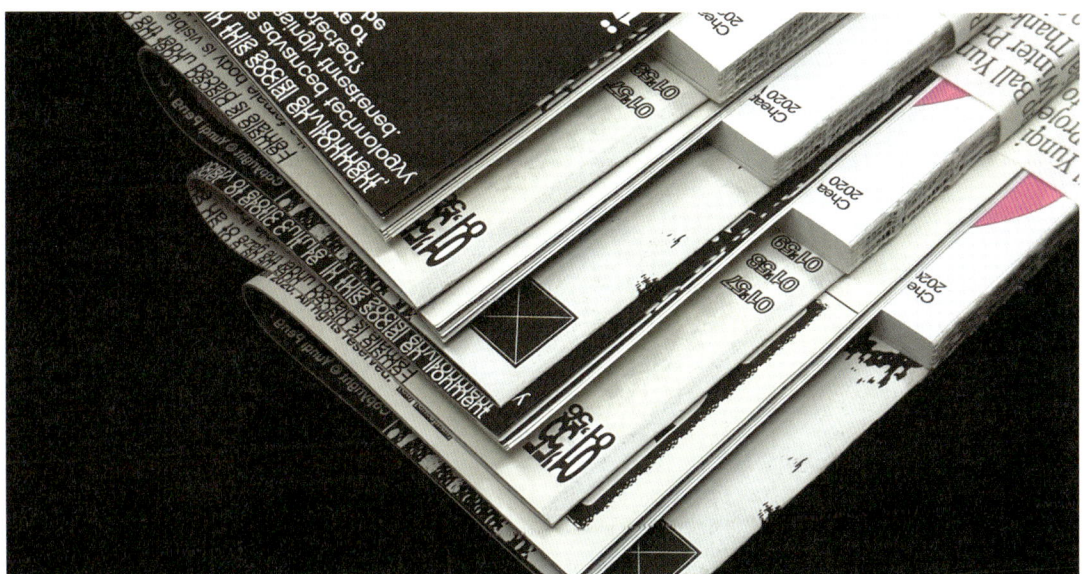
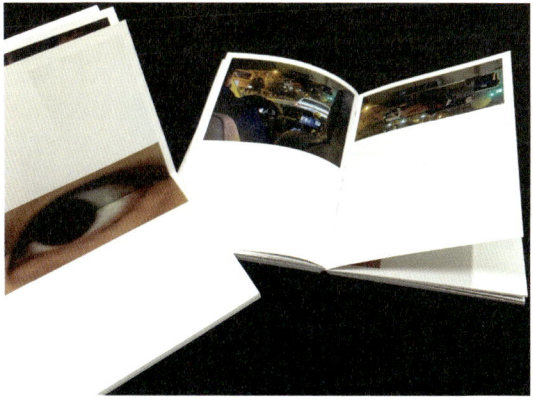
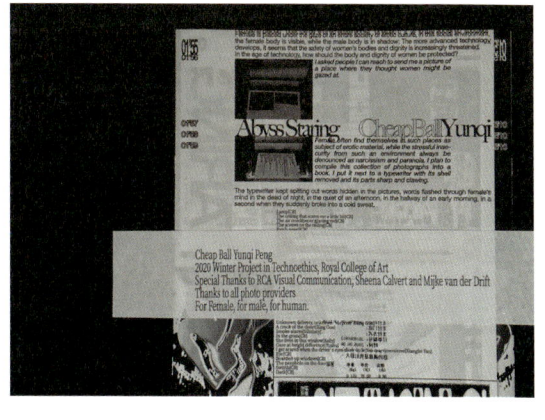

● Desginer: Cheng Xin, Yuki（Xinyue Wang）　　Language: Chinese and English

A Visual Archive of Drying out in Shenzhen's Urban Villages

The creative team acts as an observer, presenting, guiding and focusing on objects and people, connecting the city and the urban village. This project focuses on the phenomenon of hanging and drying in Shenzhen's urban villages, and the slow-paced creativity of the residents. Led by documentary research and presented in the form of a visual archive of information, the project conveys the precious qualities of the urban village residents who create according to their local conditions, trying to improve their hanging and drying way.

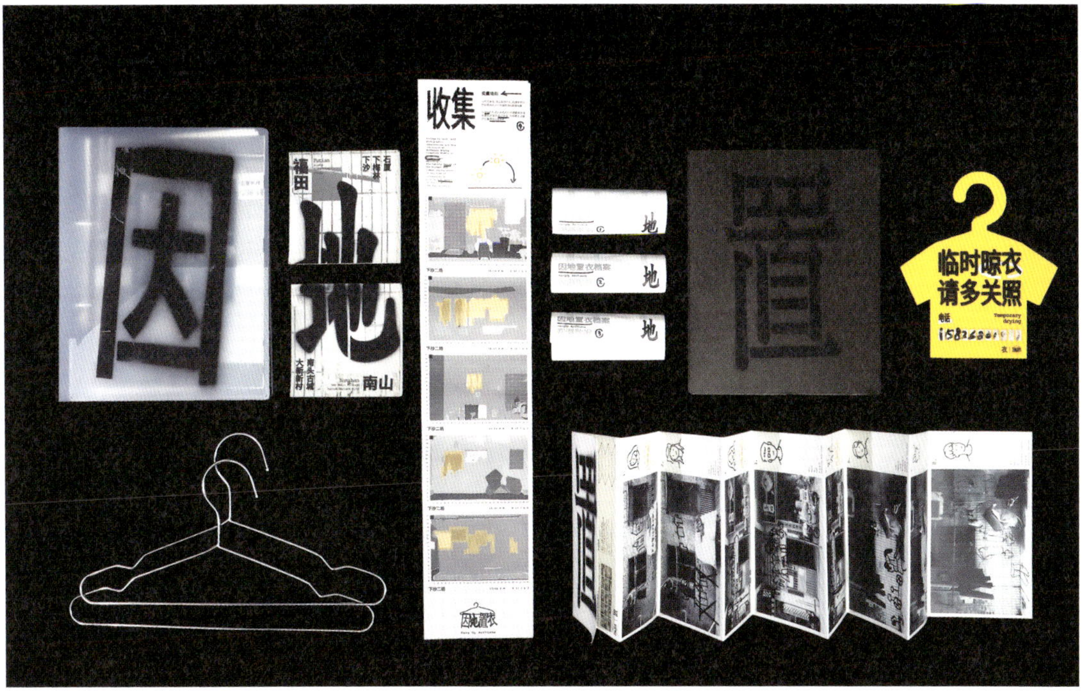

○ After experimenting with a variety of binding styles, they decided to use coil binding, which has a more archival feel, and to combine it with the structure of the shelves, so as to echo the theme of the special binding and to present a visual representation of documentation and information gathering, while at the same time relating it to the keyword "dry out". The content of the booklet is organized in points of view to show the origin, the main idea, the development process and the experimental concepts of the project, with a focus on textual documentation and information transfer. The large-print information on the front and back cover is in a spray-painted font, which is appropriate to the geo-visual iconography of the project's urban village setting, while making the main core keywords clear and recognizable. The layout of the interior was designed using structural reorganization to design the specific positions of the main title and the main text, so that when they are split into separate pages they can form a continuous textual message, allowing the split pages of the publication to function as a poster and to clearly convey the main idea of the project.

Format	100 × 100 mm
Paper	White Card 150 gsm
Print	Digital Printing
Binding	Multiple Folds (handmade)

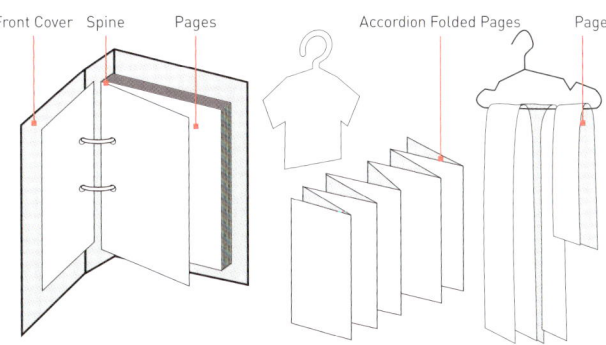

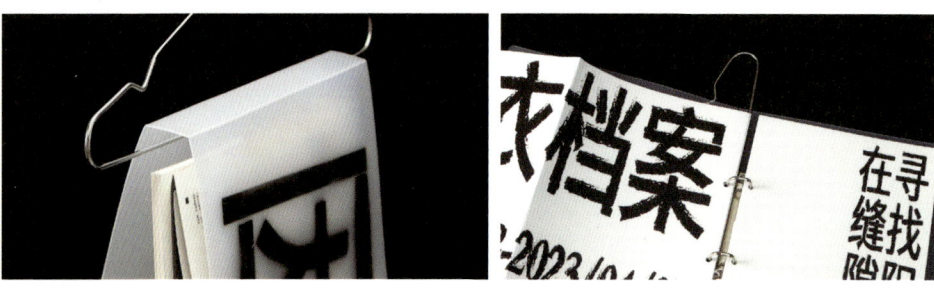

○ The flip-flop animation is a dynamic presentation of the research route and data, which allows us to visualize the changes in the location of urban villages and the different drying effects as the book is flipped. Presented on low-grain paper, the data report sheet continues to simulate the drying state of fabrics.

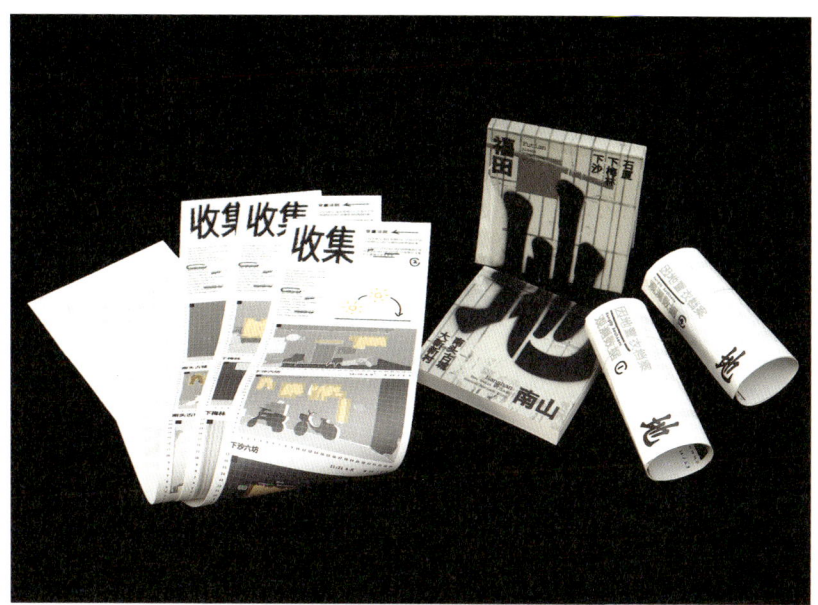

○ The co-designed card is presented in a simple form with a gingham fold, which makes it easy to integrate and read a large number of interactive results and to compare the different ways of drying fabrics.

○ Curiosity drives people to explore, discover and understand. Designers are pushed to delve deeper into user needs and behaviors to better understand their expectations and challenges. Communicating with, observing, and engaging with users reveals hidden insights that provide deeper inspiration and creativity in design. By remaining curious, the team will continue to explore the infinite possibilities of design, and create more valuable and meaningful designs for users.

● Designer: Happycentro   Language: Italian   Client: ALU Company

ALU Company Book

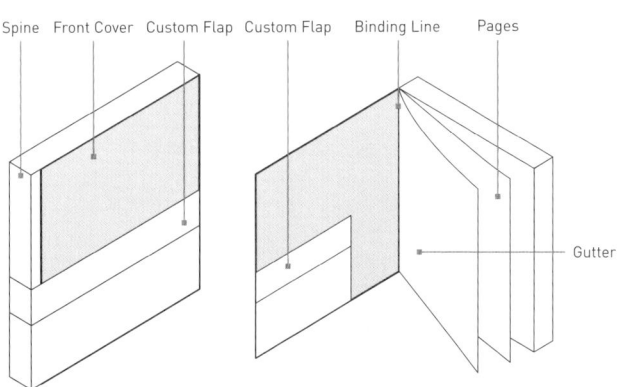

Format	200 × 200 mm
Paper	Black Cardboard, Arcoprint White by Fedrigoni
Print	Embossing, Die Cutting
Binding	Bordoni Binding

This book was designed for ALU, an international retailing company. The brief was to redesign the company profile for EuroShop 2011 where their brand new products were going to be presented. Since most of the company's products were made of basic materials like aluminum, the designers decided to use these materials as inspiration.

○ The designers then took inspiration from the material soul of these elements to develop ALU's ID. Starting from this basis, they chose to tell the brand through a series of keywords explaining their values. All the drawings and photographs in the book are made from paper cut-outs: small parts are cut out and then put together to form the whole picture. For the design of the book, Arcoprint White Paper from Fedrigoni was chosen for printing, with an embossed all-black cardboard cover, a Bordoni Binding.

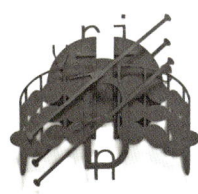
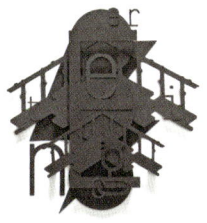
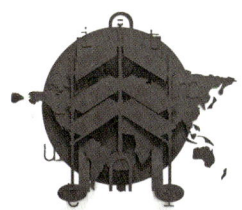

Designer: Explicit Design Studio   Language: English   Client: Notess   Page: 164

Hello Copenhagen

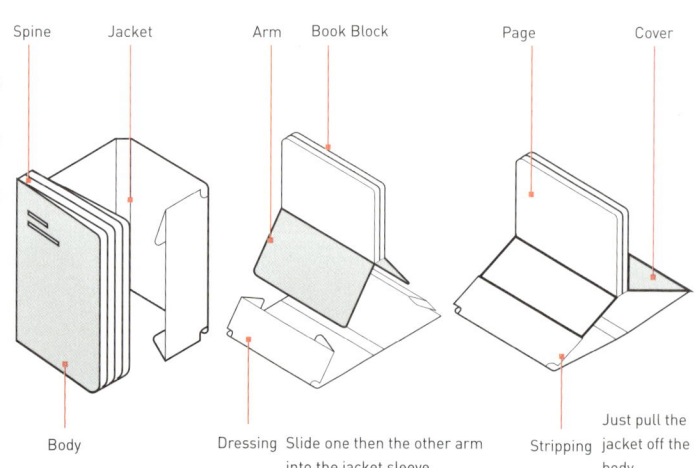

Print	Offset Printing
Paper	Covers	Keaykolour Color Sytle 300gsm, FSC certified
	Illustrated pages	SH Recycling 100 gsm, FSC certified
	Note pages	Munken Pure 80 gsm, FSC certified
Font	Westeinde by Adàm Katyi
Binding	Swiss Binding

Spine · Jacket · Arm · Book Block · Page · Cover

Body · Dressing · Slide one then the other arm into the jacket sleeve · Stripping · Just pull the jacket off the body

01

During the design and production, their goal is to create well-used, exciting, contemporary, demanding and nature-friendly products. Your sketches, drawings, and ideas love grid layouts that are subtle and can help you.

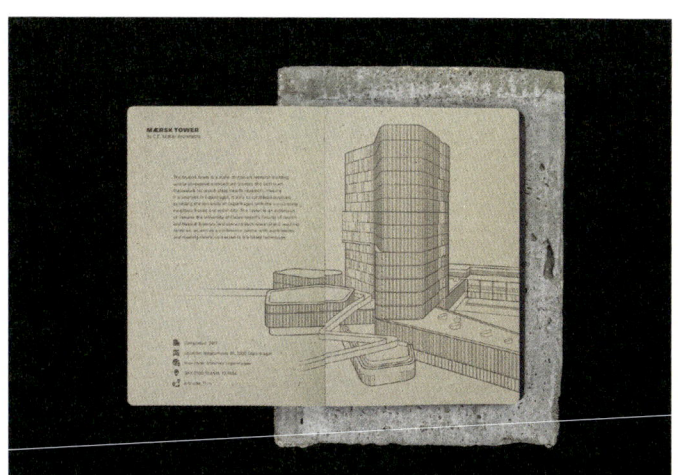

○ The notebooks are designed in line with Dieter Rams's 10 principles of good design. Not too large. Not too small. Not too thin. Not too thick. Just the perfect size for your hand and your bag. The architectural masterpieces of the cities are presented on the 32 pages centre seam. Today's materials, today's technologies, today's appearance - for today's Van Goghs and Cézannes. The fine touch Munken Pure paper from Sweden is pleasing to your eyes and your touch. The structure of the book can eligible to the owners to change their notebooks colours.

Designer: Arithmetic   Language: English   Client: Westbank

San Jose Collection

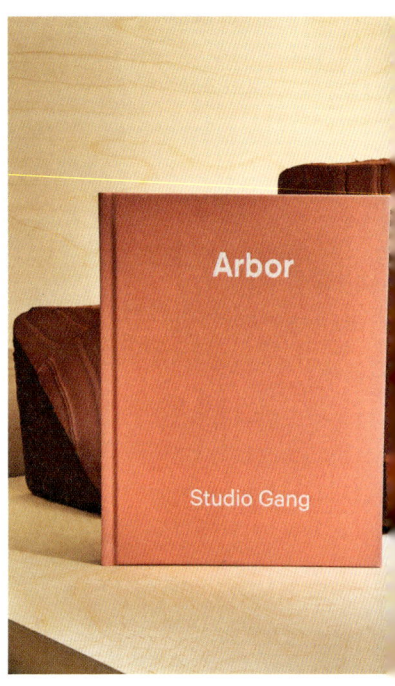

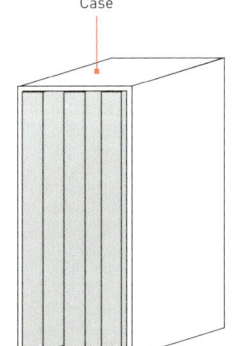

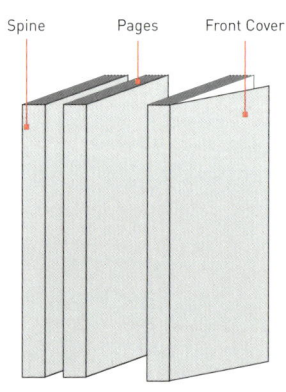

Case · Spine · Pages · Front Cover

Format	Box Set
Paper	Printed on FSC Certified Paper
Font	Calibre (*Park Habitat*), Temeraire (*Bank of Italy*), Domaine Test (*Arbor*), Cholla (*The Energy Hub*), Monument Grotesk (*The Orchard*), 224 (*Resilience Starts with Optimism: A New Ecosystem for the Third Industrial Revolution*)
Binding	Linen Bound Custom Box Set
Page	183 (*Park Habitat*), 179 (*Bank of Italy*), 153 (*Arbor*), 197 (*The Energy Hub*), 183 (*The Orchard*)

Each book in this limited-edition set represents the unique perspective of an internationally acclaimed architect for the San Jose sustainability renewal initiative. Custom printed linen covers and the individually unique layout design of each book expresses not only the innovative architecture but the spirit and harmony created by its respect for nature. The volumes metaphorically embody the unique concepts of each project through bold colour treatments, tactile materiality, unique structural elements, and considered typographic layouts.

○ *Arbor* is distinctive, with a wood screen facade that creates ideal natural light conditions inside the building. The modular angled screens, a defining architectural feature, are echoed in the project logo and blind debossed into the end pages. Bold blue is featured prominently throughout *The Energy Hub*, a vibrant symbol of electricity. Rounded typography was selected to reflect the distinct curvature of the architecture. Chapter breaks are defined by soft gradients of vibrant blue light. The gradient light source rotates on each chapter break spread, a metaphor for the sun rotating around the structure. Inspired by the citrus orchards that lend the project its name, golden-orange is prominent in the design. The offset layouts featured throughout the book are a reflection of the gridded facade of staggered terraces, echoing *The Orchards* architecture. Inviting the reader to reimagine the future and welcome nature back into the city.

○ The key of *Park Habitat* is the "green lung," an open space that travels from the ground floor to the top of the building, inviting light and air to permeate the structure. A pull-out feature inside the book mirrors this functionality, showcasing the architectural feature and serving as a metaphor for the "green lung." The book design of *The Bank of Italy* explores the concept "book as an object." The ink black linen cover bleeds into a full immersion of black edge painting, an homage to the singular printing press colour of the time.

● Desginer: Xinyi Liu, Xuemin Song   Language: Traditional Chinese   Page: 32

Sister&Sister

Paper   Colorful Paper
Font   Handwriting
Binding Binder Clip

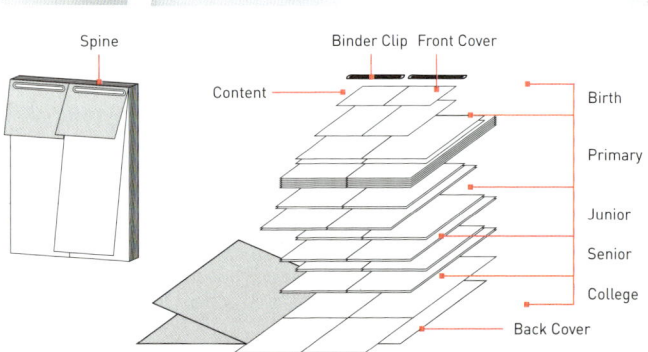

Sister&Sister embarks on a profound journey, delving into the intricate facets of identity, individuality, and the extraordinary bond shared by identical twins. The project is an exquisite tapestry woven from the personal diaries and cherished family photographs of "Da Da" and "Xiao Xiao," spanning the expanse of their lives from childhood through to adulthood. *Sister&Sister*'s book structure weaves these moments together, showcasing the intricate tapestry of sisterhood and the beauty of our individuality within shared experiences.

○ The narrative masterfully captures the twin's duality: their distinctiveness and commonalities, as well as their capacity to coexist symbiotically yet independently. It's an exploration of the multifaceted nature of their relationship, where sameness and uniqueness dance in harmony, offering readers an engaging glimpse into the captivating world of these remarkable sisters. *Sister & Sister* is a testament to the bonds that tie them and the intricacies that set them apart.

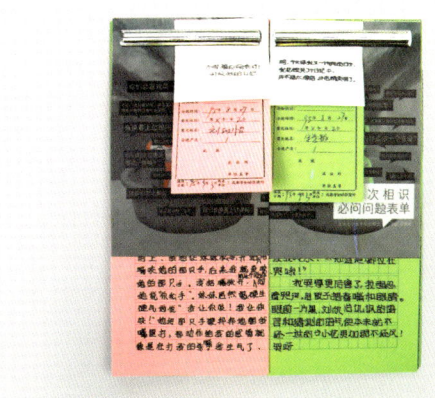

○ A cleverly designed visual narrative with a striking red segment dedicated to the elder sister, and a vibrant green segment devoted to the younger. These two parallel threads invite readers to explore their intertwined lives simultaneously, evoking a palpable sense of shared moments and experiences. Each page becomes a portal to a specific juncture in time, unveiling the twins' lives with breathtaking clarity. This engaging book, anchored in 2000s nostalgia, creatively blends diaries and photos, bound with vintage binder clips for a nostalgic. It uses color coding to distinguish between the older and younger identical twin sisters and employs their ages as a timeline. This setup enables a fascinating exploration of the twins' reactions to the same events at the same age.

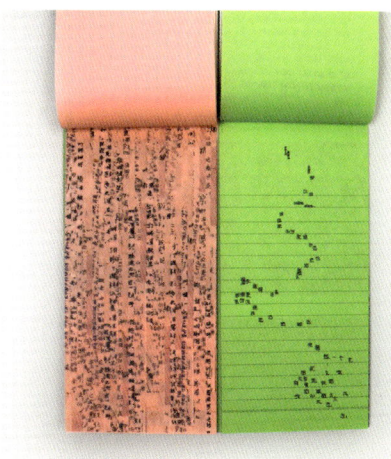

● Designer: Vanissa Foo   Language: English   Page: 70

Zhongshan on Paper

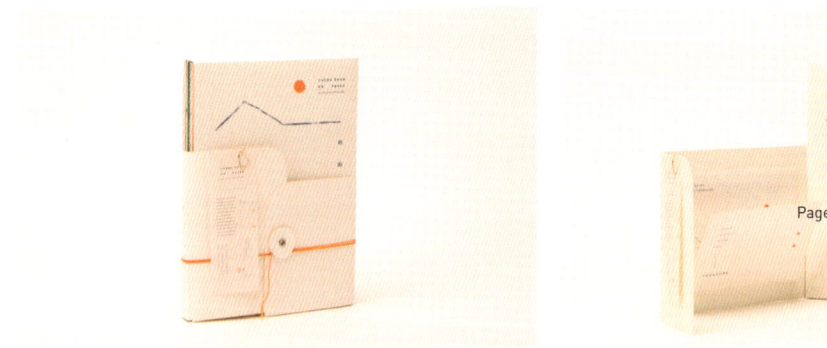

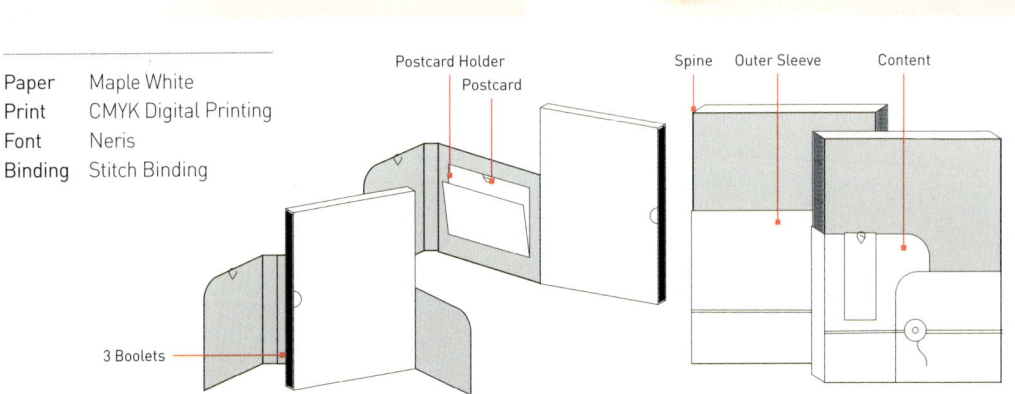

Paper   Maple White
Print   CMYK Digital Printing
Font   Neris
Binding Stitch Binding

This project illustrated the author's personal experience in Zhongshan building with an unusually observant eyes. The book records the unusual and bizarre incident through her drawing sketches. These little things are turned into creativity, inspiration and crazy thoughts. This set of publication contains 3 books which are 3 locations, namely Kokfar tea, Tommyle Baker, and Piu Piu Piu, a map and postcards.

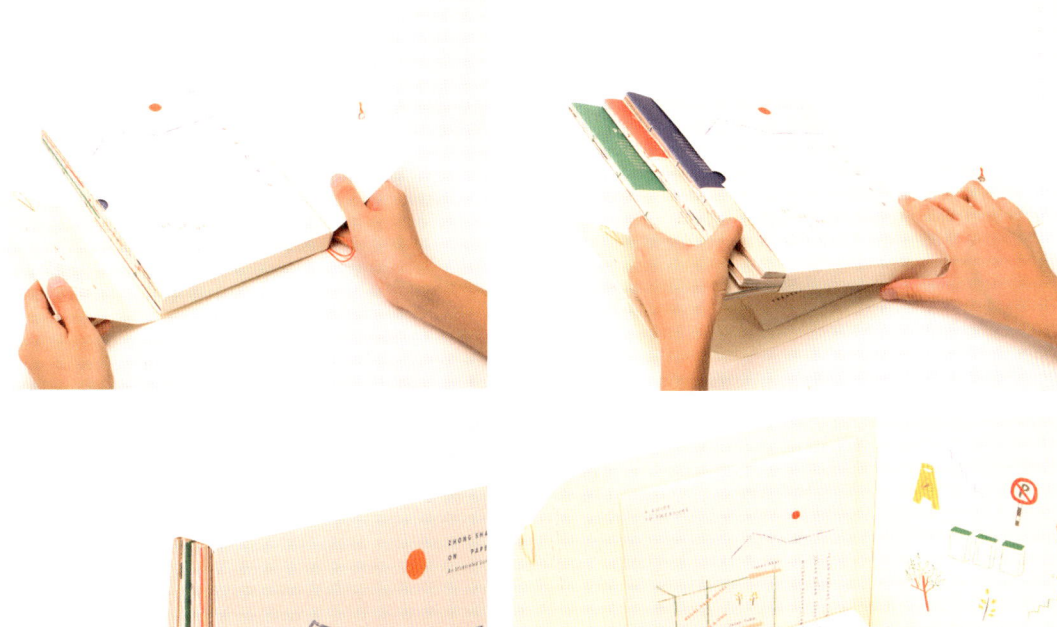

◯ The book's outer structure is inspired by the architecture of the old Zhongshan building, known for its clean and white aesthetics. The interior of the building is comprised of small individual shops, such as cafe, bakery shop, etc. Throughout the books, there are prints or leaflets attached to certain pages, serving as surprises for readers as they flip through the pages. This experience mirrors the feelings of exploration when visitors enter the Zhongshan building.

● Desginer: Wuthipol Ujathammarat   Language: English and Chinese

COVER UP

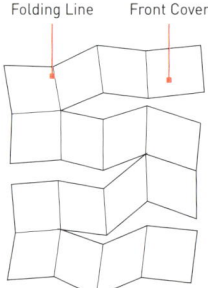
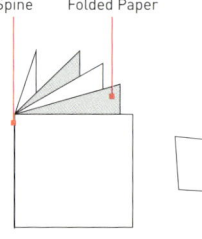
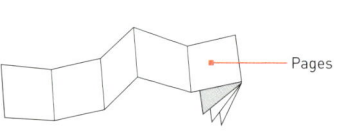

Format	100 × 100 mm
Paper	White Card 150 gsm
Print	Digital Printing
Binding	Multiple Folds (handmade)

The intention behind his handcrafted photographic pamphlet "Cover Up" is to resurrect the forgotten charm and danger that beautify this chaotic metropolitan with a disconsolate aesthetic through persistent crafting of mosaic tiles. "Cover Up" is a visual reflection on potential dangers that are hidden within the charm of exterior architectural structures. They may be beautiful in the eyes of many, but they will keep peeling and falling off through time without a doubt .

○ Thai photographer, Wuthipol Ujathammarat, notices the insignificantly strange and outdated details of exterior tilework that is blanketed upon numerous urban structures in districts of Taipei. Excessive use of tiles on urban structures is believed to reason more a functional matter than a decorative. Taipei often experiences high humidity from the wet weather, these exterior tiles help to seal off the entire buildings to keep the moisture out. The falling of mosaic tiles from exterior walls and facades is now a life threatening hazard to all pedestrians travelling below. Net cages, which appears to be a temporary solution, are now installed and added to buildings to prevent the fallen tiles from causing further injuries and damage. Yet the questions on safety measure still remains.

Designer: Toby Ng Design Language: English Client: K11 MUSEA Page: 170

Inside Muses

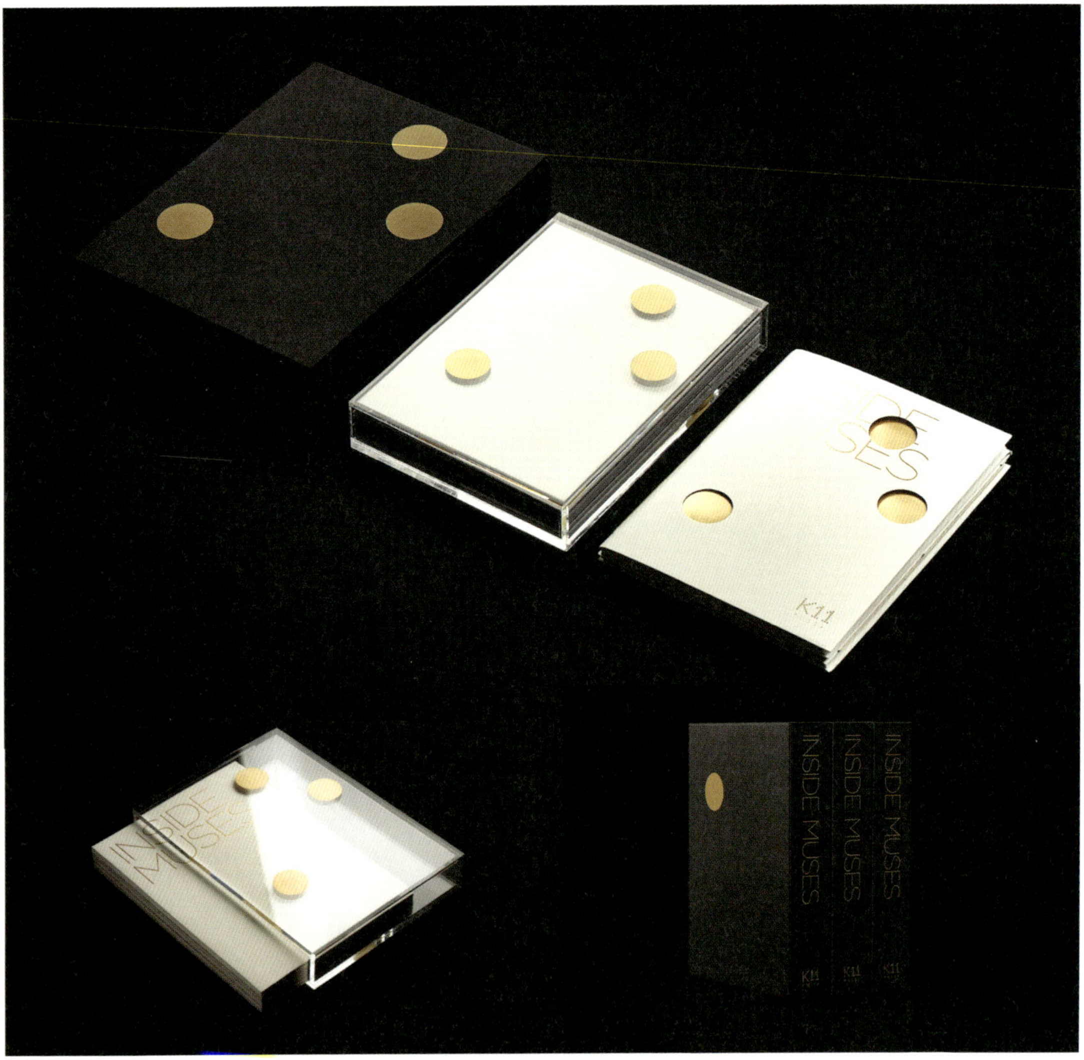

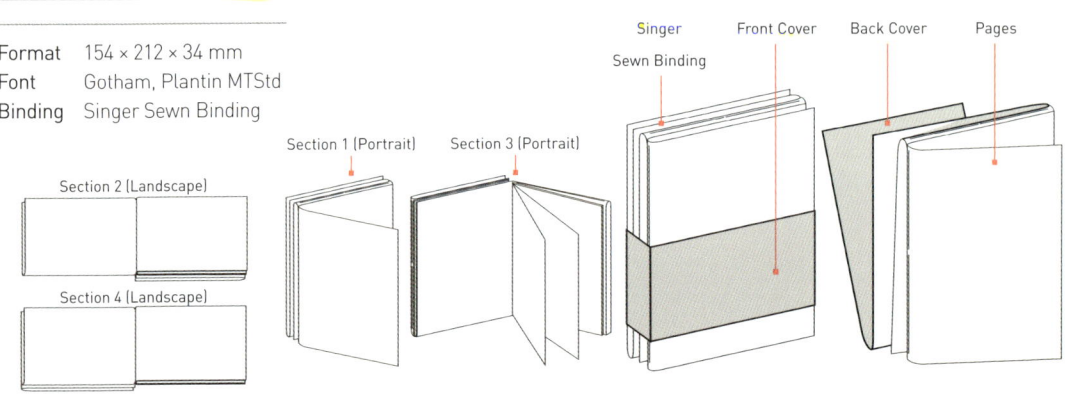

Format   154 × 212 × 34 mm
Font   Gotham, Plantin MTStd
Binding Singer Sewn Binding

Characterised as a Muse by the sea, K11 MUSEA is more than just a retail mall. It is a cultural destination that overlooks Hong Kong's spectacular skyline from the unique vantage point of East Tsim Sha Tsui. Contemporary art and design are advocated throughout the retail and dining experience creating a vibrant space that brings each visitor on a sensory adventure. Prefacing the unique retail concept, *Inside Muses* is created as a publication that would feature key pieces from the four muses of K11 MUSEA: Architecture, Furniture, Nature and Art.

◯ Reflecting the spirit of discovery, the reading experience of *Inside Muses* is guided by an unconventional book format which uncovers new perspectives at every physical turn per chapter. Referencing the logo design of K11 MUSEA's parent brand, K11, the cover design of *Inside Muses* is elevated with shimmering gold graphics in the shape of geometric circles that represent the sensuous spheres of the four muses. Both regular and executive editions of the book are exquisitely crafted to depict the fine quality of K11 MUSEA. The regular edition is assembled with intricately hand sewn-binding while the executive hardcover edition is encased in a premium crystal acrylic box, reminiscent of the vitrines that display objects d'art. The unique reading experience of *Inside Muses* draws elements of surprise, igniting curiosity as readers are encouraged to journey through adventure and discovery.

Designer: Toby Ng Design   Language: English and Tradition Chinese   Client: SIE Fund   Page: 65

SIE Fund Portfolio

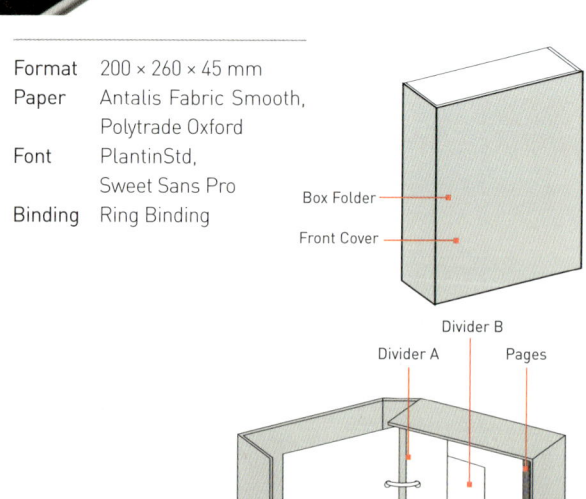

Format   200 × 260 × 45 mm
Paper   Antalis Fabric Smooth,
          Polytrade Oxford
Font   PlantinStd,
          Sweet Sans Pro
Binding   Ring Binding

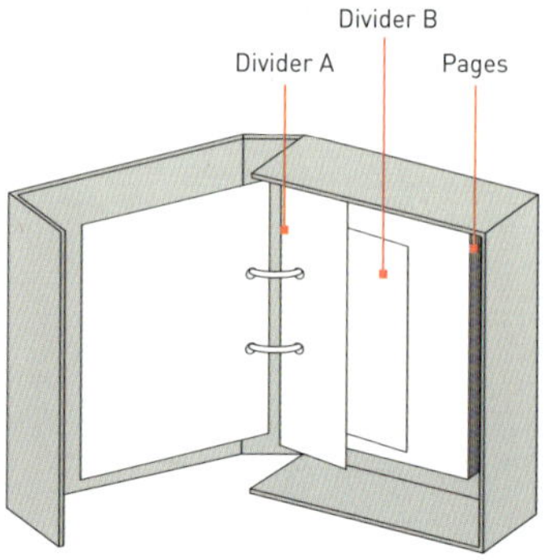

The Social Innovation and Entrepreneurship Development Fund (SIE Fund) focuses on cultivating and supporting social innovation to undertake issues of poverty and social exclusion within Hong Kong. To foster a socially beneficial ecosystem, the SIE Fund provides social entrepreneurs with a wide pool of resources for research and capacity building to uphold the entire life cycle of innovative programmes.

◯ In order to illustrate the work and impact of the fund, a portfolio box based on the Social-Inno Box (which houses videos telling stories of the fund's work) has been devised to depict areas and projects that have been backed thus far. Three bold graphic arrows characterize the priority areas of research, capacity building, and innovative programs as overarching outlines of the portfolio. Contained within each area, color coded sections are arranged to represent different sectors of society assisted by the aid of the SIE Fund. A boxed ring binder format that encases the content allows for flexibility to change and curate sections according to the needs the user while accommodating to the ever-growing list of projects undertaken by the SIE Fund.

Designer: Vanissa Foo   Language: English   Client: Humana Studio

Humana Theatre Zine

Humana Theatre Zine is a self-published publication that combines the art of imaginative performance with graphic illustration. The objective of *Humana Theatre Zine* is to showcase the celebration of performance and art in a fresh and imaginative way. The design features vibrant and bold color choices, along with geometric patterns, creating a maximalist theatre. The author hopes to provide an engaging and memorable experience for readers.

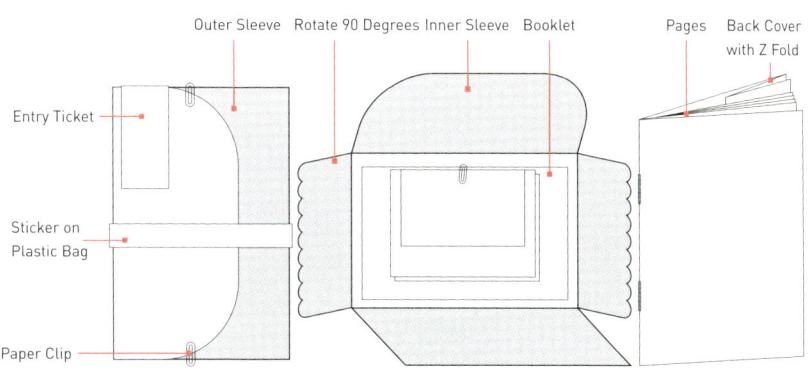

Paper	Munken, Mohawk Navajo, Meridien Silk
Font	Coquette, All Round Gothic
Print	CMYK Digital Printing
Binding	Staple Binding

○ The outer packaging includes an entry ticket, which grants access to the theatre show. The packaging sleeve can be transformed into a mini theatre, adding an interactive element to the experience. A playbill serves as a guide to the entire theatre program, providing an overview of each of the 16 performances, including title, choreographer, and performers involved. Additionally, there are two prints as souvenirs. Each performance likely has its own page within the booklet, which is filled with full illustration of geometric shapes and bold color combinations, creating a modern and whimsical aesthetic.

HIDE

Find the hidden thoughts between pages

Reshape the reading experience and guide readers to take the initiative. We are used to reading explicit text, but some designers take a different approach, hiding information between the lines for the reader to discover. This way of hiding information can stimulate the emotional exchange and interaction between the reader and the book, or the author, stimulate the reader's curiosity and imagination, and increase the enjoyment and engagement of reading. By changing the way of reading, readers can change from passive input to active output and participate in it more actively, which helps readers to better understand and absorb the content. The author's emotions and experiences are sealed in the words and images, they are like echoes in the valley, through the barriers of time and space, to be heard, understood and felt by the reader in the quiet moment of reading.

● Designer: [e] De SIGN   Language: Chinese   Client: Chongqing University Press   Page: 384

Museum of Life

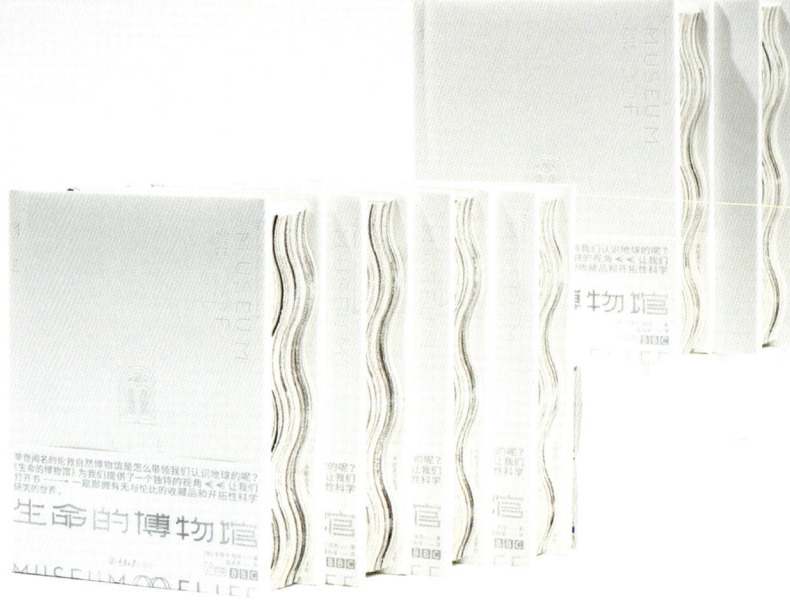

Format	135 × 157 mm
Paper	Xuesha Cherry Blossom
Print	Foil Stamping, Die Cutting, CMYK Printing
Font	Self-Design, Source Han Sans CN
Binding	Hardback

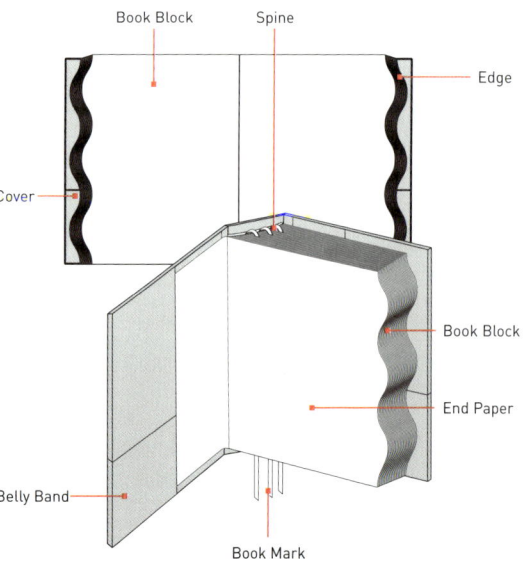

The creative team wanted to make the book feel like a museum, while to show the spirit of life in a more subtly. Therefore, they finally thought of designing the book as a wave-shaped cutout, so that when flipping through the book, it can show the flow of life. The red, white and blue book band symbolizes the arteries and veins (inspired by the logo of barber store); the typography uses the guide system and text file summarization, as if they are in the museum of life.

○ From the outside to the inside, the book uses a lot of pure white, and only prints the information in the form of hot stamping, wanting to visualize the feeling of people walking in the museum, but also expresses the idea that natural life is a little bit bigger than it seems, and that we need to pay attention to nature to see it unfold in your eyes in a different way.

● Designer: Jiang Song   Language: Chinese and English   Client: Suzhou Museum   Page: 694

The Painted Screen: Past and Future

This is an exhibition album about Chinese screens. It consists of two parts: ancient and contemporary. The ancient part consists of literary theory, while the contemporary part consists of screen-related art works created by nine contemporary artists.

Paper	Silk and Art Paper
Font	Song, Times New Roman
Binding	Sewn Binding

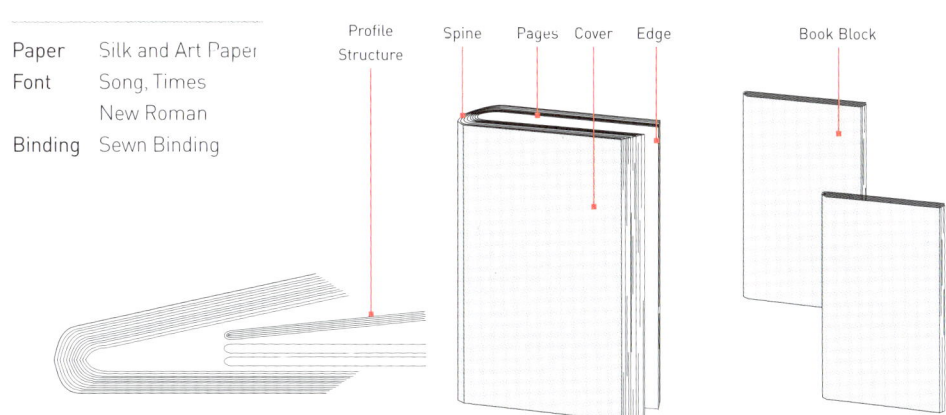

○ The book folio chooses a ratio of length and width similar to the screen and adopts the concept of "book in book" to reflect the theme of the ancient and contemporary exhibition.

○ The cover is made of silk that is associated with the texture of the screen. The main and sub-volumes of the books correspond to the exhibition contents of the ancient and contemporary sections respectively. The concept of "book in book" conforms to the intention of the exhibition to integrate the dialogue between the contemporary and the ancient, and expresses the unique symbolic meaning of the screen inside and outside.

● Designer: Zhipeng Xie, Jiangping Liu, Xiaoman Chen   Language: Chinese   Page: 78

The Plant Tenants

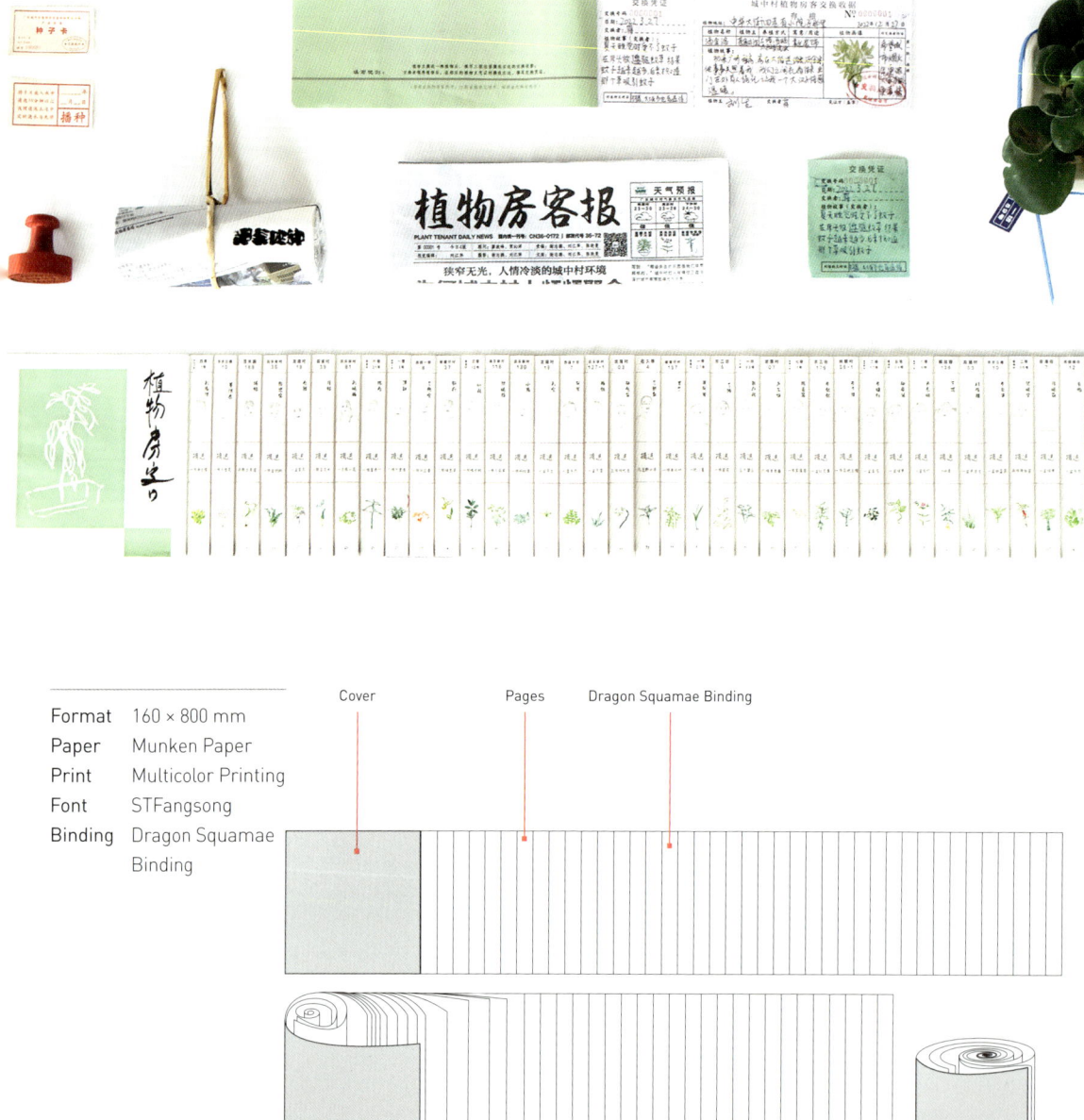

Format	160 × 800 mm
Paper	Munken Paper
Print	Multicolor Printing
Font	STFangsong
Binding	Dragon Squamae Binding

The Plant Tenants project uses plants in the urban village as a medium to enliven the communication between people in a light and fun way. With the consent of 36 villagers in the village, the design team asked for 36 plants and collected the stories behind each plant; and recycled bottles and cans from the village, which were redesigned as planting containers and coded by door number to form 36 brand new potted plants for urban villages. Special exchange devices were made to attract villagers to exchange potted plants with their stories of urban village plants, thus obtaining 72 stories, which were designed into this book of 72 tenants' plant storytelling.

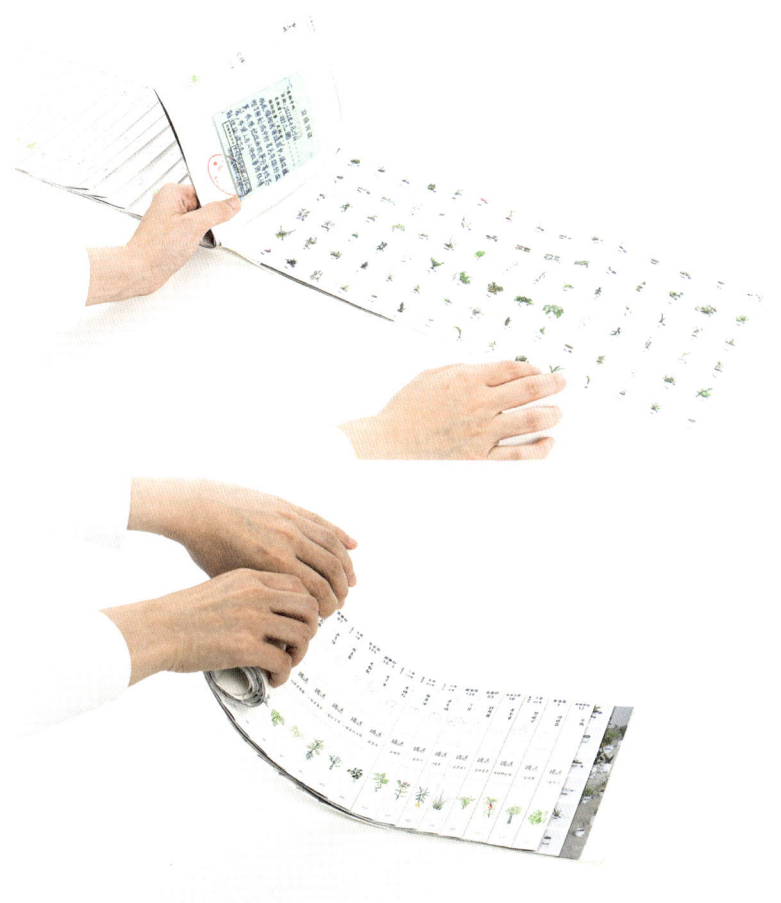

○ They used similes and metaphors in the book. The unity of a close community relies on the outstanding favors owed to each other, so the team designed a receipt book to restore the concept of "owed" and "returned" favors; and a Dragon Squamae Binding with the arrangement of the favor gift book and merit list to encourage and record the stories of the 72 tenants in the book in the form of traditional rituals. The two are rolled into tubes and packaged in *The Plant Tenant* newspaper with the project concept and process, with a string for easy carrying, forming a set of humane reading materials for the residents of the village.

○ The residents' simple but nice gesture of passing plants to strangers is, in their opinion, a great merit. Therefore, the team designed the outer red color of the book in the form of a merit list, which conveys the good feelings and affirmation of the residents who gave plants and exchanged stories. At the same time, using the structure of the inner pages of the Dragon Scale Binding, some of the space on the inner pages serves as a catalog search function, making it easy for readers to quickly access different characters. Adopting the inner page pair analysis and folding lines to fill in the information of the plant giver on the left side and the plant receiver on the right side, the interaction of a pair of unfamiliar residents is effectively presented in a single paper plane, which facilitates readers to understand the correspondence of the characters and to obtain a more multi-layered experience of the reading space.

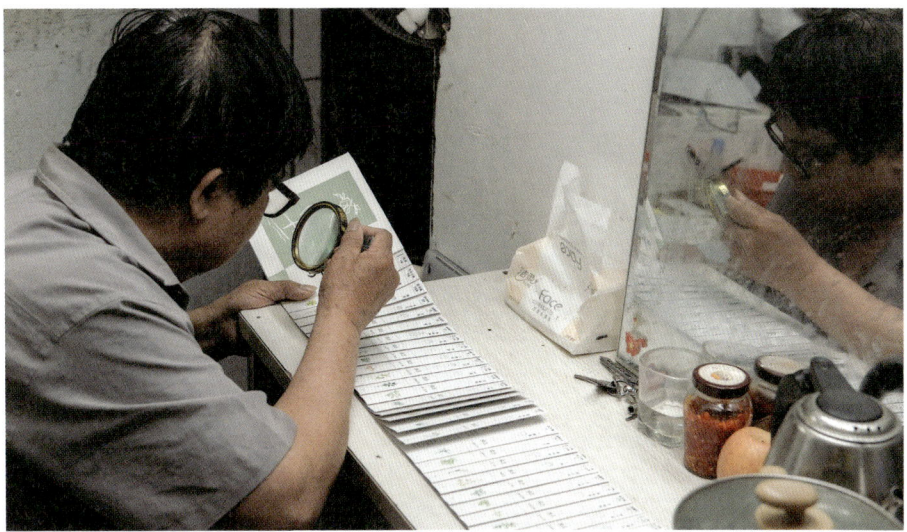
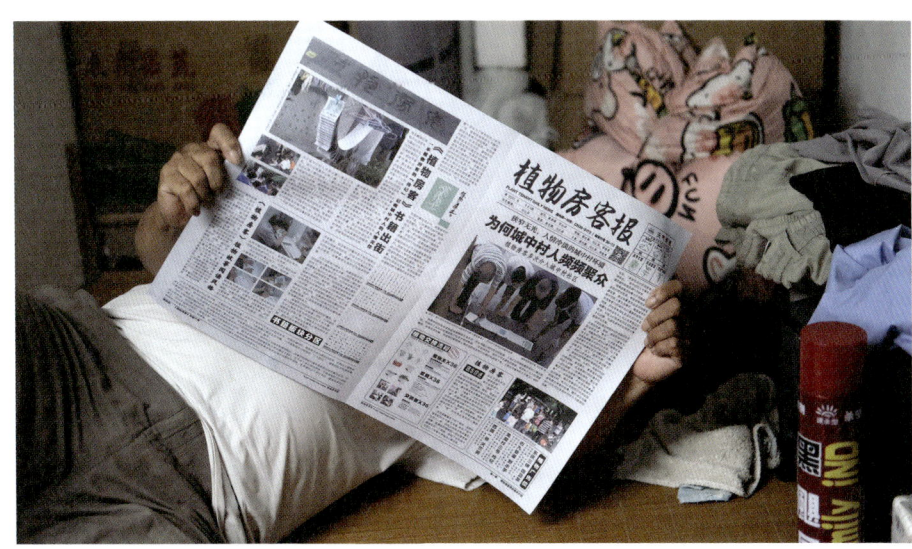

● Designer: out.o studio   Language: Chinese, English   Client: out.o studio   Page: 124

Reference vol.02

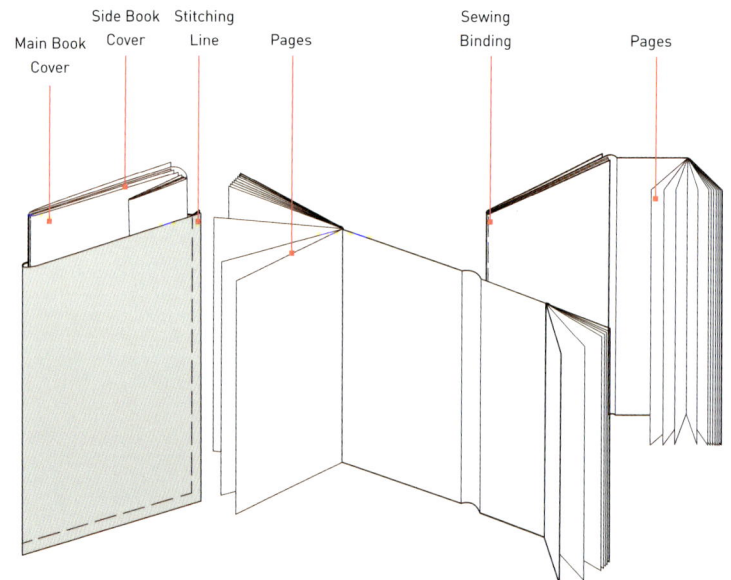

Format	160 × 280 mm
Paper	Sakura Snow Semi-transparent Paper 135 gsm, Arjowiggins Matter Andina-grey 80 gsm, Meiji Red Specialty Paper 130 gsm
Font	Source Han Serif JP, ABC Laica
Binding	Sewing Binding, Double Volume Folio

REFERENCE is an exploratory graphic design publication, similar to a paper podcast, in which the participants in the discussion serve as a reference for each other. Each issue proposes a topic for discussion, and different designers create their own ideas on the topic. The second issue is a collection of phrases about love. Using others' understanding of love as reference, it discusses love, depicts love, and falls into love.

○ The binding of the issue is in an envelope cover, which distinguishes it from a direct flip book format, and gives it a more intimate feel in line with the theme. The foiled paper of the book jacket and the transparent UV on the back cover attempt to create an intimate reading by hiding the text of the book amongst the paper and making it non-directly recognizable. The overall hierarchy of graphic and textual discussion is organized into left and right columns, allowing the reader to prioritize and focus on either the graphic or the text, depending on their habits, so that they can immerse themselves in the information at hand. The text retains the oral habits of the discussants and the time records generated by the software to convey a sense of authenticity and personal involvement in the discussion.

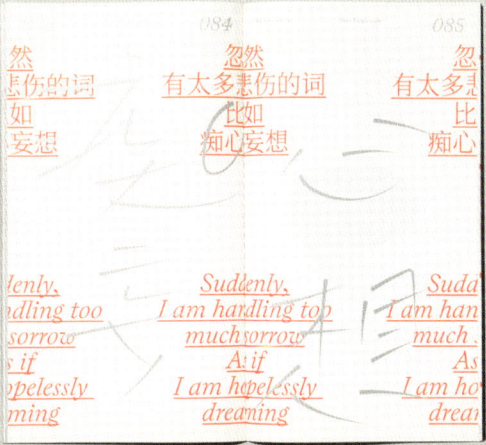

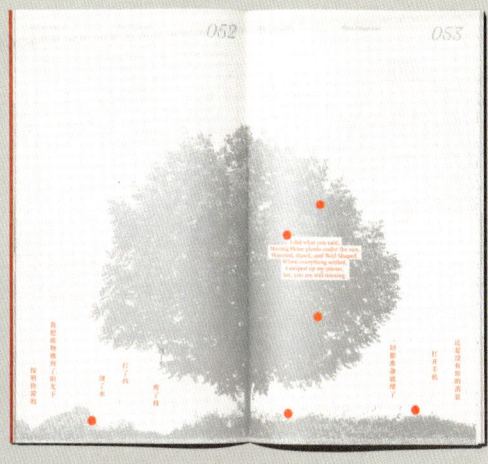

● Designer: Elizabeth Novianti Susanto   Language: English   Page: 12

Lecture Notes 02

Paper   Cover | Botany Natural 230 gsm
           Insert | Rives Design 120 gsm
Font   Knockout Fonts | Fonts by Hoefler&Co.
           Hoefler Text Fonts | Fonts by Hoefler&Co.

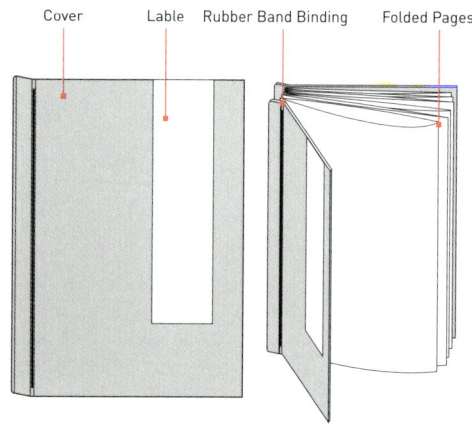

Cover   Lable   Rubber Band Binding   Folded Pages

The book, a hybrid of traditional lecture notes and an experimental art book, features a variety of design elements, including typography, layout, and layers, to create a visually appealing and informative resource.

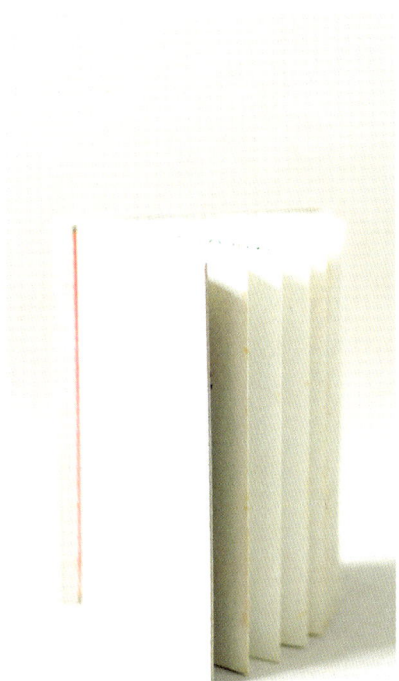

◯ The publication is a distillation of thoughts and reactions on innovation and experimental layout, infused with the playful patterns and eclectic aesthetic of the Memphis design era. The layout is systematic and lucid, yet infused with playful and experimental air, unfolding as the reader turns the page. The designer used rubber bands as a binding technique to make the pages as flexible as possible, so the reader can easily add extra pages. The fact that the reader can easily add or remove pages suggests that the book is not a fixed or static object, but rather a living and evolving work of art.

Designer: Zephtang Design   Language: Chinese, English   Page: 219

HUMAN

This book is a reflection on life and the world after the loss of a beloved one, and it holds the theme that "only death is an inevitable choice that we can never avoid."

Format	270 × 410 mm
Print	Fine Art Printing, Brush Coating, Fore-edge Gilding
Paper	Meilin Paper
Font	Toppan
Binding	Manual Brushing Glue on Tongzi Pages

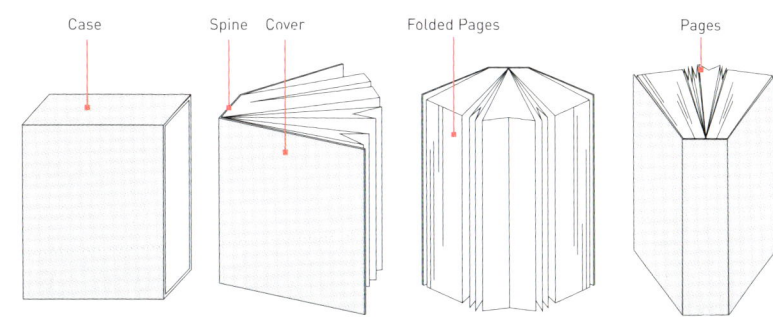

○ *Human* utilizes a binding design of Tongzi Pages as well as interleaved pages, with a lot of shaped cut-outs throughout the book, or jumps between different materials. Tongzi Pages are a type of traditional Chinese binding, namely double-page paper is folded horizontally in half, with the crease towards the fore-edge and the opening of the fold towards the book binding. Therefore the team wanted to utilize this to reflect the heaviness as well as the layers in this book. The significance and inspiration of these designs come from the fact that it is an anthropomorphic book, which seeks to present all the documents, certificates, and things that a person may use and record throughout his or her life. In order to maximize the information and to restore this characteristic of documents that can be extracted and passed on, they have made dotted lines on the shaped cuts, which can be torn down to become independent pages that can be passed on.

Designer: Sangwon Haman Jo   Language: English   Page: 59

Number of Participants: 2

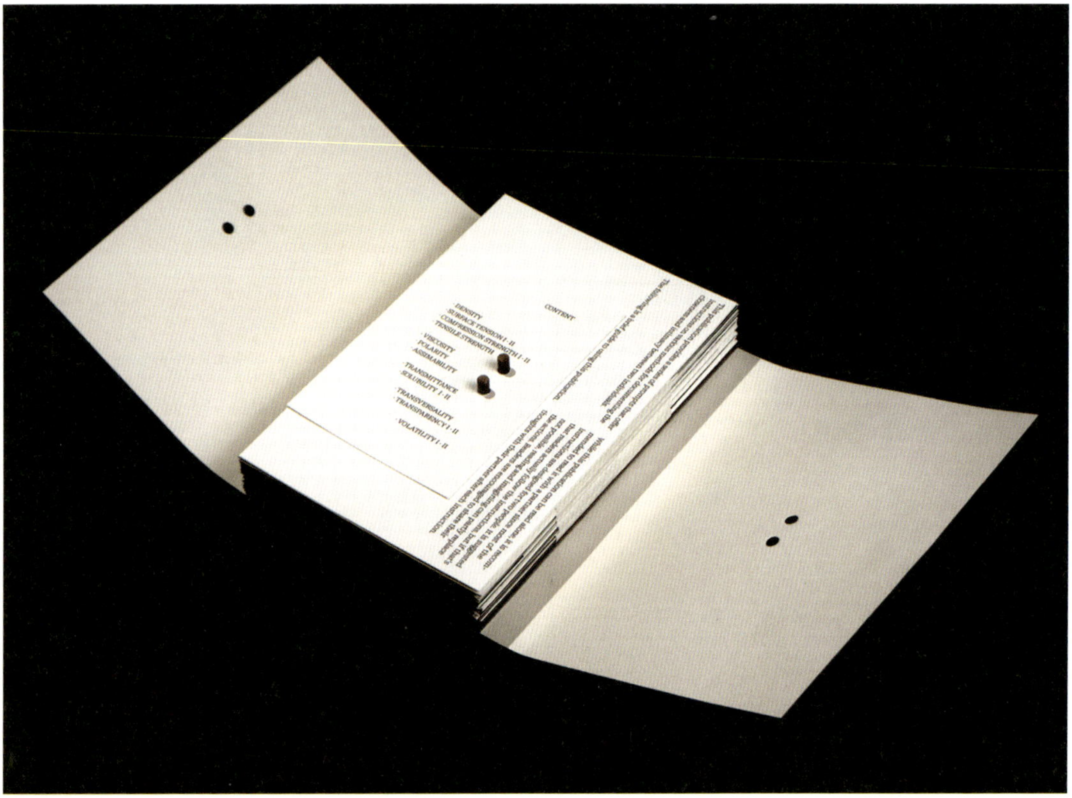

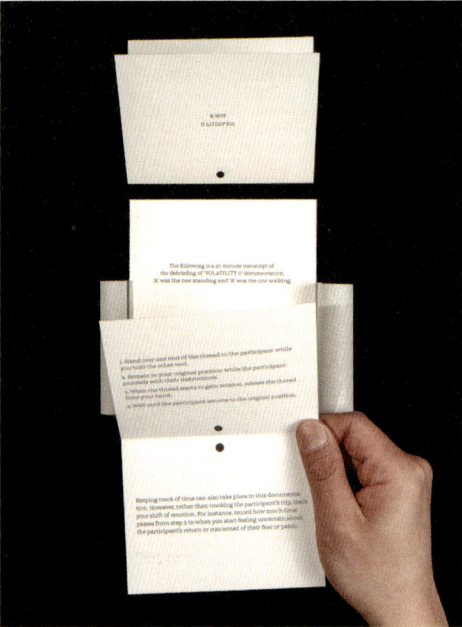

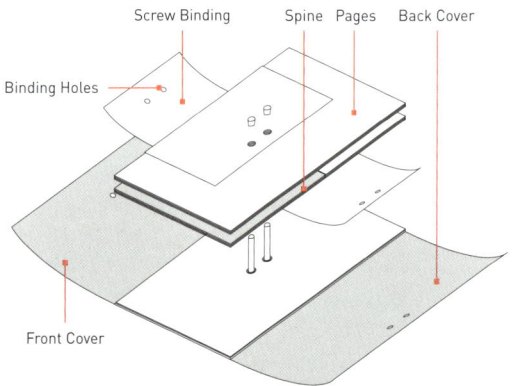

Print   Digital Printing and Inkjet Printing
Paper   Various (including photo, tracing, cardboard, and book papers)
Font   Main-Mala, Sub-Shree Devanagari
Binding   Iterated Screw Binding

This book is an anthology of performance instructions designed to guide readers in observing the dynamics that exist between two individuals. The performances curated in this book borrow the form of step-by-step instructions, introducing pragmatics as an approach to understanding the complex structure of awareness and its embodiment. Each instruction is named after different qualities of materials, such as Tension, Viscosity, and Transparency, which helps readers relate the materiality of intangible awareness to the physicality of matter.

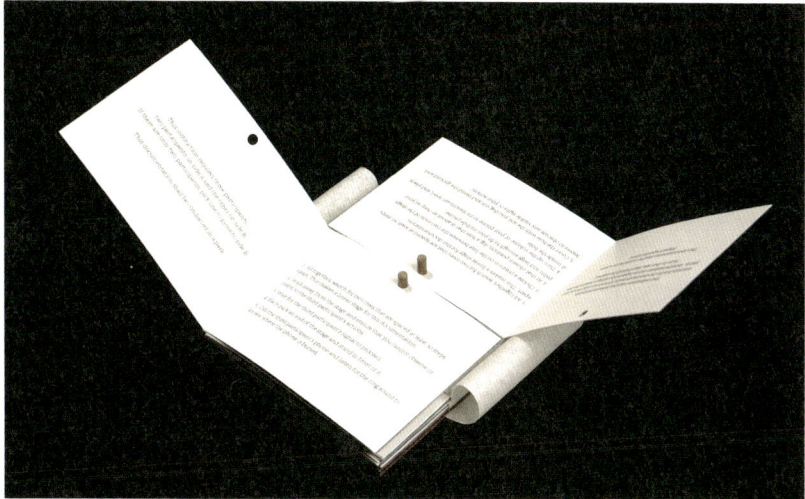

○ This book's design challenges the potential extension from writing to bodily experience. It aims to encourage active participation in the performances. The book's structure adopts a non-binding method, utilizing a one-sided open pole (commonly referred to as a screw) and spreads with punch holes. The pages are the size of cards and detachable, suggesting that readers keep them handy to prompt themselves with the possibility of participation. Furthermore, the book has two sides, Side A and B, physically separated with its structure. Readers are encouraged to invite another participant and collaborate in the performances. The instruction prompt cards feature various foldable designs that cooperate with the structure of the instructions, dramaticising the reading-participating experience.

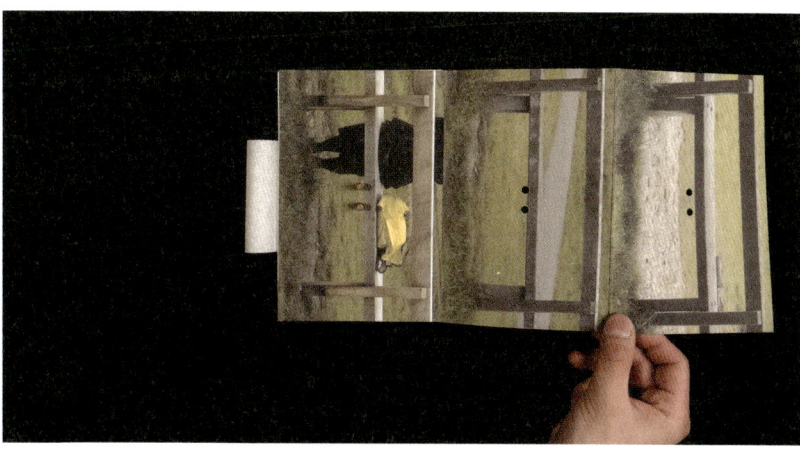

● Designer: Ng Kai Wei   Language: English   Page: 93

The Art of the Insect

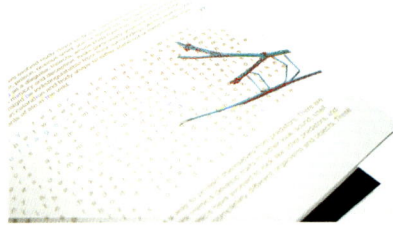
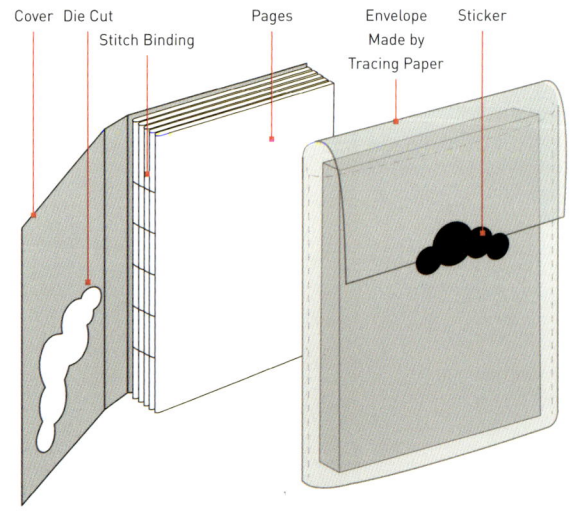

Print   Digital Printing
Paper   Mohawk Superfine
Font   Neue Haas Grotesk Display Pro
Binding   Stitch Binding

Insects, the unsung heroes of our natural world, have long captivated with their astonishing diversity, captivating colours, and enigmatic behaviours. Yet, in the midst of their intricate beauty and vital ecological roles, these tiny creatures are often overlooked or even reviled by many people. Venture into a realm of insects' world, *The Art of the Insect* shed a light on the incredible diversity and complexity of these tiny creatures and provides a chance for audience to explore by themselves.

○ Within its chapters and pages, the book introduces and celebrates different kinds of most beautiful insects where audience get to learn more about the natural world and further cultivate a deeper appreciation for the small wonders that surround them. There are total of three items in the book, which are the main book, *The Art of the Insect*; the mini book, *The Strangest Insect Behaviour*; and a series of bookmarks. Drawing inspiration directly or indirectly from the insects, the graphic element and visual execution of this book pay homage to the creatures. Every design facet, from color palettes, shapes to page layout and typography details, echoes the behaviour of the insects and even their survival strategies against predators.

○ Having different size of books, some surprise elements or extra leaflets in different pages, bookmarks are to create a more interactive experience within the readers.

Designer: Copyright Reserved Studio   Language: Bahasa Indonesia, English   Page: 36

Domestic Disturbance 2

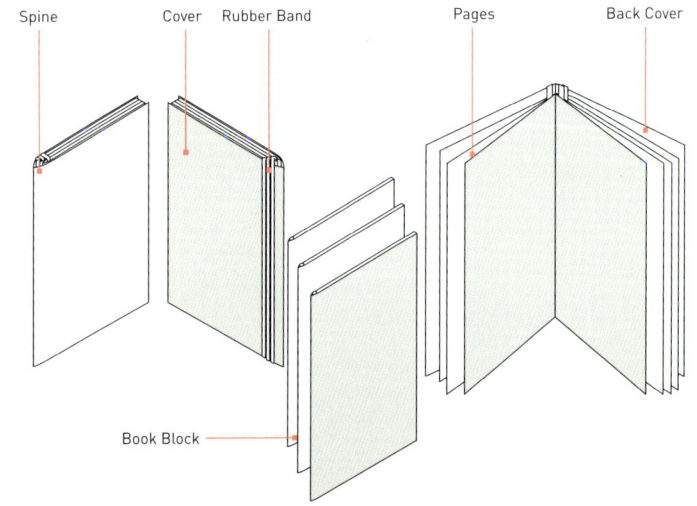

Format	176 × 250 mm
Print	2 to 4 Colors (ricebran and soy ink).
Font	Frankfurter, Hiragino Kaku, Roslindale, Longinus, Helvetica
Binding	DIY Booklet Folded with Rubber Band

Domestic Disturbance stripped down each contributor's conformity, norm and behaviour to explore their predisposed state of mind and personal desire. Each edition is filled up with three zines created by 8 designers and sold as a bundle of collective thought in a single binder. The studio predictably has to maintain and create visual formation to help the job run smoothly. Everyday, they eliminate their wants to not let any behaviors in contrary to the unwritten rules out in the wild. There has always been an implicit guide when it comes to how to design, in which a predisposed state of mind has no place, let alone personal desire.

○ In this zine, the creative team aims to strike a balance between personal nature and instinctive behavior, in which the audience can engage spontaneously, assembling the piece they like. Furthermore, they want it to be a very easy-yet-fun process and experience since the thought process depends on what we (and the audience) are as a person while we make the best of our condition. No edition is similar to each other because the audience takes roles in assembling their editions.

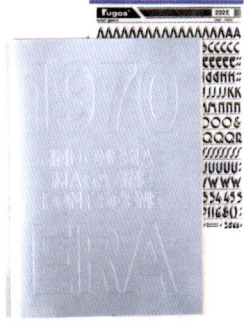

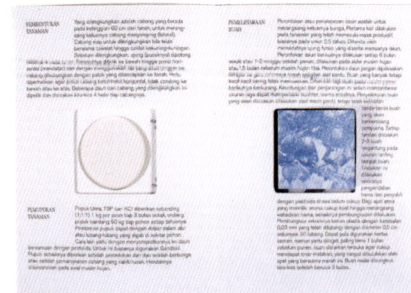

Designer: Robbin Ami Silverberg Language: English Page: 82

From Dreams to Ashes

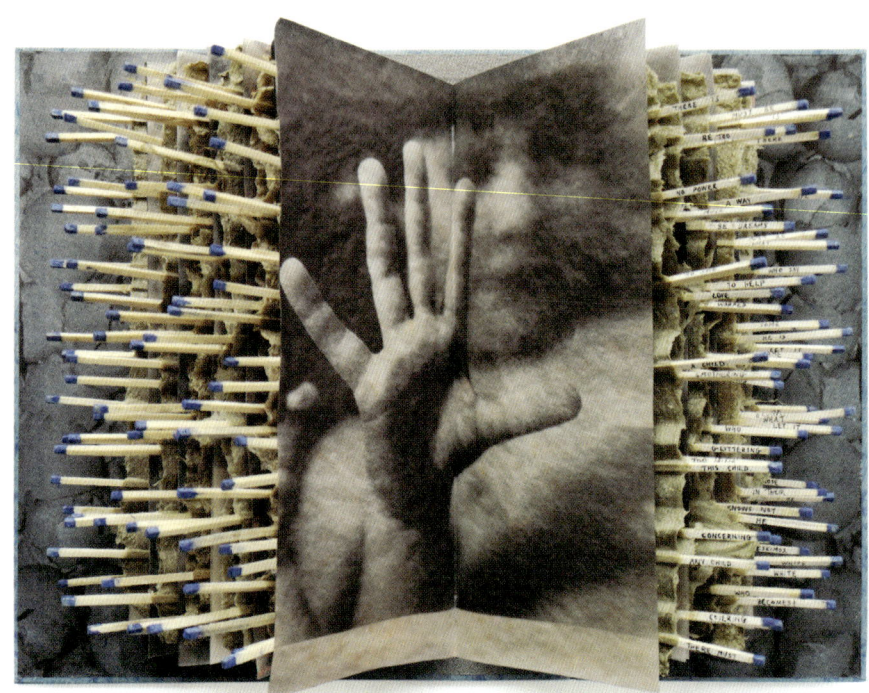

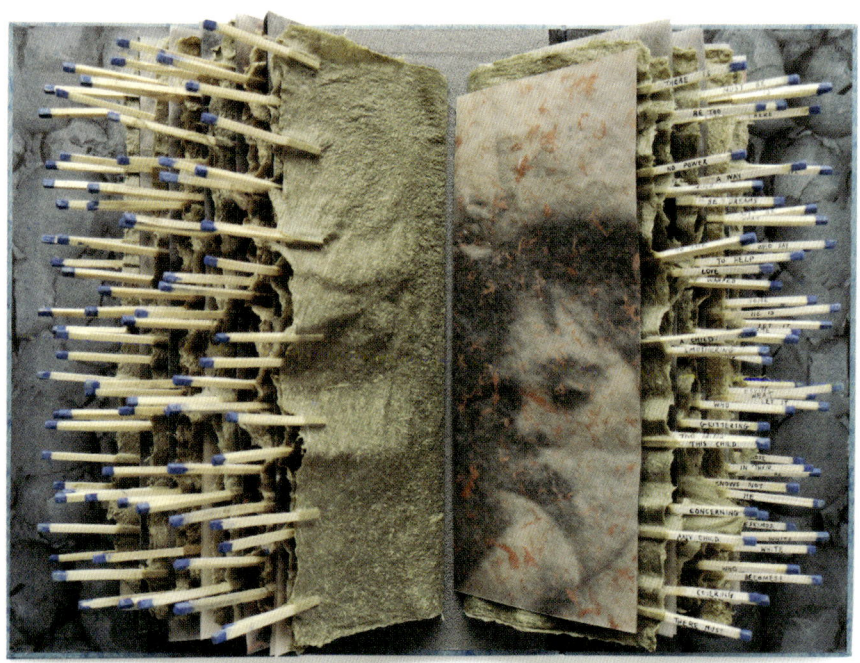

The main book has its pages sewn to book cloth glued down onto the spine board. The designer chose this binding due to the fragile nature of the paper. The book's prose is based on a nightmare about vivid and prophetic dreams, which was hand-written on matches and embedded into the fore-edges of the mugwort paper. The two materials, mugwort and matches, offer fantasies and destructions simultaneously. The interspersed photographic images of young boys add a bitter-sweetness to the dream sequence. The second book, *Taking Hold of the Night*, is printed on translucent papers, so the prose text based on a month of the artist's actual dreaming, layers and overlaps with the photo images.

○ Mugwort fiber made a brittle paper hard to fold, sew and bind but conceptually was essential to the work. Another challenge was figuring out the most effective way to present the ideas & emotions connected to the dreams & nightmares. What helped most here was realizing that the materials could represent the ideas within.

Print	Archival Inkjet Printing
Paper	Dobbin Mill Papers,
	Book 1	Handmade
	Mugwort Papers
	Book 2	Handmade
	Abaca Papers
	Box	Cotton Rag
Binding	Case Binding
PS	Book 1	30 Pages
	Book 2	52 Pages

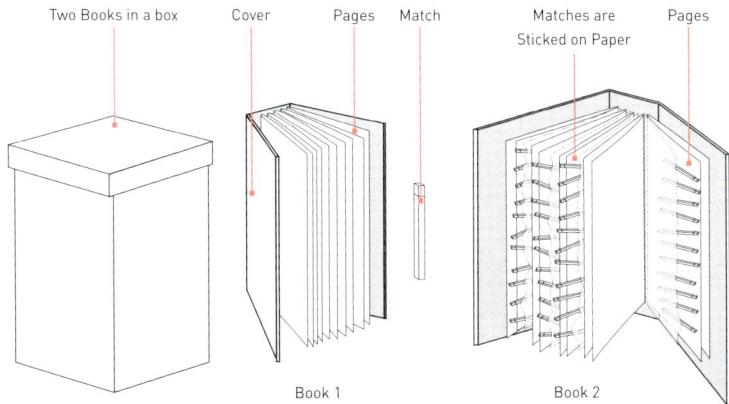

Designer: Marta Guidotti   Language: Italian and English   Page: 286

/ū/(r)-nation (Your nation / not your nation)

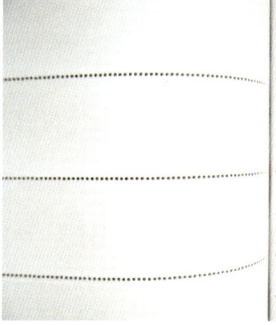

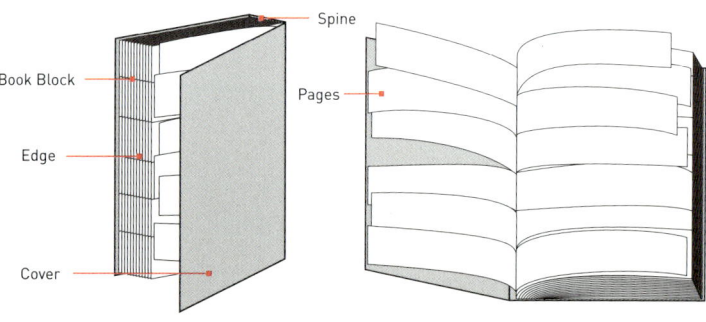

Format   165 × 220 × 35 mm
Paper   Cover | Plike-black
         (Cordenons) 140 gsm
         Inner | uncoated 90 gsm
         GSK
Font   Ping, Peter Bilak
Binding Paperback

This book explores the themes of identity and nation through letter shapes and book design. It envisions the possibility of creating a utopian nation tailored to each individual through a dynamic system that embraces diverse singularities and identities.

○ Within the pages of this book, the mottos of all nations, including those without one, are collected and reassembled through a process of deconstruction. This results in a unicum defined by the nations' mottos and the colors of their flags, and each reader's input. The generation of new sentences and forms, achieved through the overlapping and merging of letters from the original mottos, serves as an expression of mixture and plurality. Readers are encouraged to participate by rearranging the word order of the mottos up to them, through a cutting system. This allows each person to affirm its vision without erasing the identities of others, resulting in an indissoluble coexistence that contributes to the construction of individual and collective identities.

Designer: Lim Zhi Yee   Language: English   Page: 104

A Journey to the Moon

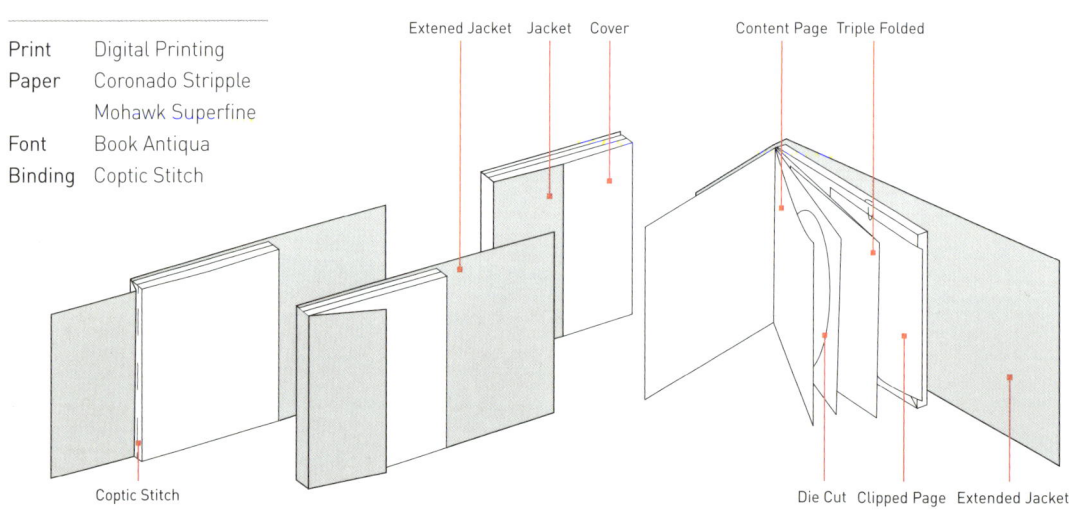

Print   Digital Printing
Paper   Coronado Stripple
          Mohawk Superfine
Font   Book Antiqua
Binding   Coptic Stitch

Extened Jacket   Jacket   Cover   Content Page   Triple Folded

Coptic Stitch   Die Cut   Clipped Page   Extended Jacket

A Journey to the Moon is an experimental visual book that takes readers to explore the wonders of the moon. The designer has always been fascinated by how the moon looks from afar, on this project she took the opportunity to explore the different aspects of the moon, from historical to scientific & including cultural beliefs.

◯ The designer particularly chose a square format to design the book the initiative is to make it as comapct as how holding a moon would feel like. Small but mighty. The inside of the book brings readers through by having interactive pages that is designed to feel the texture to seem like we (the readers) are a part of NASA, landing on to the moon.

Designer: Sandra Teschow   Language: German   Client: Science Notes Magazin   Page: 284

Nacht

Format   115 × 160 mm
Paper   Book Cover | Römerturm Cardboard Black 270 gsm
         Content | Circleoffset Premium White 100 gsm
Font   Primo Serif

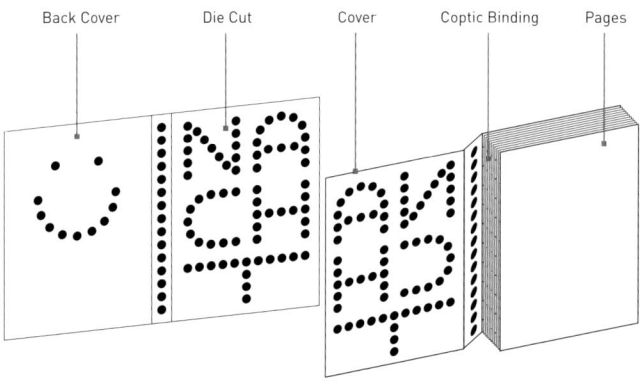

Just as man brought light into the night, the design brings light into the dark book. By illuminating, or lighting up, everything that is important. Text, graphics, photographs and illustrations glow from the black pages.

○ Headlines have a slight glow effect. The images, illustrations, and graphics were designed so that the black tone either matched the black tone in the background, creating a smooth transition between subject and background, or so that a distinct difference in black tones was visible to separate subject from background where necessary. The introductory pages are identical in layout, the type area follows a strict grid, and the typography is clearly and uniformly set. The cover also brings light into the darkness. Holes reminiscent of cones of light have been punched in the cover, revealing the page behind. When you turn the page, the theme of the magazine shines out at you.

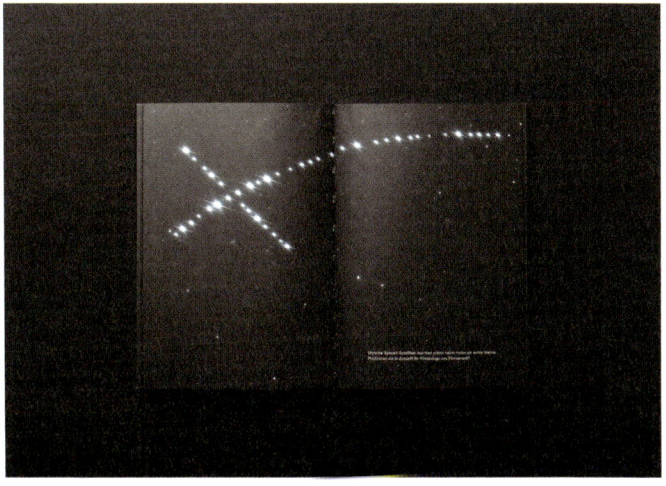

○ The play of day and night follows a constant rhythm. This rhythm forms the basis for the book design. The pages always follow the same structure, the font sizes are identical, the layout is the same on all pages, and pictures and illustrations were designed and edited in the same way. There are no deviations from the rule, because even the night always appears in the same rhythm.

● Designer: Wuthipol Ujathammarat   Language: English

in•scape

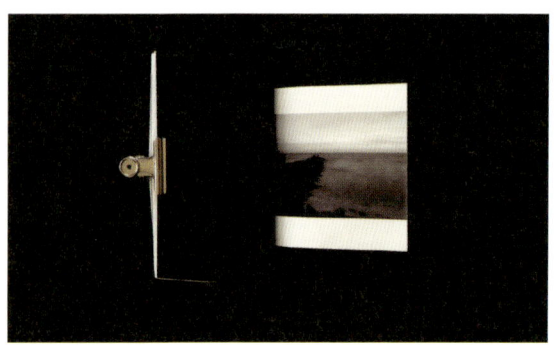
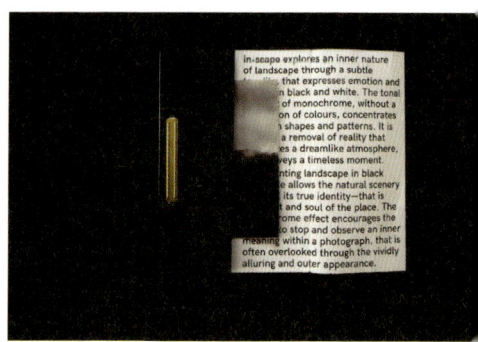

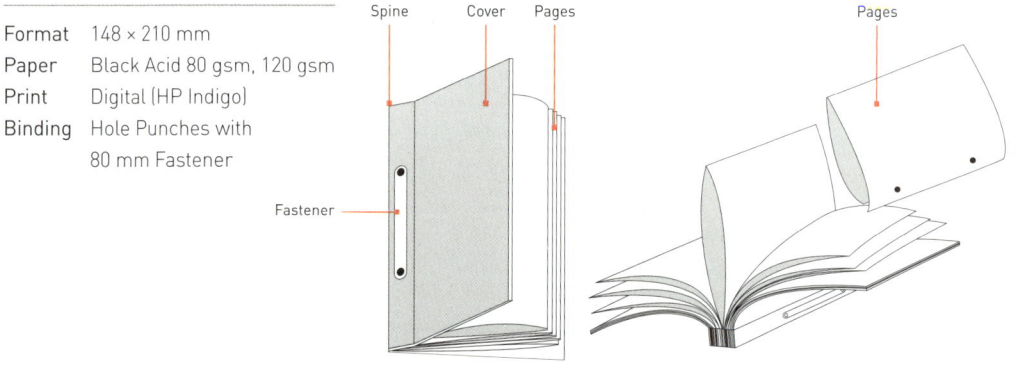

Format   148 × 210 mm
Paper   Black Acid 80 gsm, 120 gsm
Print   Digital (HP Indigo)
Binding Hole Punches with
         80 mm Fastener

in • scape unveils an interesting way of seeing natural landscape. It inspires the readers to closely observe the emotions and thoughts, that are expressed through sequences of black and white images. The use of French fold design encourages the readers to seek and peek, seeing what else there is to discover. It blends the reading experience with the actual storyline both visually and interactively. Your eyes are drawn more to natural shapes, forms and patterns, revealing an authentic essence of natural scenery with emotions, feelings and thoughts.

● Designer: Wuthipol Ujathammarat   Language: English

Little Yellow Spots

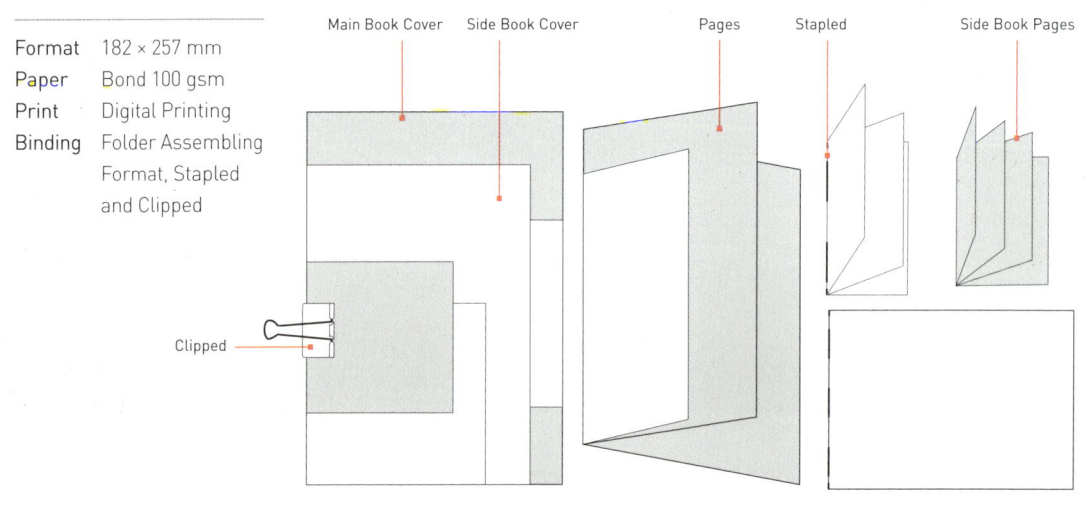

Format   182 × 257 mm
Paper   Bond 100 gsm
Print   Digital Printing
Binding Folder Assembling
         Format, Stapled
         and Clipped

Clipped

Main Book Cover   Side Book Cover   Pages   Stapled   Side Book Pages

To question a widespread repute for tidiness and orderliness usually associated with Singapore, Thai photographer Wuthipol Ujathammarat finds himself startled by an excessive number of bicycles left scattered disorderly on its city streets. His photographic publication *Little Yellow Spots* captures unfamiliar streetscapes, carelessly dumped with dockless bicycles, as an urban art form that puts Singapore on a spot.

○ The eerie perspective the photographer emphasizes floats beyond political or ideological affairs. It introduces an alternative impression of Singapore where the dockless two-wheelers are being observed as a form of artistic mundane. His unusual curiosity reflectively creates a foreign outlook that hands Singapore with a quirky aesthetic through urban tonality and untypical street clutters. The physical bundle of work does not incorporate any literal descriptions. Instead, the readers are required to scan a QR code to exclusively access additional content about the work — much like how bike sharing works.

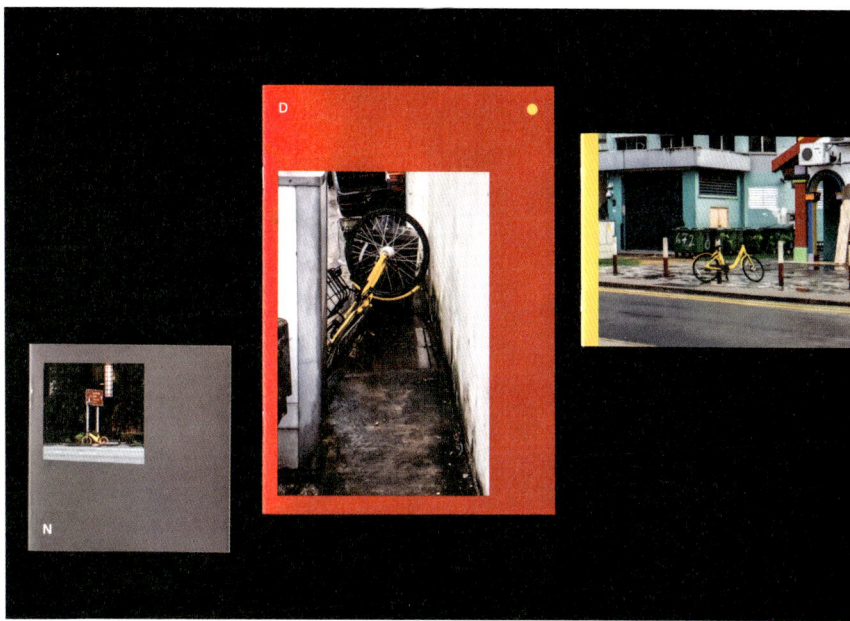

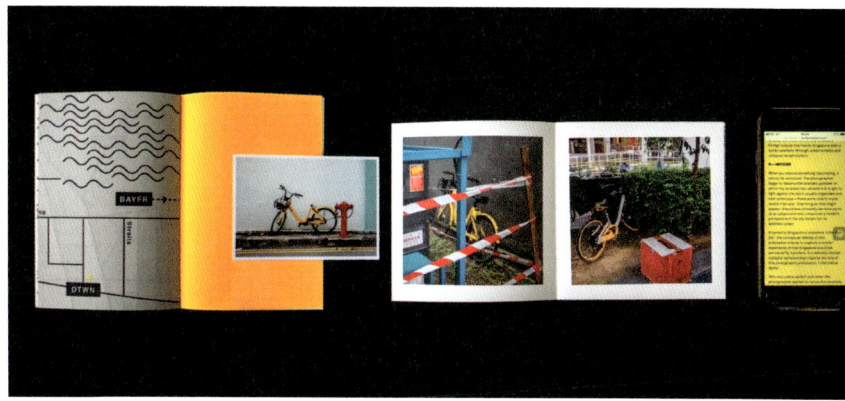

FOLD

Present the unique folds on the paper

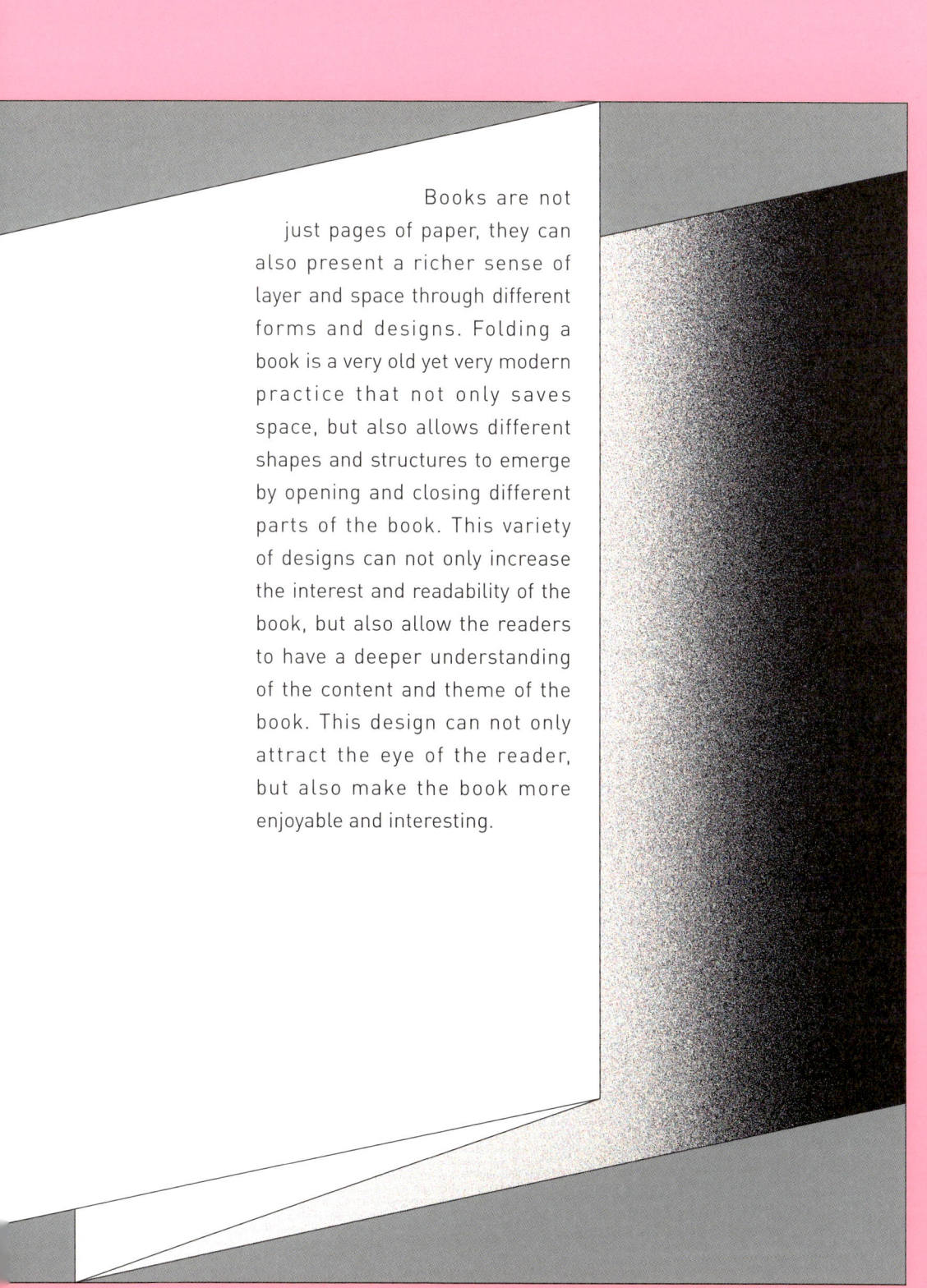

Books are not just pages of paper, they can also present a richer sense of layer and space through different forms and designs. Folding a book is a very old yet very modern practice that not only saves space, but also allows different shapes and structures to emerge by opening and closing different parts of the book. This variety of designs can not only increase the interest and readability of the book, but also allow the readers to have a deeper understanding of the content and theme of the book. This design can not only attract the eye of the reader, but also make the book more enjoyable and interesting.

Designer: United Design Lab.   Language: Chinese   Page: 20

Form of Love

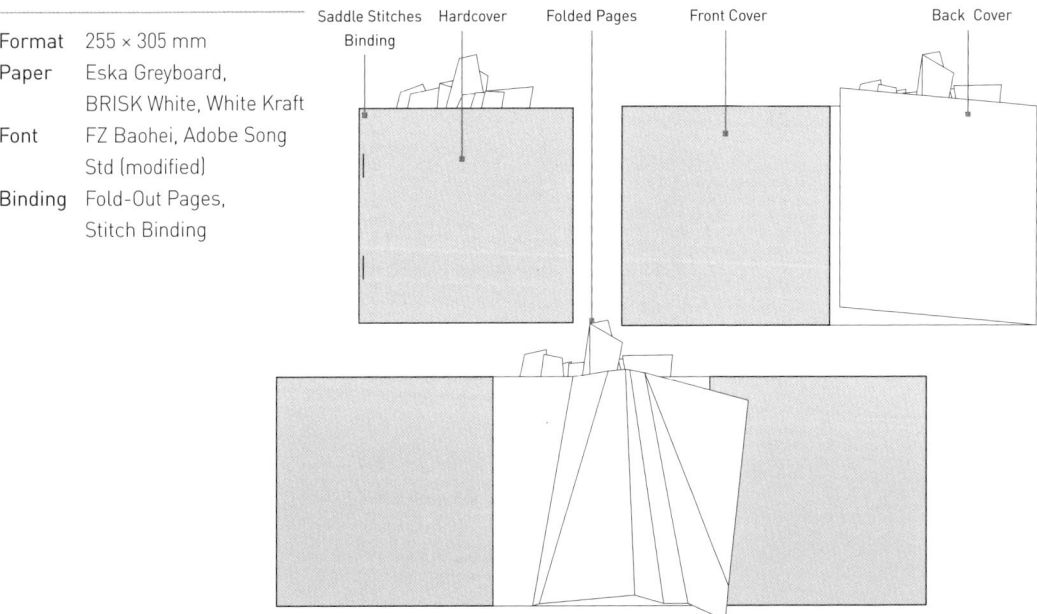

Format	255 × 305 mm
Paper	Eska Greyboard, BRISK White, White Kraft
Font	FZ Baohei, Adobe Song Std (modified)
Binding	Fold-Out Pages, Stitch Binding

"What is love" is a question that gives people a hard time, because there is no such thing as a model answer. There is more than one kind of love, and more than one form of expression to it. Valuing a person is love, and so is cherishing a belonging. The reason why the creative team made this Zine is to give the subject of "what is love" back to the audiences.

○ One of the designers creates the images based on her interpretations of different kinds of love and depicts it on the contour of the character "爱(Love)," and the other designer responds to it based on his understanding of the images and translates it into texts. 10 groups of design represent the 10 strokes of the character "爱(Love)." There are far more forms of love than ten. What they can do is merely capture the fragments and moments of it, and state it out.

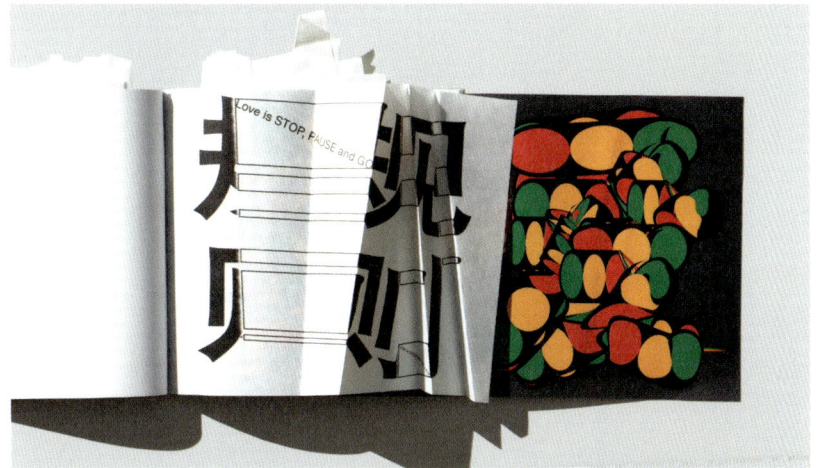

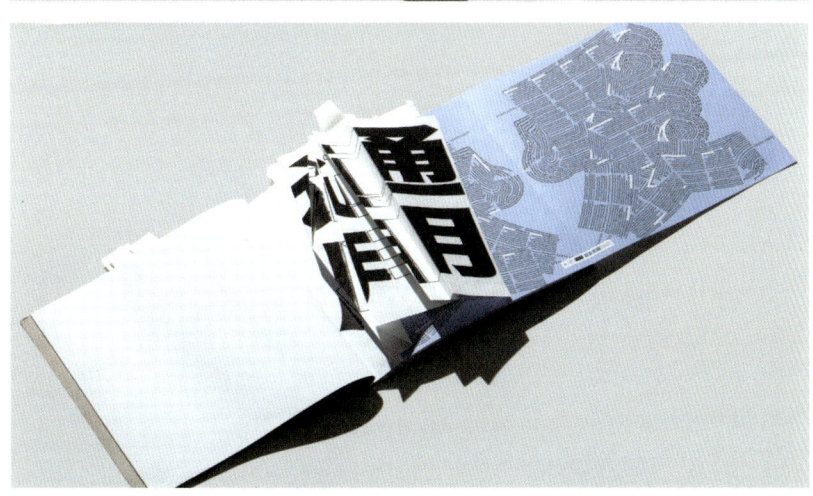

Designer: Belinda Ulrich, Louisa Kirchner, Alessia Oertel   Language: German   Page: 30

Buch der Körper

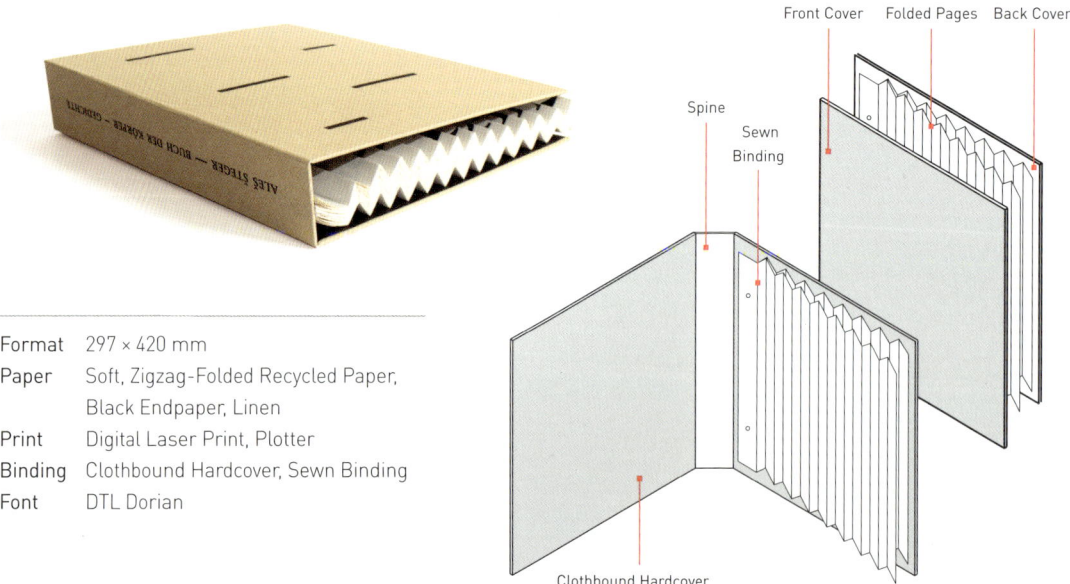

Format	297 × 420 mm
Paper	Soft, Zigzag-Folded Recycled Paper, Black Endpaper, Linen
Print	Digital Laser Print, Plotter
Binding	Clothbound Hardcover, Sewn Binding
Font	DTL Dorian

Buch der Körper emerged from a collaboration with Louisa Kirchner and Belinda Ulrich at Muthesius University of Fine Arts and Design in 2017. It delves into the boundary between functional book design and artistic expression. Extracts from Aleš Šteger's poem "Buch der Körper" fueled their exploration. This poem is a study of the interplay between body and language. Themes of love, pain, confusion, and loneliness are its core.

○ Writing is in the form of short prose, often ending abruptly. They use En-dash and Em-dash to show a change of thought and bridge associative words. Repeated dashes serve as a motif on the cover and across the book. Dashes complement and contrast when applied to folded pages. Designers wanted to give the poem a warm and robust look and chose the Antiqua serif font DTL Dorian, which has a low stroke contrast and long ascenders and descenders. To amplify emotional impact, they chose a zig-zag page folding technique. This approach disrupted the uniform typeface and introduced spatiality. The exterior boasts a classic, solid book cover, juxtaposing the delicate interiors. Use of sand-coloured linen on the cover reminiscent of skin tone. The poem was printed on soft-structured, recycled paper. The book concludes with a black endpaper. Golden book screws hold the book together.

○ The zig-zag folding wasn't arbitrary; it mirrored "Buch der Körper's" emotional depth. The folding amplified emotions, engaging readers in a tactile journey. This structure transformed the book from words to a sensory experience. The rhythm of folding disrupts uniform typography, inviting reflection. It echoed the poem's emotional flow, adding another layer of meaning. The folding is a dance between form and theme. It's our way of breaking conventions to craft an experience that resonates intellectually and sensually.

Designer: Toby Ng Design   Language: English   Client: New World Development Company Limited

The Pavilia Hill

The Pavilia Hill is a luxury bespoke residence in Hong Kong and curated by Cultural Entrepreneur Adrian Cheng under New World Development's project, The Artisanal Movement. The design pays tribute to nature and artisanship. Its interior and landscape designs are all based on Wabi-Sabi, a Japanese aesthetics and worldview centred on the acceptance of transience and imperfection.

Format	200 × 280 × 12 mm
Print	CMYK, Debossing
Font	PlantinStd, SweetSansPro

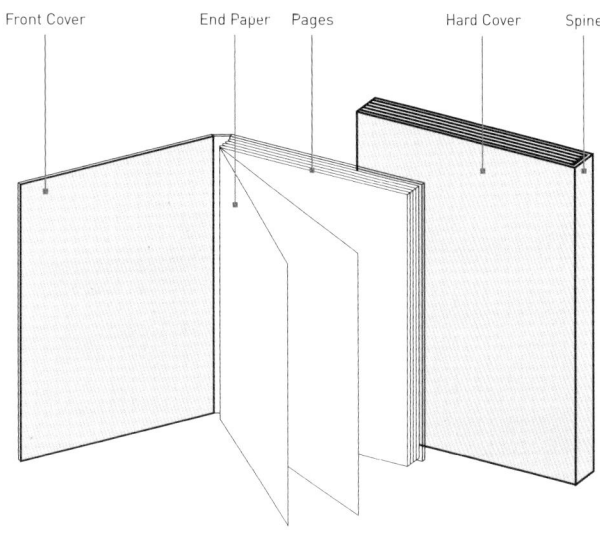

○ Based on the principles of Wabi-Sabi, the designer designed a visceral and texturally rich book to reflect the serenity of the main feature of this residence, the Tranquil Zen Gardens by Japanese Zen priest and landscape architect Shunmyo Masuno. A raw stone texture was chosen for the book's hard-cover, to resemble the special stone sculptures' sublime presence in *The Pavilia Hill*. In addition, by deploying various printing methods in combination with a selection of 10 types of texturally rich fancy paper, the final effect created a striking visual impact and sensual experience for readers of the book.

● Designer: Zephtang Design   Language: Chinese, English   Page: 20

To the River

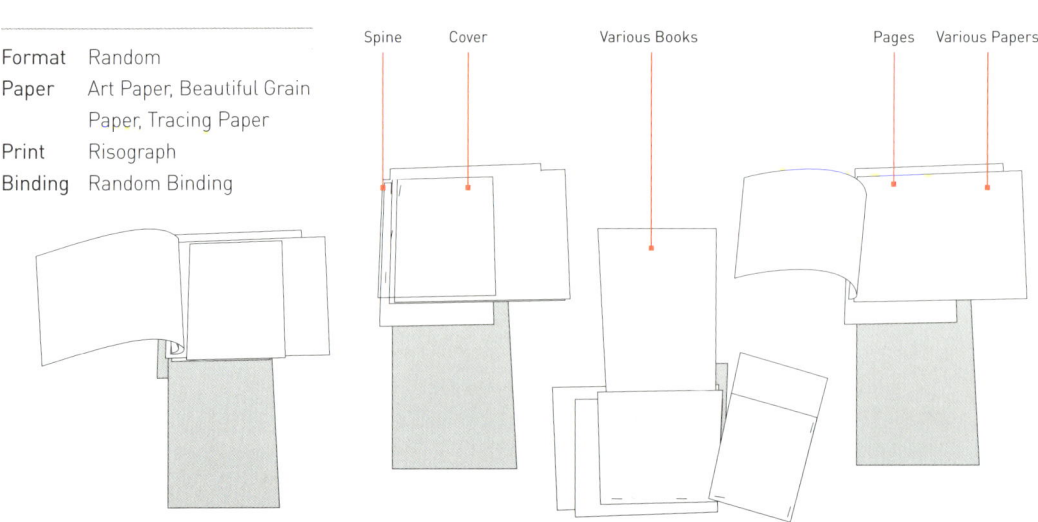

Format	Random
Paper	Art Paper, Beautiful Grain Paper, Tracing Paper
Print	Risograph
Binding	Random Binding

Spine   Cover   Various Books   Pages   Various Papers

This work is designed to introduce typographical errors and typographic rivers, or to make readers realize more quickly that reading rivers isn't actually scary. Readers can learn about the causes and effects of typographical errors and typographic rivers, as well as how to avoid or fix them. The creative team also thought that the piece itself would be an important part of understanding how to typeset *To the River*.

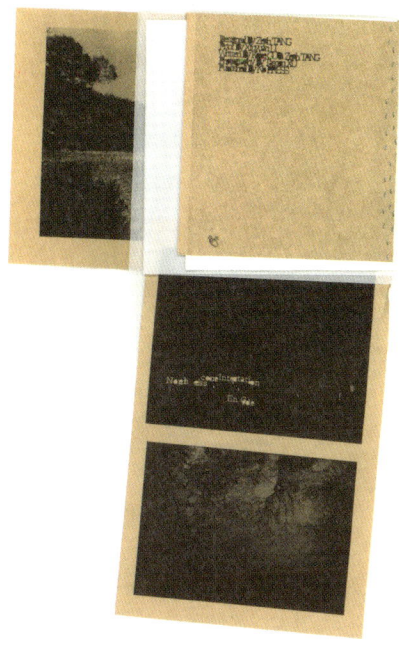

○ In the design, the designers have made extensive use of extreme misprinting and split typography, and these split typographies and misprints make up a different paper presentation, which in the eyes of many designers or printers is substandard, but the creative team wanted this to be accepted correctly by the reader. This is a new topic and possibility that can be explored for the design as well as the printing industry.

○ The creative team tried to use graphic aesthetics to corroborate the relationship between typographical errors and typographic rivers of correctness and incorrectness in the reading process. In terms of graphic design, a large number of experimental graphic elements were used to create more uncertainty and randomness through the RISO printing method, thus presenting a unique visual effect. In terms of fonts, a variety of different styles of fonts are used to create a unique reading experience through typography. Through this series of works, they try to express the endless possibilities and diversity of reading.

Designer: Atelier d'Alves   Language: English   Client: Rampa   Page: 50

A Garden at Night

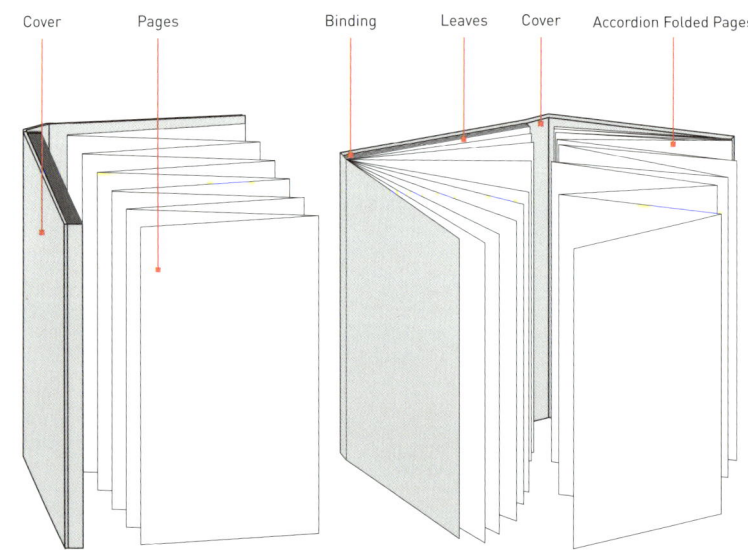

Format	120 × 190 mm
Paper	Munken Print White 115gsm
	Pop Set Black 240 gsm
	Mirror Vinil
Font	Stellage, Stellage Display
Print	Offset Print

A Garden at Night, an art exhibition by the artist Tiago Madaleno, is based upon the story of a garden that Kurt Schwitters (a Dadaism artist) had in its childhood and the tragic event of its destruction. The main objective of the book was to reflects upon some of the exhibition's main topics: the Garden, the life and work of Kurt Schwitters and the concept of "Text Expanded into Space." The book invokes the idea of the wanderer, so familiar to the philosophy behind the English garden, to reenact this dialogue between body and landscape.

○ The book is divided into two paths: one is composed of text, where three authors write about Gardens, Kurt Schwitters and Text Expanded into Space; the other is a mirror accordion folio that plays with reflection, montage and perception. One of the reasons why the designers chose that is connected with the idea of the double and the story of Schwitters and Pierce. The other reason was a play with the concept of landscape and the tensions between formal/informal, order/chaos, composition/wildness.

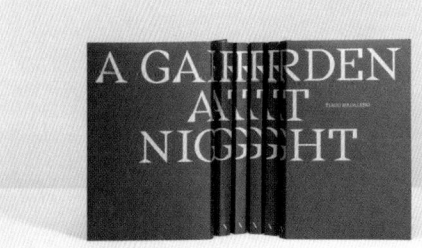

◯ The main idea was to propose an infinite landscape through some kind of provisional picturesque. Using the mirrored surfaces, the book could go against the stability of the panoramic view, so many times associated with the full-length frieze of the folio, and be able to explore the infinite reflection of the painted trees. In that sense, the book invites the reader to compose, even if it is always an unstable composition, forever changing, according to the reader's position and the way the book is displayed in space.

Designer: Robbin Ami Silverberg   Language: German, French and English   Page: 31

Abriss

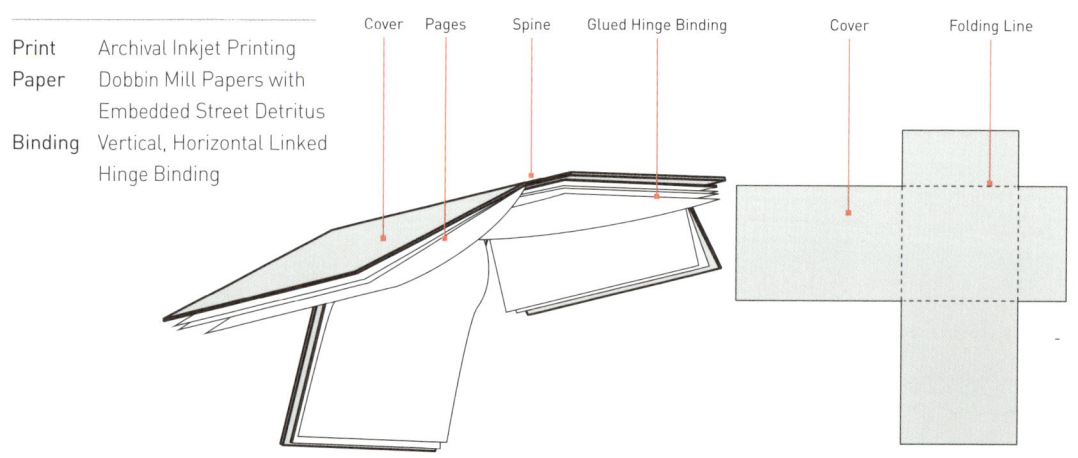

Print	Archival Inkjet Printing
Paper	Dobbin Mill Papers with Embedded Street Detritus
Binding	Vertical, Horizontal Linked Hinge Binding

Abriss (kante) is German for the tear-off edge or stub. *Abriss*, a nonlinear combination of installation, performance, and the book is a result of her ambulatory mapping of New York City. The author calls this practice Anamnesis – which means the opposite of forgetting – or as Socrates determined: What one perceives to be learning is the recovery of what one has forgotten.

○ Since 2009, the author has created hundreds of postings, which she has placed in specific locations around the city. Each copy in the varied edition contains the exact text and images in the same sequence. Still, they differ in materials: to activate the substrate, each page contains paper detritus that she collected on an earlier walk and then incorporated into the paper she made at Dobbin Mill, either as inclusions or actual pulp. These postings engage the viewer in a discourse on the psycho-geography of place and memory. The glued linked hinge binding allowed her to use single sheet pages while both vertical & horizontal pages/flyers lay flat. The book structure closed is el-shaped.

Designer: Robbin Ami Silverberg Language: English Page: 34

Memory Walk

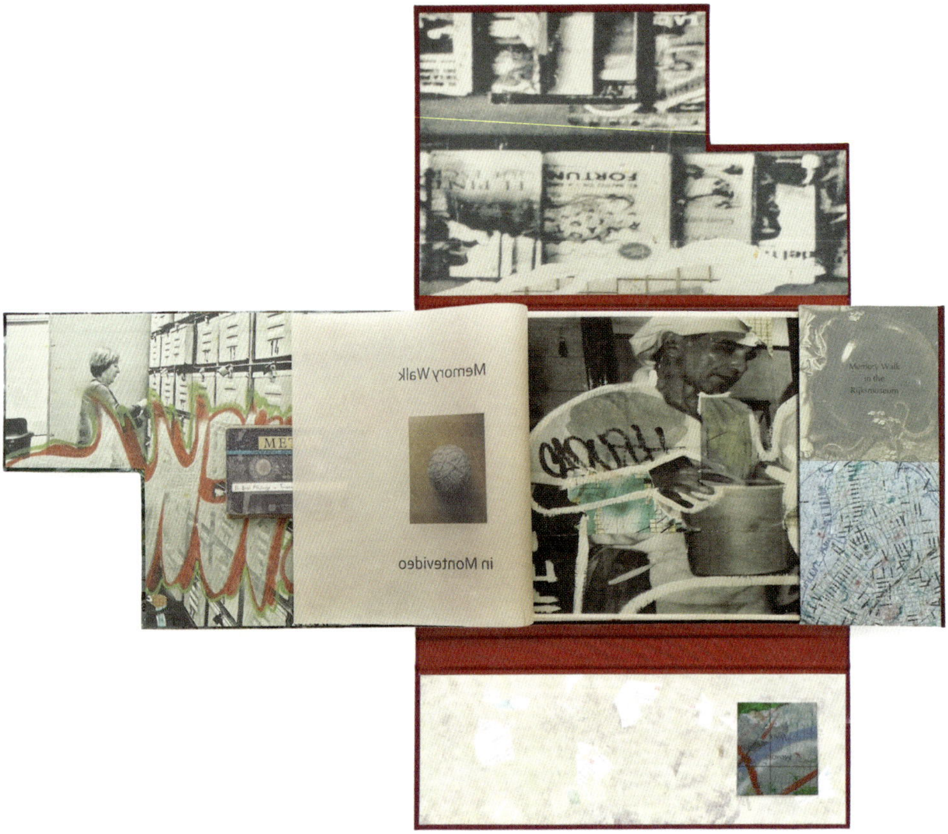

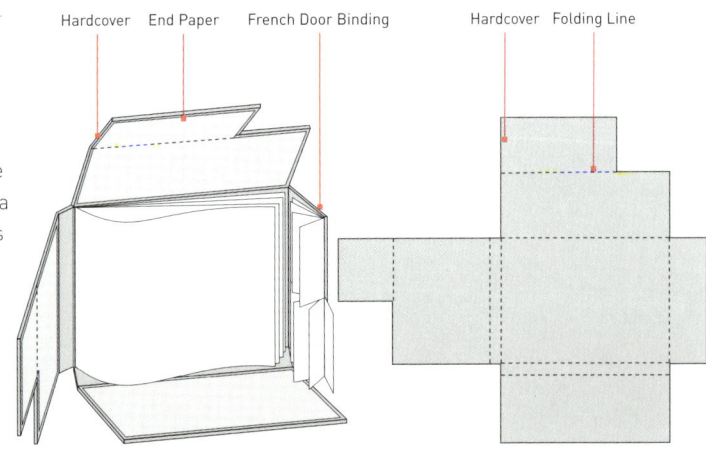

Print	Archival Inkjet Printing
Paper	Dobbin Mill Papers, Cotton rag Paper and Abaca Papers with Embedded Map Pieces
Binding	French Doors Binding with One Side a Stab Binding, the Other a Pamphlet with Throwout Pages
PS	14 Pages for Stab Binding, 20 Pages for Pamphlet

The memory palace is an ancient mnemonic device that works with architectural space in one's mind. This book presents three different memory palaces designed as walks: the streets of Montevideo, Uruguay, the designer's home & studio in Brooklyn, and galleries of the Rijksmuseum in Amsterdam.

○ As such, spatial and temporal memory converges in this French Door structure, consisting of a stab binding of layered translucent papers on the left and a pamphlet with throw-out pages on the right. The designer repurposed a set of her handmade papers that had been painted using two robots (Artbots built by Käthe Wenzel, Berlin) for another project. She added painted lines of movement that indicate the travel from one object to another. Finally, each edition copy has a different embedded tape recording of music. The images, the objects, and locations all function as visual poetry ... and the movement through spaces & pages of the book creates a dialogue and poetic logic for the reader to enjoy.

○ Designing a structure that could follow a range of possible forms of reading was a challenge in this book. Portions needed to have layers, to suggest the act of remembering, while others, foldout pages that changed the text or image layout, just as the sequence of ideas changes thoughts as they develop. In addition, the designer wanted papers that had different sounds as the pages turned.

Designer: Esra Melody Butcher   Language: English   Page: 160

Lord of the Flies - Special Edition

Format	Cover	Panels 90 × 180 mm (Full length 560 × 180 mm) Leaves	105 × 148 mm (A6)
Paper	Recycled Paper
Font	Akzidenz Grotesk, DTL Documenta, Bitstream Vera Sans
Binding	Accordion Binding

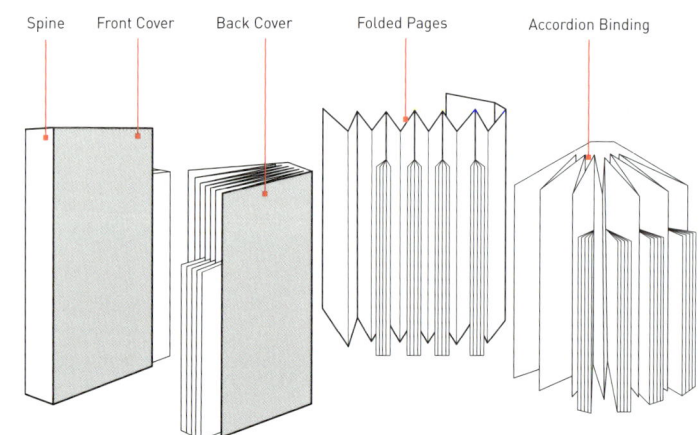

This special edition book has designed for the sixtieth anniversary of the novel *Lord of the Flies* by William Golding. The novel in 1954 tells the story of a group of young boys stuck in an inhabited island after a tragic plane crash. In time, they try to govern themselves by establishing rules and a system to maintain order. Since they were running from war, catastrophic events led them to believe there might not be any adults who survived. As a result, the struggle of building a mini civilization with no adult supervision leads to violence and brutal acts.

○ Being stranded on an island and the internal conflict of characters was the designer's main inspiration. To convey this, she wanted to take a very manual approach, therefore distorted text and images using a scanner. The book was designed to look like an island, and the chapters which were printed on a smaller format page represents the youth of the boys. Chapters are separated by panels created by folding the cover; as the cover of the book stretches out, each panel has an image taken from the black and white film directed by Peter Brook, based on the same novel. The distortion of the images and the texts cue the boys' corruption; while each chapter and its panel represents the boys, isolated from each other with their ideas, but somehow still stuck to each other, on this one big island, which is the body of this book.

Designer: Ivy Chen   Language: Chinese, English   Page: 52

A Room of One's Own

By redesigning the first and last chapters of Woolf's book, we explore how typography affects the narrative experience. While conveying Woolf's vibrant language and brilliant metaphors, the designer wanted to create an atmosphere of "private conversation," using the physicality of the book to create a conceptual space for interpreting the notion of "freedom of mind" mentioned in the book. In this project, both Chinese and English typography are used in an attempt to establish a harmonious parallel typographic system.

Paper	Cover	Summerset Texture White 300 gsm
	Inner Page	Unknown 100 gsm
Font	Spectral Regular, Basic Sans
	ExtraLightHelloFont, DianFangSong Bold,
	FZFangSong Regular , Baskerville Regular
Binding	Singer Sewn Binding
PS	The Chinese and English versions are bound in left and right folios separately. Each chapter is in a separate volume, 28 pages for Chapter 1, 24 pages for Chapter 6.

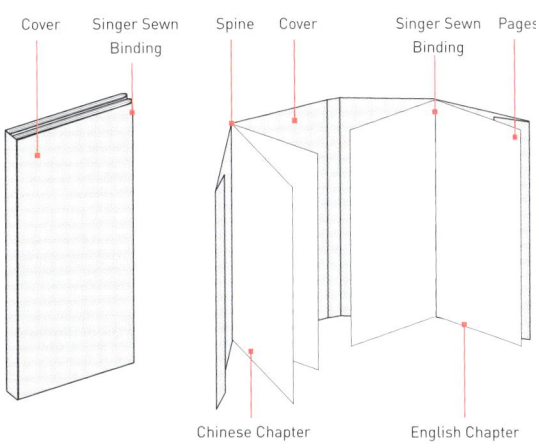

○ The designer's original intention was to design a book that is easy to carry and easy to read for young readers, like a small room to carry around. For the interior page layout, based on the shape of the long vertical strips, the designer chose to tuck the footnote part directly inside the text as a pause and rhythm, so that readers can avoid feeling bored by reading the lengthy paragraphs consecutively.

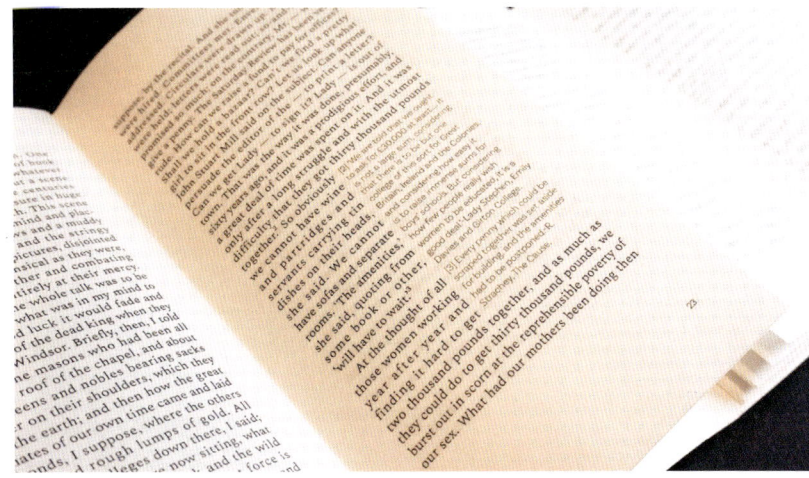

Designer: Ana Leite, Eduarda Fernandes, Luana Barbosa, Thiago Liberdade
Language: Portuguese   Page: 144

Nostalgia Is a Magic Eraser for Atrocious Truths

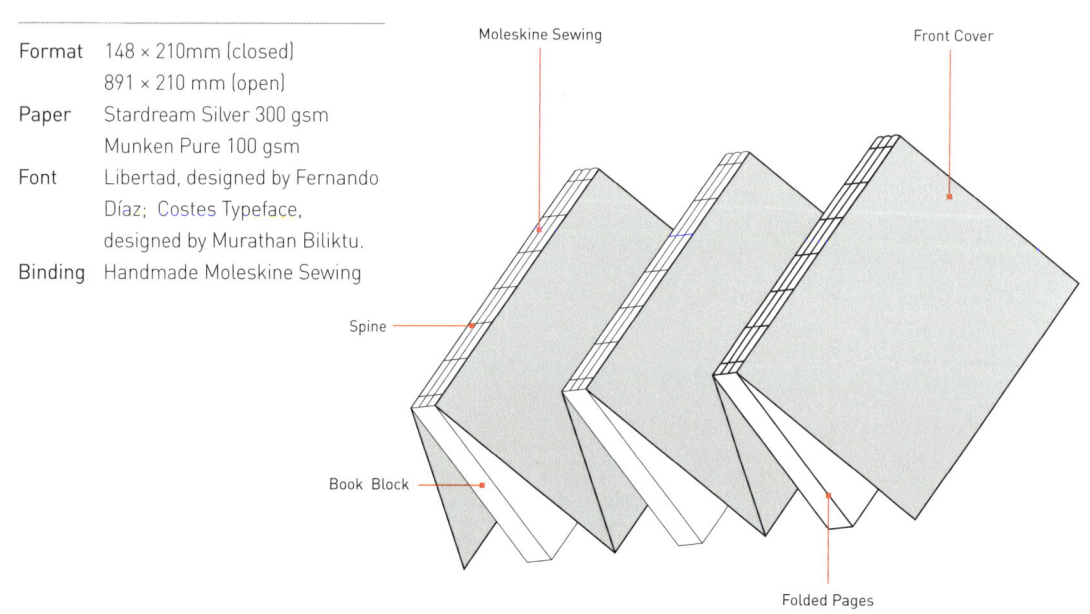

Format	148 × 210mm (closed)
	891 × 210 mm (open)
Paper	Stardream Silver 300 gsm
	Munken Pure 100 gsm
Font	Libertad, designed by Fernando Díaz; Costes Typeface, designed by Murathan Biliktu.
Binding	Handmade Moleskine Sewing

The mythical space that was the nightclub Frágil at Bairro Alto, Lisbon (PT), which had its heyday in the '80s and '90s saw many of those who became Portuguese rock stars, artists, and actors pass by. Frágil became a community, a space for sharing and trust. In the context of the pandemic, with the closing of these spaces, there was an urge to go back to the past and remember the crazy parties. This photobook arises from revisiting the past through texts and images made available by Frágil in an online photographic collection. This photobook is composed of 3 books, one for each past decade.

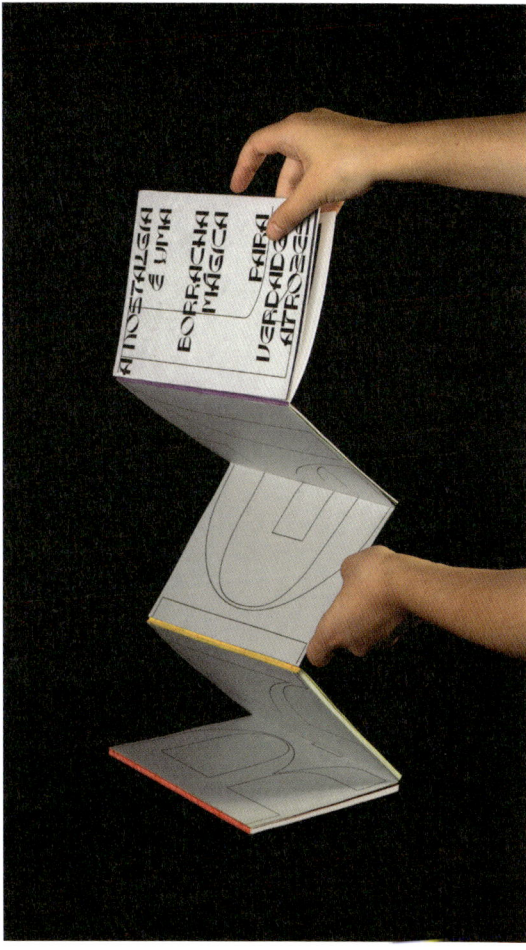

Designer: The Third Studio   Language: Spanish, English   Client: Francisco Ramirez   Page: 148

Ojos Que No Ven

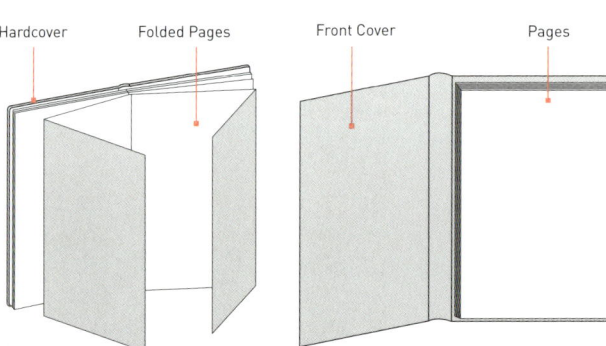

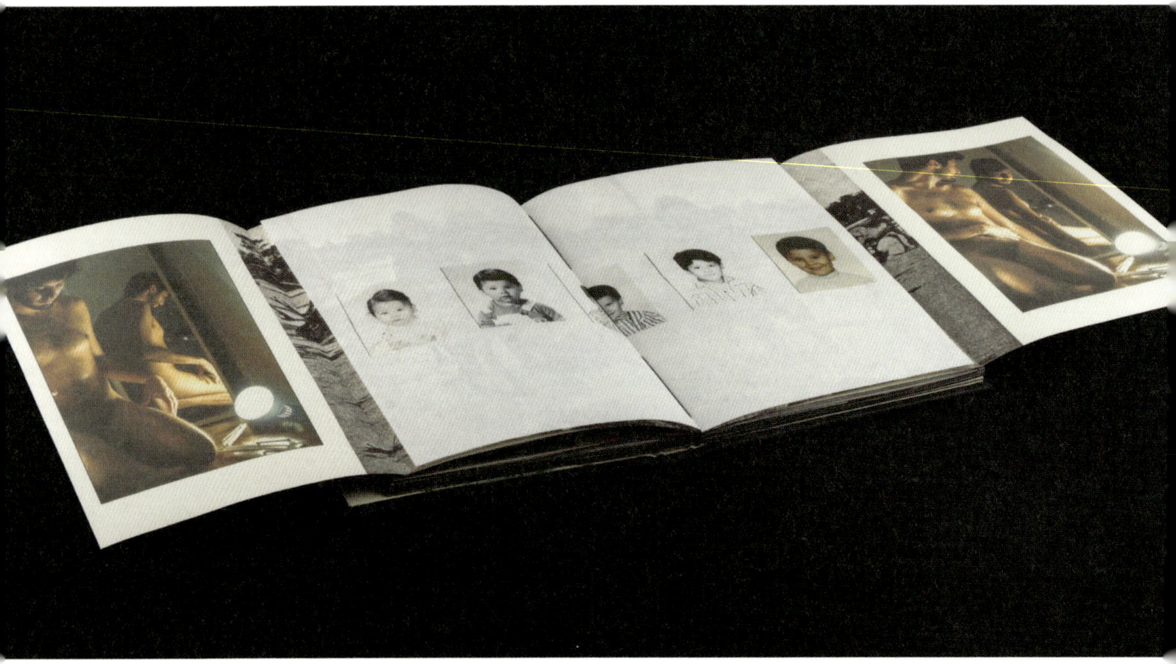

Format : 250 × 210 mm
Paper : Mantequilla 90gms, Superfine, Softwhite 118gms, Feltmark Ivory 216, Antique Vellum Black
Font : Alegreya

The title is taken from the saying "ojos que no ven, corazón que no siente," meaning that what you don't know can't hurt you, or basically out of sight out of mind. Using their personal experience as a microcosm to exemplify the issues around themes of sex, violence, and gender. The book exposes that these issues have been willingly ignored by society at large but turning a blind eye on these problems only causes more hurt.

○ The project started from the concept of "obscene" what is out of the scene, what cannot be seen. for this reason the book is a black object, the cover is printed with UV ink on black paper, which invites the reader to use a light source to see the cover. It is for this very reason that the edges of the book are also painted black. A binding was decided that would allow an opening of 180 degrees so as not to interrupt the reading of the photographs. One of the most important characteristics of the project is that the reader has to break some pages to access the written testimonials of the author, something that tries to emulate the emotion the author experienced and that works as an example of how not only with the texts and images stories can be told; the materials, the design, even the binding serve to reinforce a narrative.

Designer: Ivy Chen   Language: English   Client: Individual project   Page: 12

The Hole

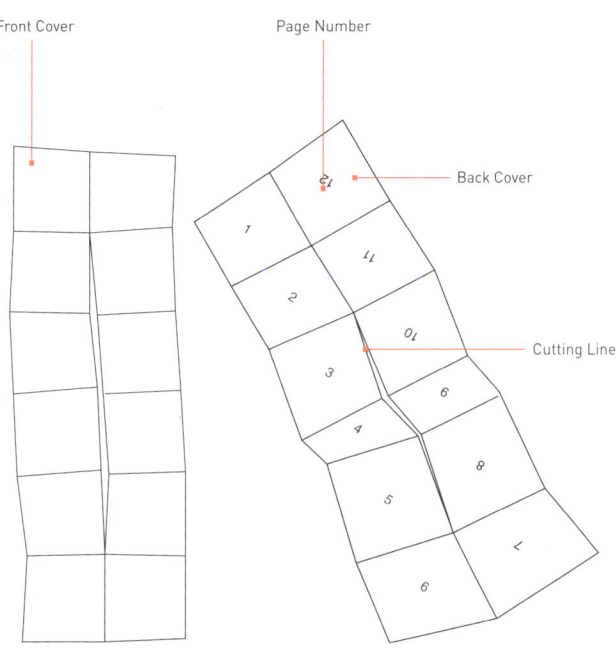

Front Cover
Page Number
Back Cover
Cutting Line

Print   Digital Printing
Paper   Recycled Paper 80 gsm
Font   Basic Sans
Binding Cutting, Folding

If a hole suddenly appeared in the ground, would you throw in a stone? Based on Shinichi Hoshi's short science fiction story "Hey - Out," the designer planned an interactive exhibition on environmental protection themes for children and designed for exhibition. Children can learn about the that playfully. This publication is an instruction for the event, the designer wanted it to be structurally simple and less expensive to produce, she came up with the idea of a booklet that can be done with a paper. Meanwhile, this booklet which folds up into a square can be read from different angles, which is interesting as well.

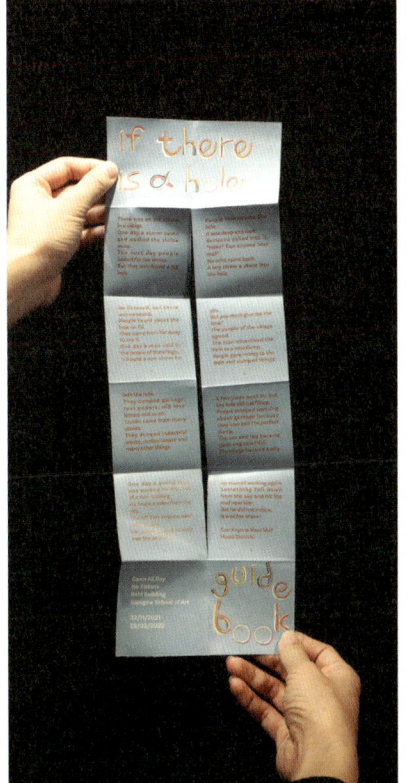

● Designer: Wuthipol Ujathammarat   Language: English

Lollipop Utopia

Format	148 × 105 mm
Paper	Wove 120 gsm
Binding	Hand Folds (handmade)
Print	Risograph

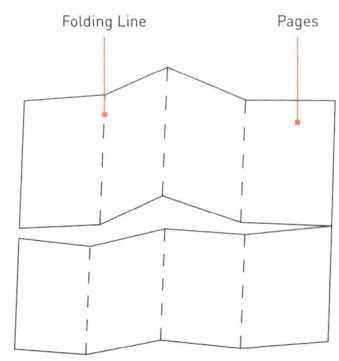

Folding Line   Pages

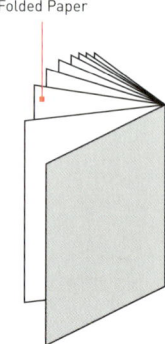

Folded Paper

Lollipop Utopia is a reflective response to his previous publications, *Day Mundane* (2017) and *Popsicle District* (2020), that offer a peculiar and yet unique perspective of Singapore, a foreign city the author grew to love. It documents a saturated aesthetic of the urban landscape, where his visual interpretation of Singapore expands beyond reality through "risograph"—a printing technique known for its vivid palettes. The outcome is so ridiculous that it creates an illusion of a polychromatic lollipop utopia.

○ Through graphical composition, he chooses to highlight the unexplored details and aspects in which the urban structures, textures, and colours collectively complement each other. This minimalist vision also brings together a metaphorical perception of a lollipop utopia where vivid aesthetics are uncovered by eliminating the noticeable details, typically associated with Singapore.

Designer: Wuthipol Ujathammarat   Language: English

Made Obscure: The Visual Maze

Print   Digital Printing
Format   74 × 105 mm
Paper   Eggshell 120 gsm
Binding Hand Folds

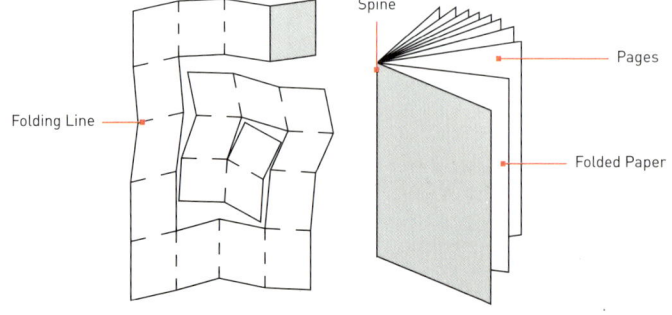

Stumbled, stared and startled. The designer wondered if these walls could talk. The unanswered visual interpretation of these coloured walls in a Bangkok district of Samphanthawong, commonly known as Chinatown, curiously dazzles his endless imagination. This book unveils a puzzling visual adventure that playfully illuminates the obscureness of exterior palettes in Chinatown, where a rare perspective is only offered to those who observe. A palette within its urban vernacular can be glimpsed as an artform, linking the "lost and found" aesthetic to form a visual interpretation of Chinatown.

○ Through a frisky photography experience, this artistic papercraft conceptually reenacts a sense of wayfinding; whereby the pages fold out and about like a maze map. It also correlates with the concertina design of the zine, reflecting on how streets and alleyways in Chinatown are tangled and branched off into various directions like a labyrinth. You are encouraged to fondle with the obscure folds, zig and zag through the visual sequence, and ask the question: could the palettes seen in Samphanthawong be a reflective notion of its Chinese heritage and flavourful culture?

● Designer: Clip Zero   Language: Chinese, English   Client: Individual project   Page: 12

Kamikakushi Spring Zine

Font Cover

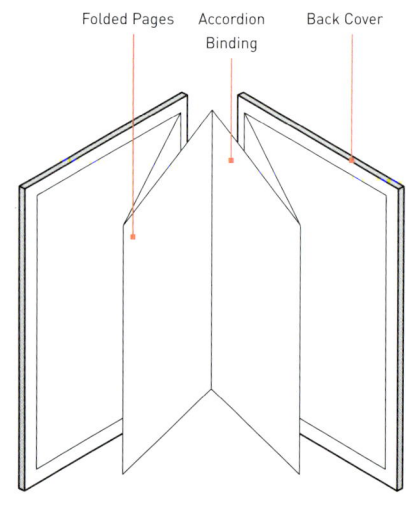
Folded Pages   Accordion Binding   Back Cover

Format   148 × 210 mm
Paper   G . F Smith Parch Marque
Binding Accordion Binding
Font   Original Handwriting Typeface
Print   Risograph

This zine is an extension of the designer's personal project, the *Kamikakushi Museum*. Based on the concepts of nature, mystery, and magic, she sought inspiration from some extinct plants to create a magical botanical illustrated book that fits the setting of *Kamikakushi Museum*.

○ Initially, she used handmade prints for engraving and printing to obtain the clumsy and random texture that characterizes handmade products. This was followed by a second printing using RISO, a vintage printing method with bright inks, and finally the book was bound using Accordion Binding which allows for a continuous presentation of the images and conveys an ancient, handmade texture, close to nature, and different from the conventional reading atmosphere of the book. Accordion Binding is an ancient Chinese binding method used for Buddhist books, and it adds a part of the occult visual impression to this book-binding. It helps to build up the reading atmosphere in the setting of the magical botanical illustrated book.

Designer: Linlin Yin   Language: Chinese   Client: Chinese Worker Publishing House   Page: 672

Life in the Beijing Opera

This is a book that introduces Peking Opera in the form of each play accompanied by an article and a picture. The structure of the book is designed in the hope that when the reader opens the book, it is like opening a curtain to the art of Peking Opera. *A Letter to the Reader* is a letter from Mr. Yu Kuizhi, a Peking Opera actor, to the readers, and also an invitation. The reader receives a ticket to the theater, where he or she can enter the "theater" and begin to "see the play".

Format   152 × 238 mm
Paper   Drizzle Paper 60 gsm
         Mechine-made Chinese Art Paper
         (xuan paper) 60 gsm
Font   Hanyi Xuansong
Binding Looped With String,
         Thermoplastic Binding
Print   CMYK, Spot-Color Printing

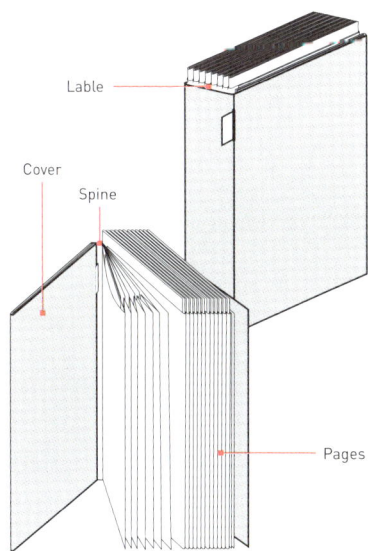

○ The content is designed as the curtain of a Peking Opera stage, the curtain is drawn to reveal the play, and behind the curtain, the characters of several major roles, including Sheng, Dan, Jing and Chou, appear one-by-one. The color of the book is designed according to the date red curtain, light green two curtains and light yellow three curtains of the Peking Opera stage, so as to bring out the atmosphere of the stage. Each play is relatively independent, and the reading unfolds and advances step by step from the title of the play, the name of the play, the type of the play, the commentary on the play the role of the play, the miscellaneous play, and the lines of the play. The paintings of the play are created in the style of Chinese painting in a pictorial style. After each play, there will be a space for a break between acts. Here readers are free to choose to enter any one of the plays, and each play is a wonderful story.

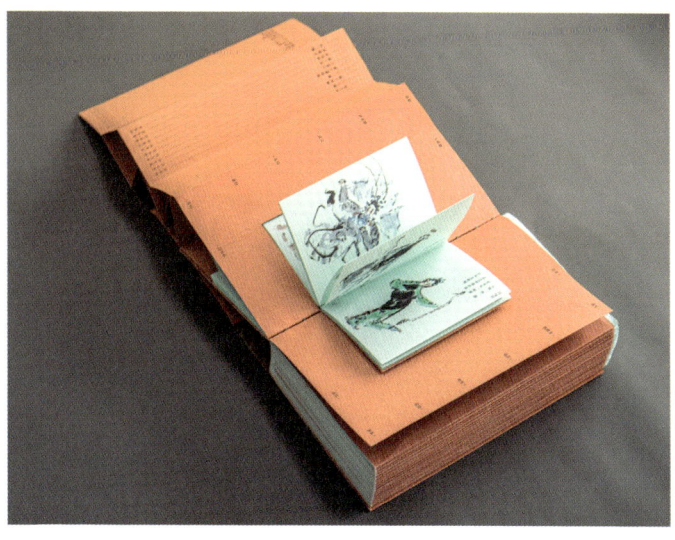

● Designer: for&st studio   Language: Chinese, English   Client: Sim SHUM Kwan-Yi   Page: 14

The Unbearable Lightness

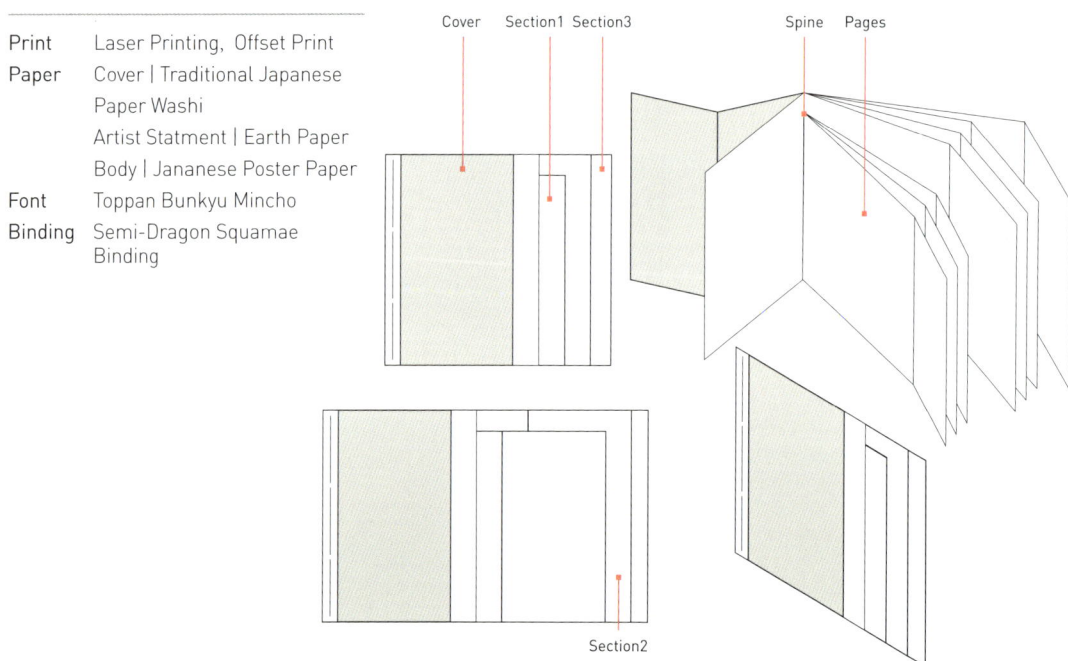

Print — Laser Printing, Offset Print
Paper — Cover | Traditional Japanese Paper Washi
Artist Statment | Earth Paper
Body | Jananese Poster Paper
Font — Toppan Bunkyu Mincho
Binding — Semi-Dragon Squamae Binding

"The unbearable lightness, and all the unmentionable truth" is the artist's exhibition. It is joined by three sections of different sizes, reflecting the three milestones of the exhibition, "The Floating Life", "The Secret Texts" and "The Inhabitant Islets," the description of each work is printed on the flip side on a semi-transparent paper, the audience could only see part of the content on the front side as if it is hidden, but the truth will still be revealed when you are willing to flip over, to discover.

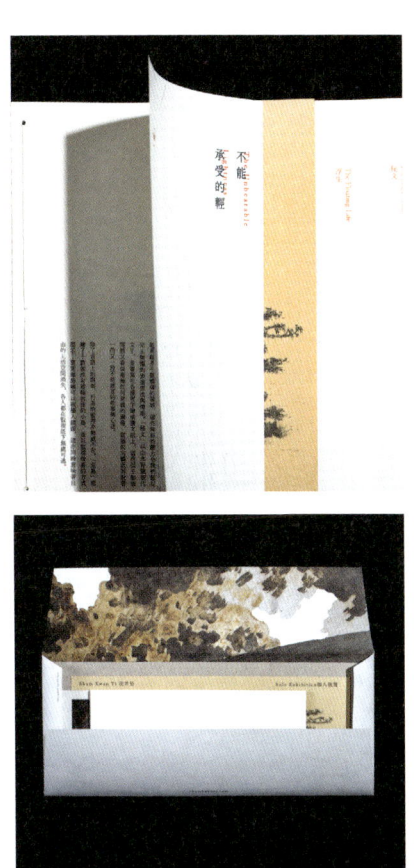

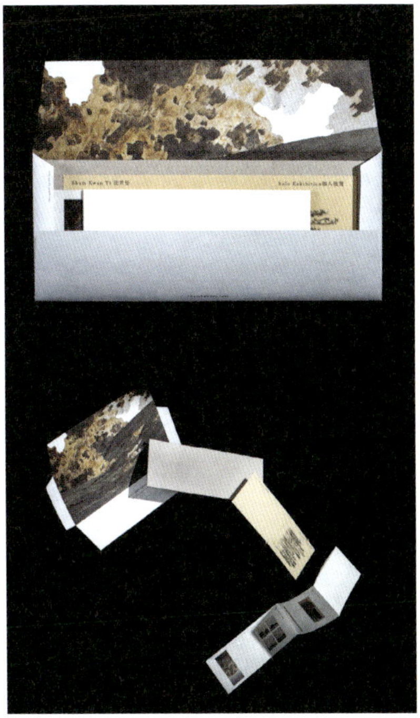

○ The book is binding with Semi-Dragon Scale Binding, with each section in different sizes and being folded, it requires audience interaction to reveal the content and also to provide a memorable reading experience. The structure is an echo of the artist's solo exhibition, which is divided into 3 parts, and the cold message of the exhibition "the unbearable lightness," is an emotional status that requires a subtle and sedimental atmosphere to channel the inner message behind each artwork. To execute that subtility, they think of a "hide and seek" concept, to fold the pages and print the works on a semi-transparent paper, as if you know something happened in a very subtle way, to trigger the audience to act and to know more about the story.

● Designer: Zephtang Design   Language: Chinese, French   Client: Scribble a day   Page: 50

Ambiguous Book

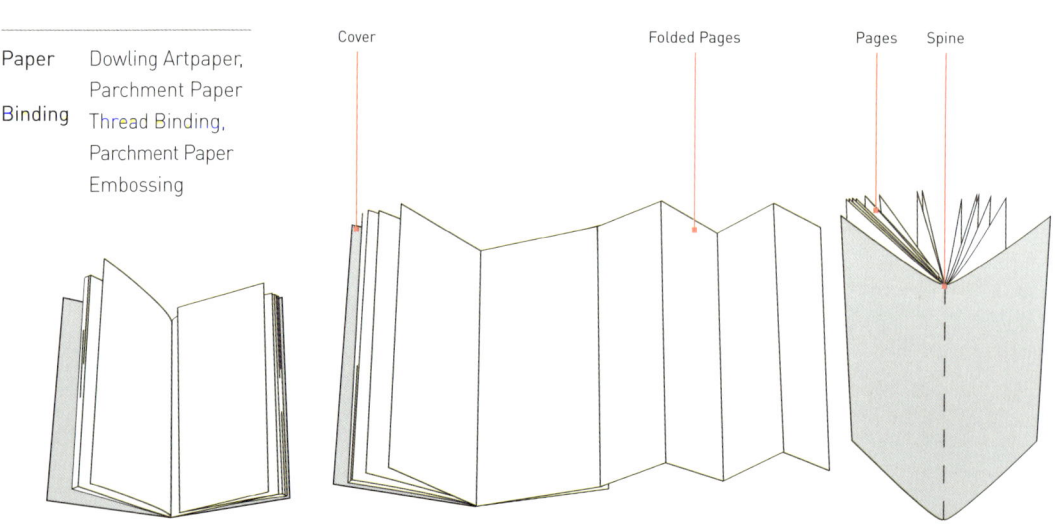

Paper   Dowling Artpaper,
        Parchment Paper
Binding Thread Binding,
        Parchment Paper
        Embossing

Cover   Folded Pages   Pages   Spine

When people receive a printed work, they usually expect to be able to read it easily and enjoyably. But *For a Group of Strange Readers* breaks with this traditional convention. It is a book design with unique text from the team on *Scribble a Day*, which contains a lot of sharp, unfriendly, and even obscure texts. The incomprehensible text was redesigned to give it more meaning, and with it a new reading experience that blurs the boundaries of design and understanding.

○ They use a lot of print marks and inks in their design, which expresses the deep impact of these words on the reader. Their design aims to make the reader not just enjoy the content of the book, but think deeply about it and even be affected by the words. The black inkjet mouth of the book emphasizes the uncertainty and "invasiveness" of the book by allowing the ink to penetrate the page. This design choice emphasizes the connotations that the author wants to convey, expressing an undefined and mysterious meaning.

○ The expressive power of the book is further enhanced by the numerous print marks and inks on the pages, a book design that aims to break traditional reading habits and lead the reader to think deeply and experience the deeper meaning behind the words. A unique reading experience will be gained, perhaps even influenced by the text. Elements such as typography, printing marks, and the use of ink will work together to create a deep, mysterious, and memorable reading environment.

● Designer: Idealform Co.   Language: Traditional Chinese, English   Client: Taipei Fine Arts Museum
Page: 220

Art Histories of a Forever War: Modernism between Space and Home

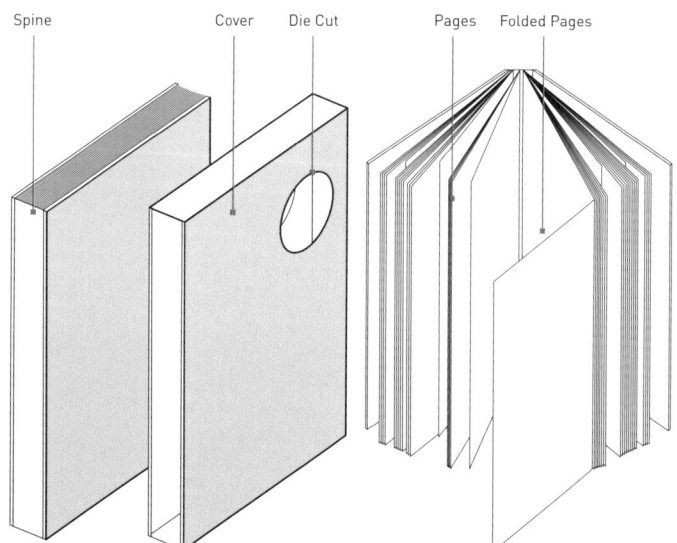

Format	190 × 260 mm
Paper	Japanese Book Paper, Venus V-Lite-Silk, Black Paper
Font	Bliss pro, Capitolina, Mbitmap Square HK, MkaiHK, VDL-YotaG M, Presicav, Wending B5 Pro MD
Binding	Exposed Spine Case Bound, Box

The exhibition is an exploration of modern art in post-war Taiwan and the enduring resonances of this historical milieu, which crystalised modern art through a series of artistic breakthroughs and debates. Three intertwined themes,"Cosmotechnicis After the Space Race," "Global Domestic," and "Aesthetic Networks of A Free World", analyze the complexity of the historical atmosphere at that time.

○ The book design reform artist Wang Dahong's work *Moon Gate*. The representative work fusion Chinese and Western modernism, bringing out the imagination of cosmic space consciousness. The inner pages are designed in two ways, Chinese and English. In order to restore the exhibition venue and bring the intertextual dialogue between the East and West, modern and contemporary.

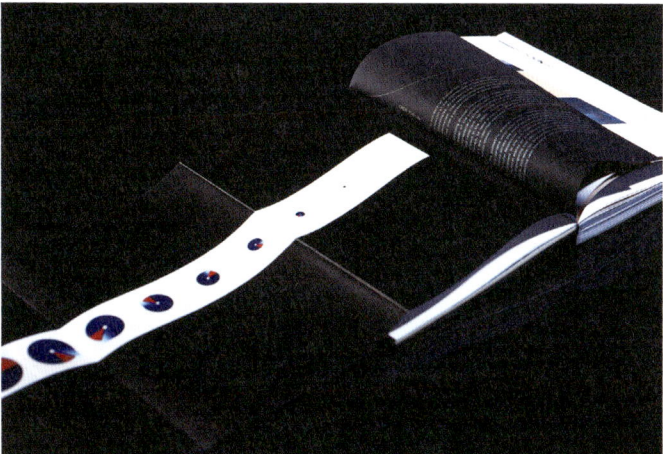

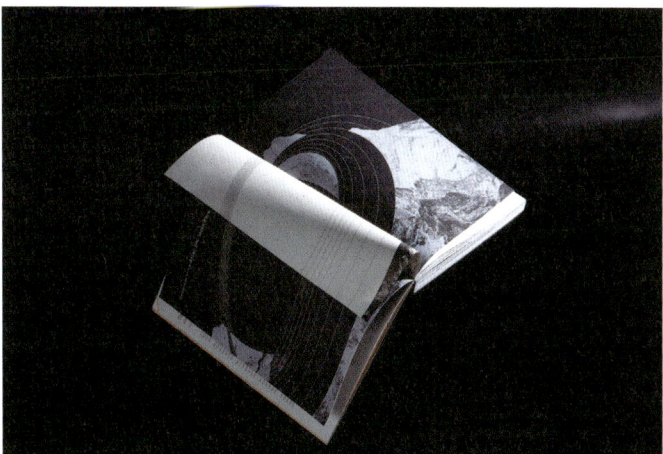

CUT

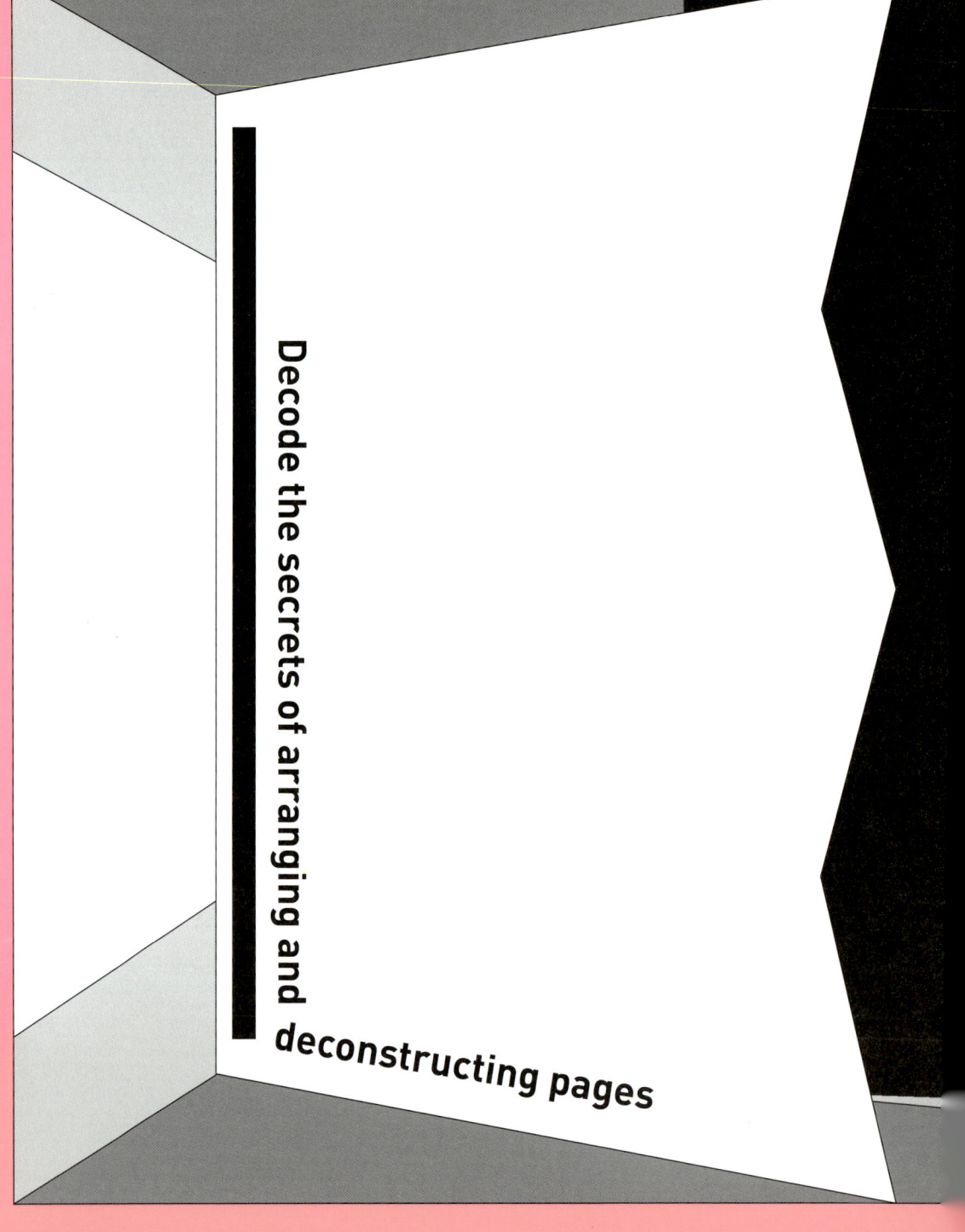

Decode the secrets of arranging and deconstructing pages

Tear or cut, it seems to be the destruction of the book, but it adds a bit of a different charm. Sometimes books become worn out by time and people, or by a particular design idea. However, this disruption is not always negative. In some cases, this destruction can bring a unique flavor to the book, making the book more personal and unique. Some artists and designers may destroy books to create new art forms and design styles. They may remove or tear out parts of the book, but they bring new life and flavor to the book. This destruction is not necessarily negative, but to a certain extent adds new value to the book.

Designer: Thijs Verbeek   Language: English   Client: Atelier Yuri Veerman   Page: 404

Book Burnings: An Anthology

Format	135 × 175 mm
Paper	Inside | Arcoprint 80 gsm
	Cover | Cocoon Offset 250 gsm
Font	Swift

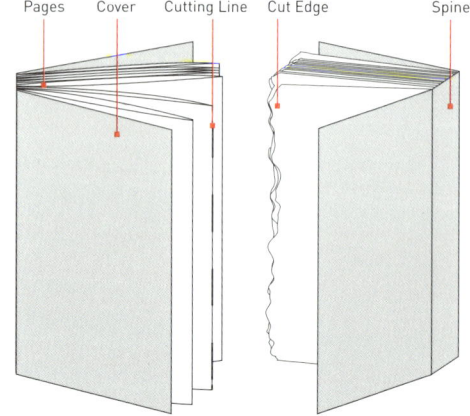

The project *Book Burnings: an Anthology* consists of a performance and book with leaflet. The project looks into the idea of a dangerous text, and why various regimes or groups of people find such a text dangerous enough to ban it or burn it. The book holds a collection of fragments from books that have been burnt or banned; the performance consists of reading the fragments around a campfire.

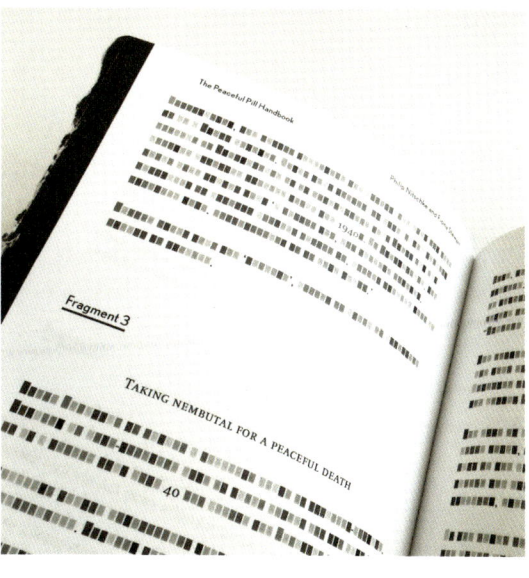

○ The publication, printed entirely in black and white, consists of 404 pages containing fragments from 20 books that have at one time or another either been forbidden or burnt somewhere. Books such as: *The Anarchist Cookbook*, *Alice in Wonderland*, *Mein Kampf*, *American Psycho*, and *Harry Potter*. The book pages have Japanese folding: each fragment is printed in coded form on the outside of the folded pages. For this purpose the designer created a typeface, built up out of squares. Starting with a very light grey "A" the letters gradually increase in intensity. Culminating in a black "Z," they form 26 shades of ash grey. After tearing open the Japanese folds a legible version of the text appears.

Designer: Linlin Yin   Language: Chinese   Client: Chemical Industry Press   Page: 432

The Blind and the Deaf

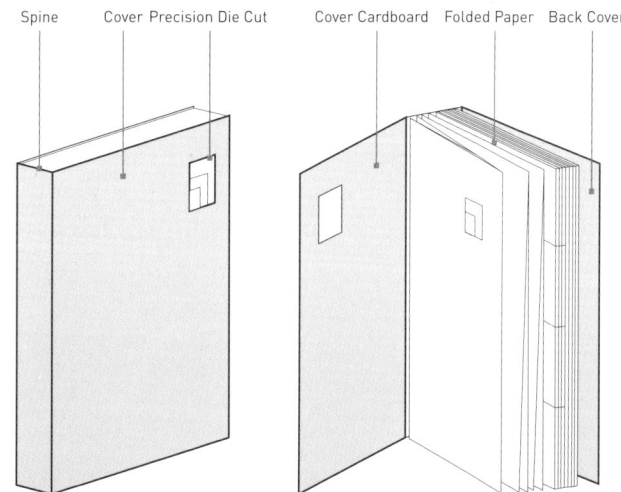

Format	133.5 x 209.5 mm
Paper	Recycled Paper 70 gsm
Print	Four-color printing
Font	Hanyi Xuan Song

Spine   Cover Precision Die Cut   Cover Cardboard   Folded Paper   Back Cover

This book documents the poetry, prose, children's stories, and photographs written by the violinist Shi Yang between his 7 to 19. The overall design is divided into two clues: looking from the outside in and looking from the inside out. The cascading effect of the cover is a passageway that takes us into Shi Yang's world from the outside, and a mirror that serves as a locus of Shi Yang's realization of his self-worth aim constant scrutiny.

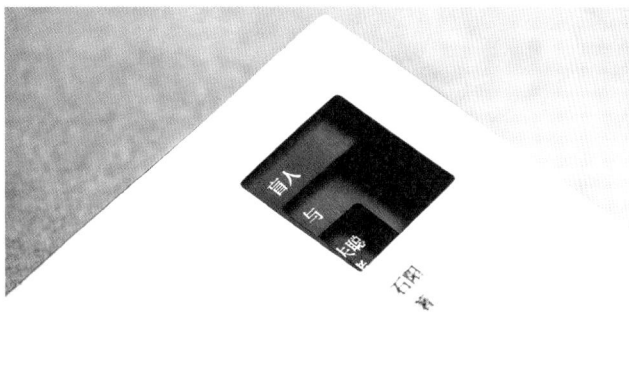

◯ The inner text is printed on recycled paper with good masking. The inner and outer layers and the two clues are like two parallel time and space, not interfering with each other if they don't cross each other, but they do exist at the same time. After losing one part, the expression of the other part will be purer and fuller.

◯ Inside, the upper cutouts of the two adjacent pages are not cut away, creating two spaces inside and outside. Outside is white, used for printing text, once the text is read out, it becomes the art of passing time; the inner hidden space is black, used for printing images, which has a three-dimensional sense and different visual effects caused by the distortion of space. Wrapping the image with words, behind the calmness is a dark surge of bureaucracy. The pages of the short poems are cut apart, so that the text, which was originally cured within the page, is free from the constraints of the main page and becomes free and dynamic. Shi Yang's struggle between tradition and modernity during his artistic growth, the contradictions and conflicts, and the compassion in his poems are released through the cutting of the pages.

Designer: Yujian Huang   Language: English, Japanese   Client: A friend   Page: 20

Shadowscapes Aaron Photo Album

In modern times, we can make photos have different atmospheres through lens filters and software color adjustments. Then, the designer wonders if it is possible to make filters reflected in physical books.

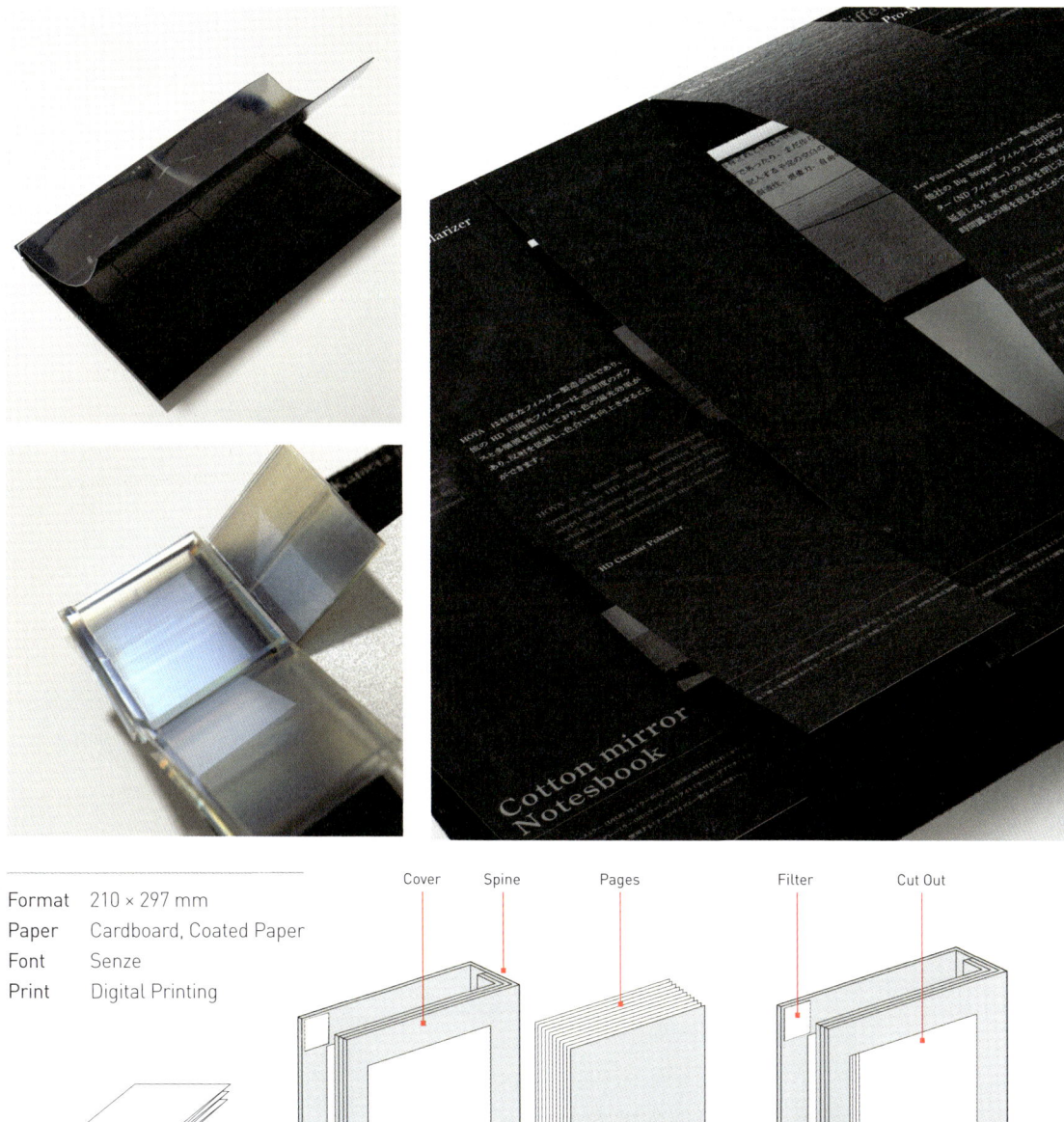

Format   210 × 297 mm
Paper   Cardboard, Coated Paper
Font   Senze
Print   Digital Printing

Cover · Spine · Pages · Filter · Cut Out

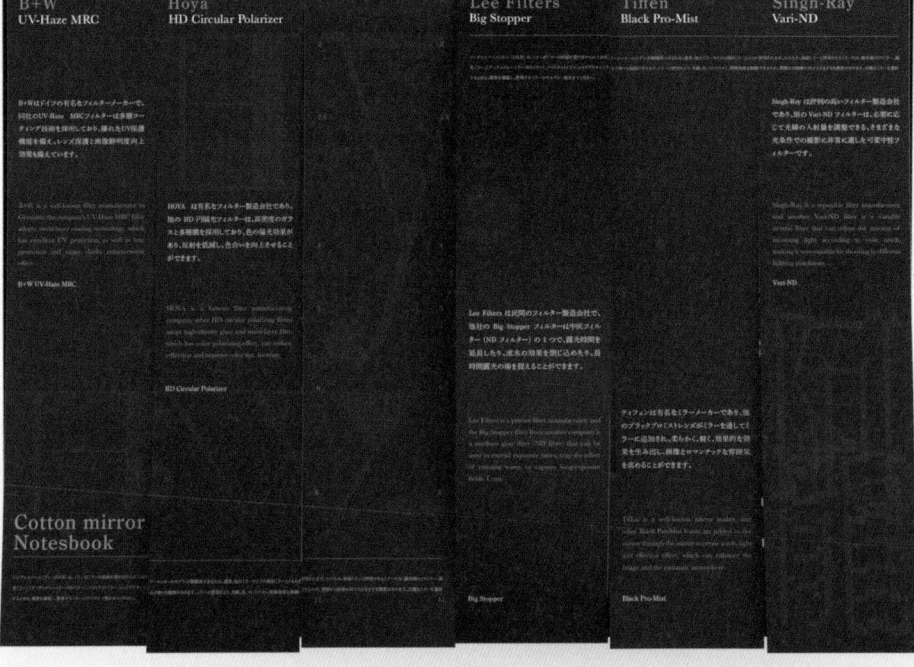

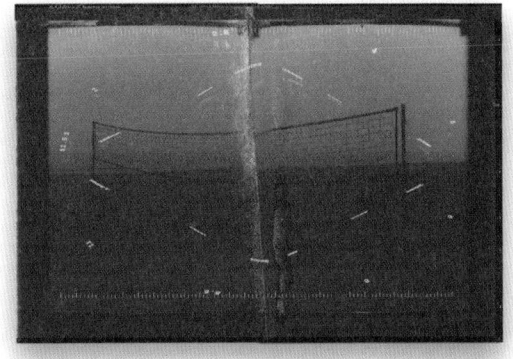

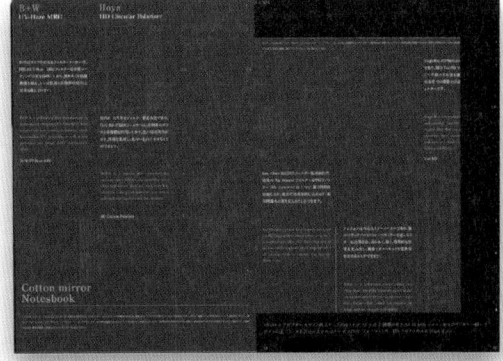
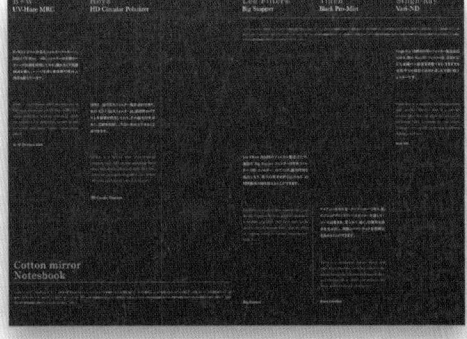

Designer: ACRE Design Studio   Language: English   Client: Park Hotel Group   Page: 16

The Real Art of Drinking Volume II

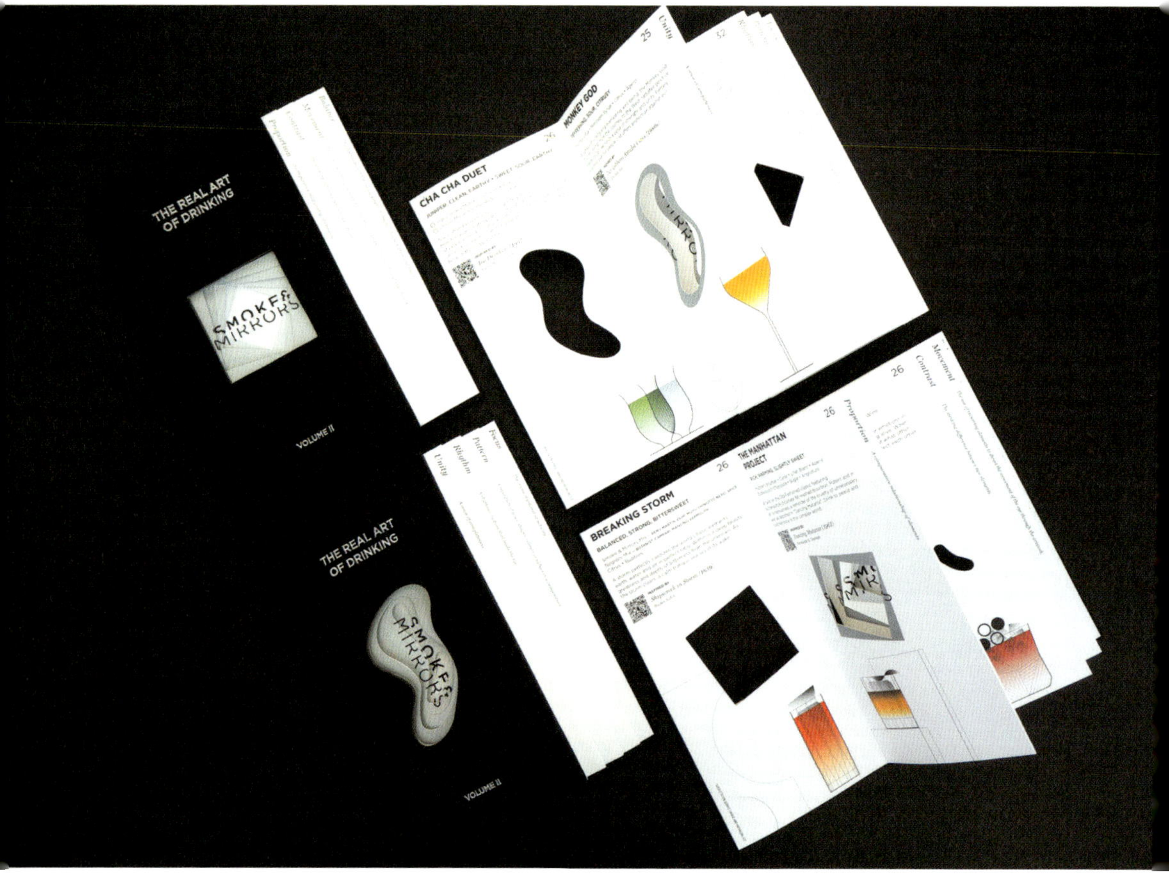

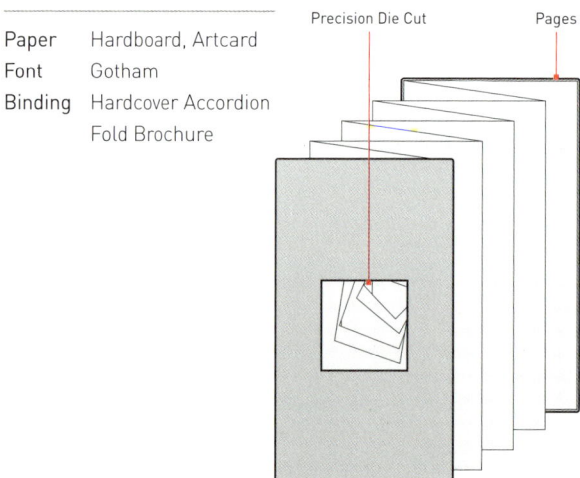

Paper	Hardboard, Artcard
Font	Gotham
Binding	Hardcover Accordion Fold Brochure

Precision Die Cut   Pages   Wrapped Cardboard   Direct Mounting

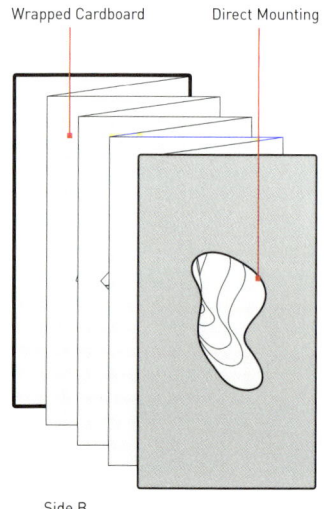

Side A   Side B

"Smoke & Mirrors" is a destination bar located on the rooftop of the National Gallery Singapore, serving creative cocktails. They wanted to create a cocktail menu that encourages exploration with easy navigation. The cocktail menu is divided into eight categories, each featuring a pair of cocktails inspired by principles of art. It features interpretations of art pieces through cocktails, paying homage to the Southeast Asian culture.

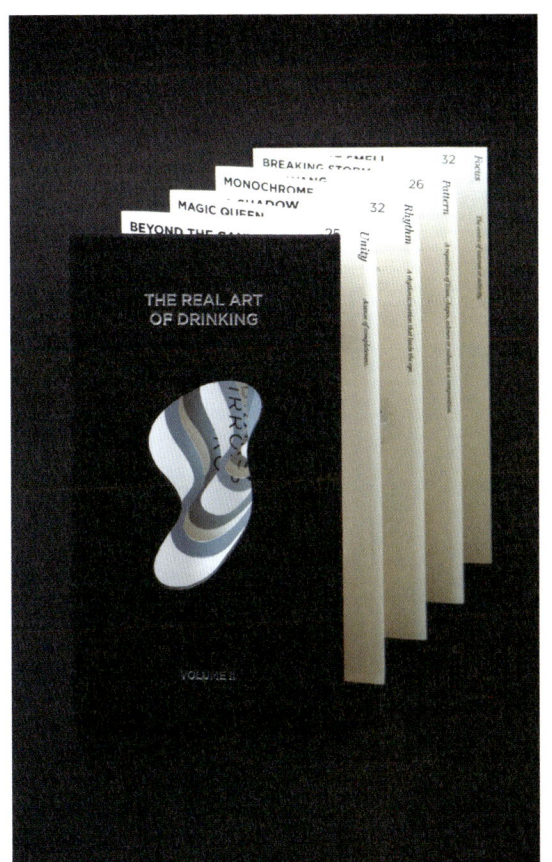

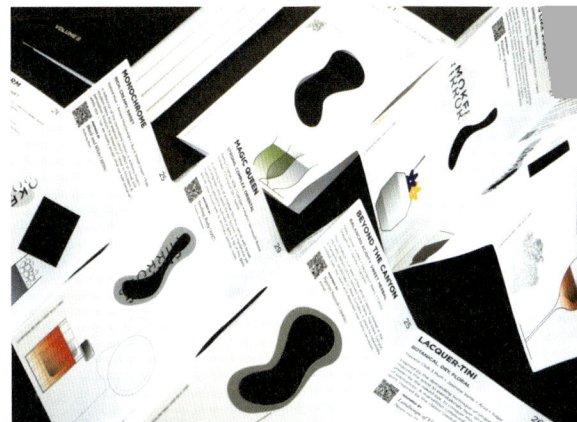

○ The main feature of the structure is the cut-outs across the pages, which forms a visually stimulating layered artwork that can be seen when closed. The accordion-fold format enables it to be browsed from either end of the menu or pulled open for an overview of all drinks with ease. Staggering the panels also allows easy navigation across the categories. The front and back covers are constructed with cardboard wrapped with a high-quality, durable fabric-like material for their tactile, premium quality.

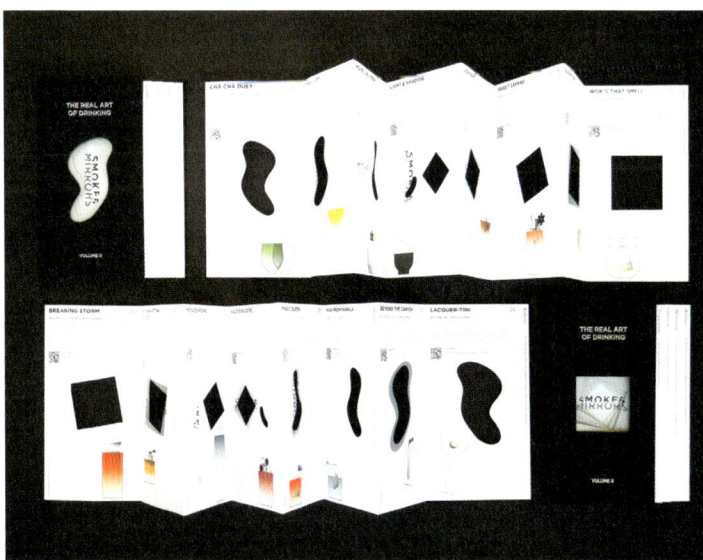

● Designer: Toby Ng Design   Language: English   Client: New World Development Company Limited
Page: 85

Artisan House

Format	205 × 270 × 7 mm
Paper	Mohawk Loop Antique Vellum, Mirror Paper
Font	AktivGrotesk, PostGrotesk

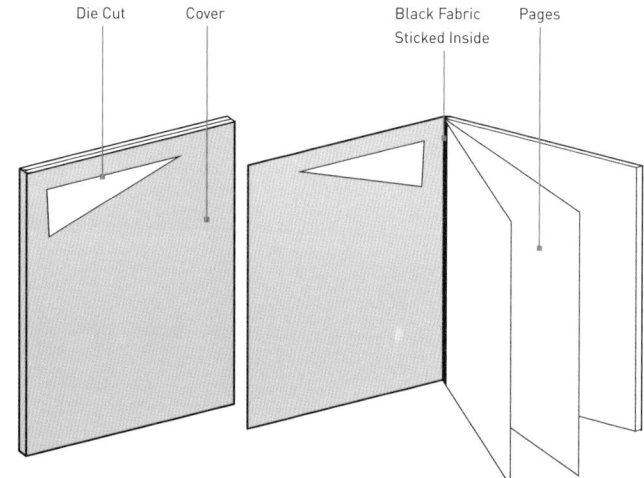

Located in the heritage neighbourhood of Sai Ying Pun, Hong Kong, Artisan House is an artistic residential project of The Artisanal Movement collection by New World Development (NWD). ARCHITECTS' vision for Artisan House is rooted in the notion of Reflections of Artistry. This is expressed on the facade through the play of reflective triangular surfaces that superimpose the experience of private living with public activities. The ever-shifting reflections of the vibrant neighbourhood create ambiguous impressions, blurring the boundary between private and public spaces.

○ The studio was tasked with creating a book to encapsulate the vision and reflect the unique character of the project. Taking inspiration from the mirrored architectural details of the building, a die cut and reflective cover was selected to front the book design. The dark color scheme was also drawn from the building itself, echoing the ambiance of *Artisan House*. A clean and simple layout was used to enhance the minimal architectural nature of the project, whilst providing a clean canvas on which the project is displayed.

Designer: Linlin Yin   Language: Chinese   Client: Chemical Industry Press   Page: 432

Minor Orthopedic Surgery

Minor orthopedic surgery is a daily routine for young orthopedic surgeons. The bookbinding features an outer cover made of fine-grained paper with white skin texture, wrapped in large red tactile paper, with a layered die-cut streamlined at the spine, strung with thin lines to symbolize the process of cutting and sewing a wound, with the effect of the cuts and seams extending to the body binding line, which is consistent inside and out.

○ The layout is designed to divide the 68 minor surgeries into 10 categories, each of which is accompanied by X-rays and surgical notes, and each of which is set up in white, red, and light red as the main color of the page according to the pre-operative, intra-operative, and post-operative sections respectively. In the preoperative section, the relevant skeletal meridian diagrams are provided to facilitate the surgeon's preparation for the surgery. In the intraoperative section, the red medium tone is used to simulate the surgical atmosphere, and the step-by-step illustration of the surgical process with the anti-white line diagrams is easy to see at a glance, while in the postoperative section, the postoperative recovery, which can be easily neglected, is emphasized by the font size change. In the editorial design, a small format is chosen to visualize the whole surgical process, with a clear hierarchy, 180-degree spreading and flipping, loose-leaf light film, and full diagrams of the human skeleton to make it as convenient as possible for doctors to read and view before and after emergency surgeries.

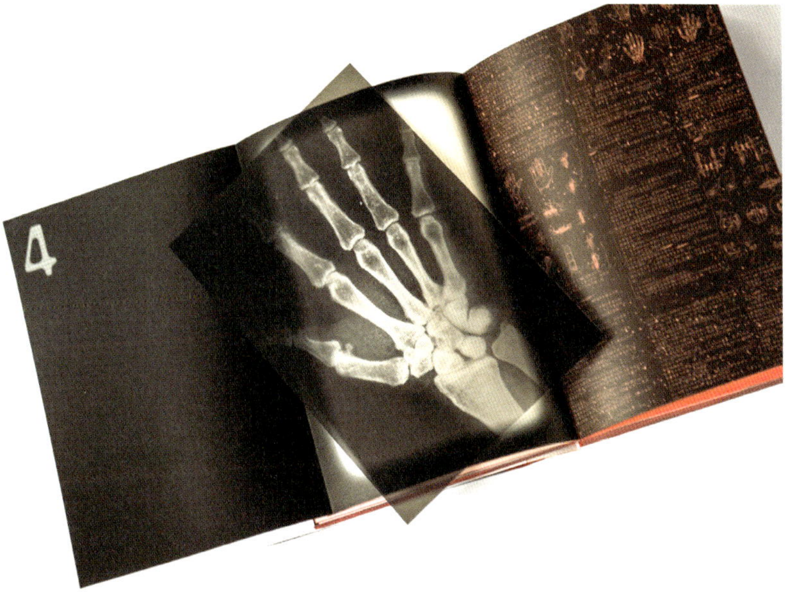

Format	148 × 210 mm
Paper	Fuji Sakura Paper 120 gsm
Print	Four-color Printing
Font	Fangzheng Langting Kan Song

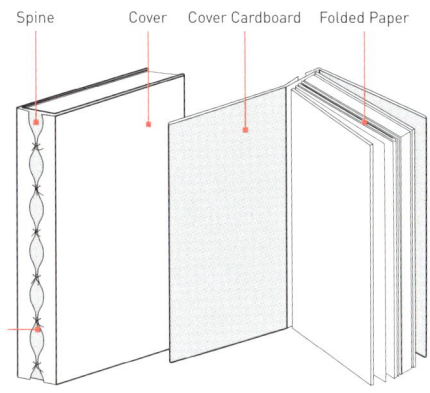

Designer: Hybrid Design   Language: English   Client: Mohawk Paper

Mohawk Maker Quarterly Issue 15: Materials

With the creation of *the Mohawk Maker Quarterly* as a celebration of makers, creativity, and the culture of craft, *the Maker Quarterly* has become an indispensable source of inspiration for graphic designers around the world. Each issue of *the Mohawk Maker Quarterly* seeks to push the boundaries of creative expression with insightful editorial features, carefully considered design and varied printing techniques on a diverse range of Mohawk papers.

Print	Offset Print, Match Orange, Match Blue, Match Green, Match Purple, Die Cut
Paper	Cover	Mohawk Keaykolour, Vellum Indian Yellow, 111, 300 gsm Text	MohawkSuperfine, Eggshell Ultrawhite, 80, 118 gsm
Binding	Sleeve Containing Multiple Objects

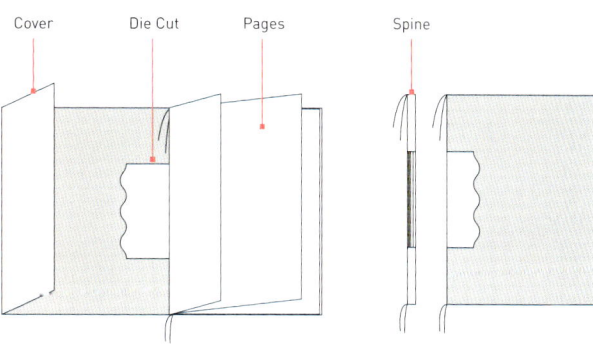

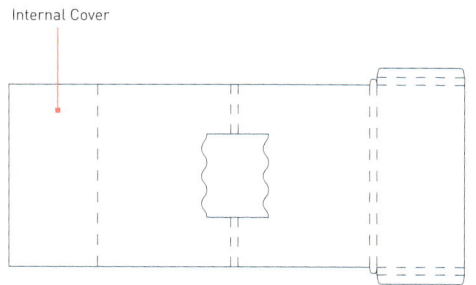

○ Materials are an emotional filter, informing how we should feel about what we touch and see. The fifteenth issue of the Mohawk Maker Quarterly focuses on the object qualities that materials make possible. Each article is realized as its own object—made of material(s) and form that help communicate its point of view. Collectively, the issue speaks to the importance of object quality in our work, and the responsibility to use these qualities not as bells and whistles, but as design elements.

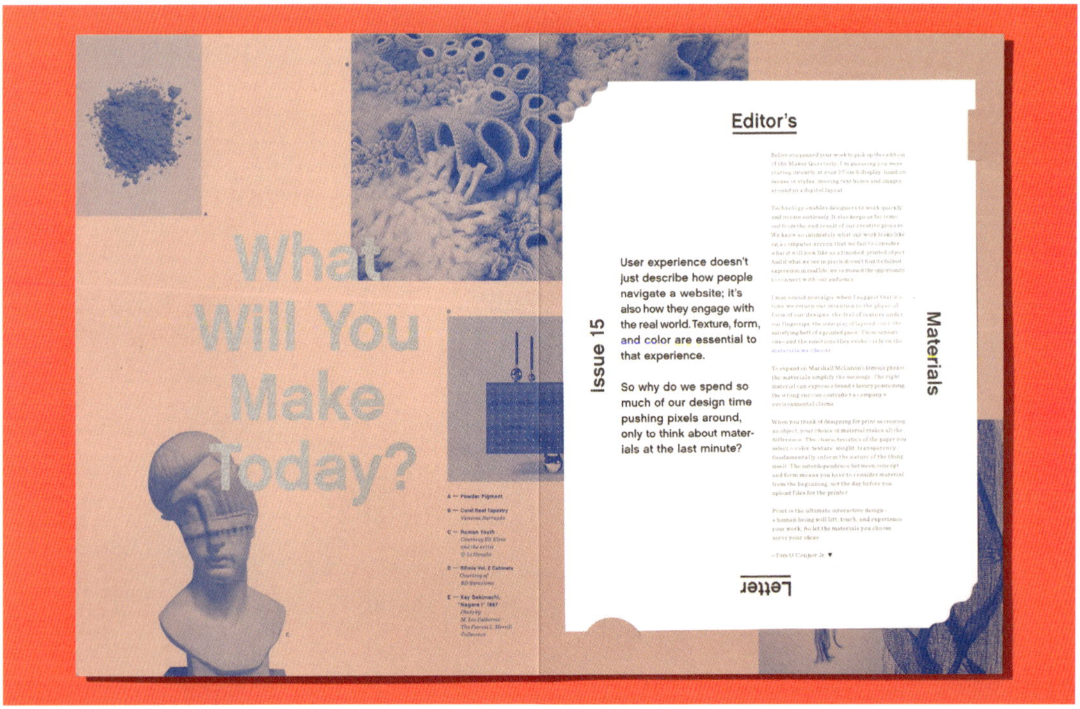

○ The structure of the book was designed to bring multiple materials together in one printed object. Each material and process was chosen to better bring to life the content of each individual piece, demonstrating that every design element deserves careful consideration. For example, the singer-sewn binding used in the article about fabric artist Kay Sekimachi was left intentionally long to emphasize the threads used in her work, while paper choices were made that contrasted a fibrous and synthetic tactility.

Designer: Hybrid Design   Language: English   Client: Mohawk Paper

Mohawk Maker Quarterly Issue 16: Community

Print	Offset Print, Match Black, Blue Foil, Silver Foil, Die Cut
Format	Band Containing Three Books
Paper	Cover | Mohawk Carnival, Vellum, New Black, 216 gsm
	Mohawk Superfine Eggshell, White, 80, 216gsm
	Ultrawhite 80, 216gsm
	Text | Mohawk Superfine Eggshell, Softwhite, 70, 104gsm
	Mohawk Superfine Eggshell, White, 70, 104gsm
	Ultrawhite, 80, 118gsm
	Mohawk Superfine Eggshell Digital with iTone
Font	Chalet, Sentinel
Binding	Stitch Binding

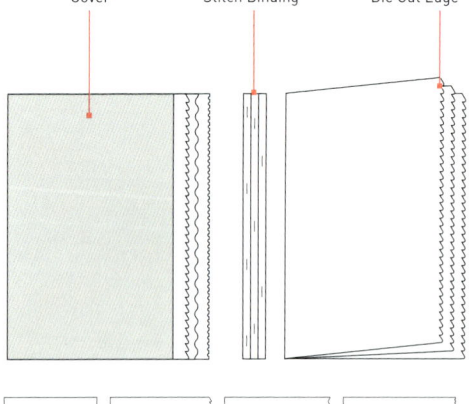
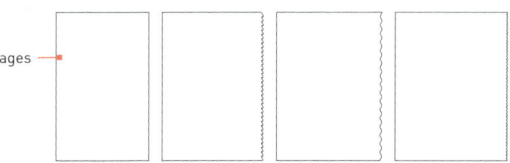

Collectively, community is a story – one we write together. Despite our differences, our voices have a gravitational pull – they converge, change form, and evolve. In this issue, the creative team explores these ideas with stories in three volumes: *Place, Voice, Time*. They reached out to the Mohawk community to assemble a diverse collection of voices from across the spectrum of art, design, and architecture – the overall goal being to connect with the communities around you – or better yet, make your own.

○ For this issue of the *Mohawk Maker Quarterly* they looked at community as a collection of stories that are at once independent and connected. Through three volumes, they explored different community points of view, giving each their own edge texture and nestling them together in a common form. The approach was designed to signal unity without discounting the differences that make our experiences unique.

Designer: Emilie Terashi Boyer   Language: English, Japanese   Page: 12

Tokyo Underground

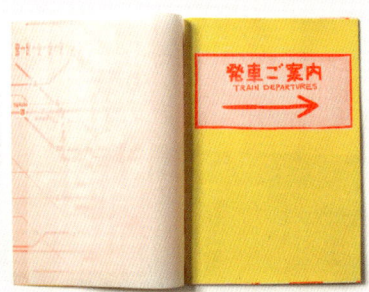

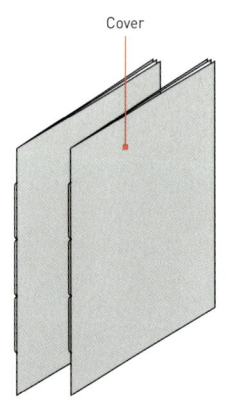
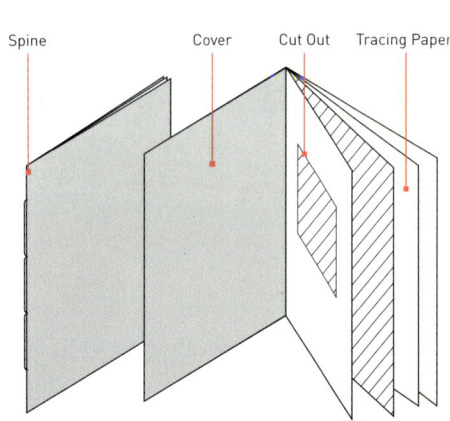

Print   Two-Color Risograph
Paper   Newsprint, Tracing Paper
Binding Handbound with
         Wax Thread

Tokyo Underground is an illustrative zine that follows a short journey through the Tokyo subway system, depicting the various carriages and their daily commuters. It is riso-printed on newsprint and features sheer tracing paper inserts and cut-outs. The zine has no words and each page speaks for itself through familiar scenes and characters which would be easily recognizable to anyone who has ever journeyed on the Tokyo subway.

◯ The book was inspired by children's storybooks which often use fun and unique structures to make every page exciting - cut-outs are a wonderful and simple way to create a dynamic experience with each page-turn, and the designer liked the idea of utilizing this with a more delicate 'adult' medium such as newsprint, which also brings out the vibrant riso inks. The designer was also inspired to add tracing paper inserts by children's tracing & coloring books - in this case, the tracing paper adds a subtle diffused effect to the page underneath.

● Designer: Jieun Hahm   Language: Korean   Client: The Open Books Co.   Page: 4,664

Bernard Werber 30th Anniversary Special Edition

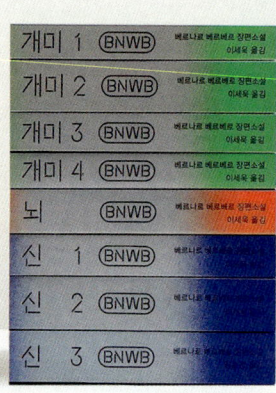

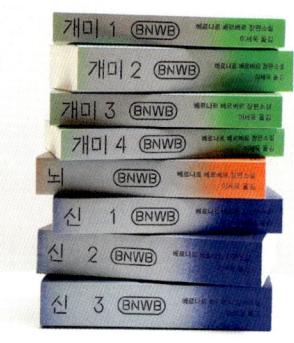
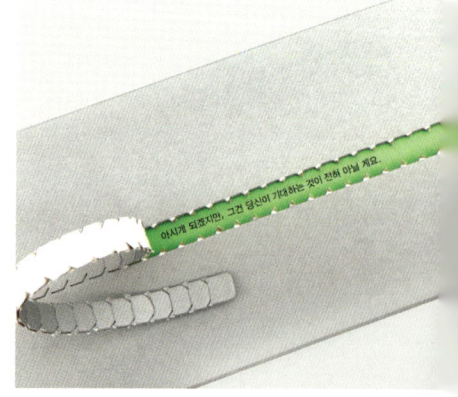

The Bernard Werber 30th Anniversary Special Edition is a lighter book set with a soft binding. It features simple typography and bold graphics that are completely different from the original book covers of the previous Korean editions. The combination of modern imagery and a futuristic story from 30 years ago helps readers immerse themselves in the story. Fans of Werber's work will also enjoy discovering the meaning behind the abstract images on the covers, such as the triangular pyramid in *Les Fourmis* and the giant eye in *Nous les Dieux*.

Print	Offset Print
Format	Book | 120 × 210 mm
	Book Set Box | 287 × 216 × 125 mm
Binding	Softbound
Paper	Gentle Face 250 gsm
Font	SM MyeongJo, Yoon Gothic, Times New Roman, Helvetica

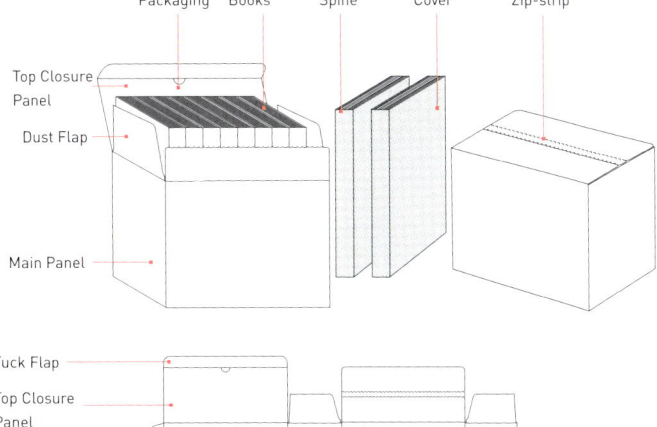

○ A special Zip-strip is added to the packaging. The first thing you see when you tear off the strip is the first sentence of the author's first novel, *Les Fourmis*, which is the author's cryptic message that runs through this special edition set."As you'll see, it's not at all what you expect."

○ The designer aimed to create a book that readers would view as a collectible. Drawing inspiration from various sources like materials and structures found in furniture and everyday objects, she approached the book's design as a product. Her goal was to offer readers an experience that transcends the common book set box, evoking the value associated with product design.

Designer: Robbin Ami Silverberg   Language: English

Duster 2

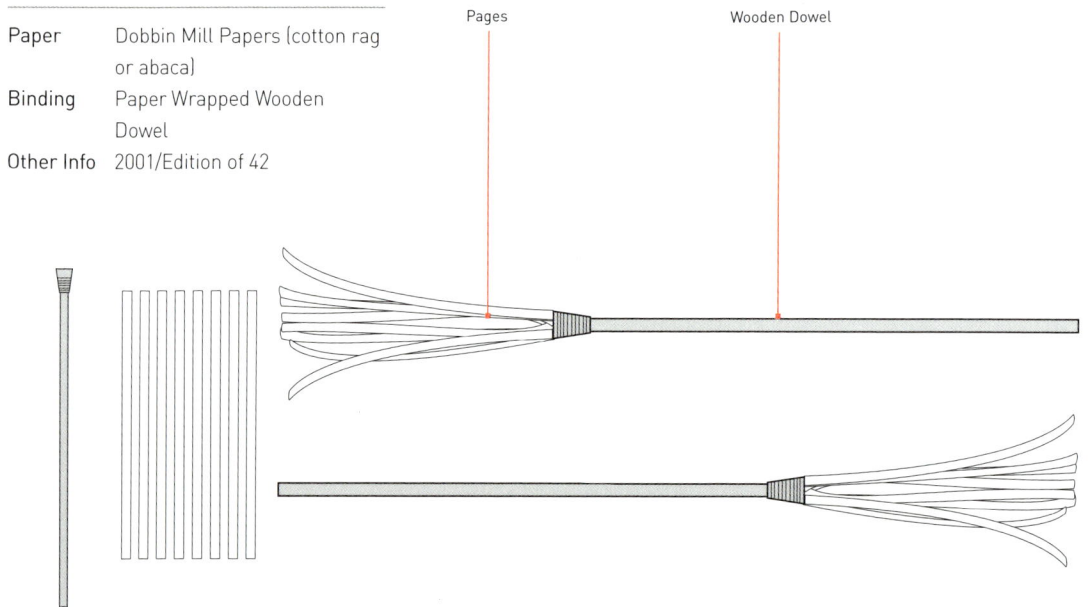

Paper	Dobbin Mill Papers (cotton rag or abaca)
Binding	Paper Wrapped Wooden Dowel
Other Info	2001/Edition of 42

Pages Wooden Dowel

The designer found a dusting brush in Kyoto, Japan, made from the pages of a cut-up block-printed book. In response to this almost confounding choice of disposable materials, she produced her edition of dusters. The text she wrote and printed on the paper strips reflects this creative reuse of a book and the philosophical issues a book-cum-duster can only elicit. Was this upcycling? Or a form of book destruction? Was this censorship or one of liberation?

○ Materials used here are Dobbin Mill papers, letterpress printed by Peter Kruty Editions, a wood dowel, and waxed flax cords. The designer had to make a duster of her own in response to the found duster. It is, therefore, an unconventional binding structure paper cut into strips and wrapped around a piece of wood.

Designer: Robbin Ami Silverberg   Language: English

Spun into Gold: First 100+ Words

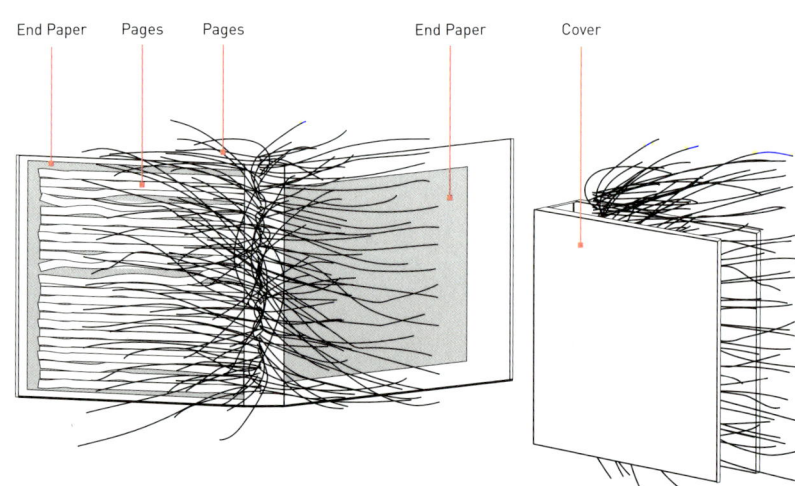

Format	Square Book in a Larger Box
Paper	Handmade Kozo Dobbin Mill Papers
Print	Archival Inkjet Printing
Binding	Case Binding

Using the traditional Japanese technique of shifu, where (washi) paper is made and then spun into thread used for woven cloth, the designer altered a sound poem she wrote consisting of more than 100 words that her daughter first learned: by harvesting fiber from (Kozo) trees in her garden, made paper from the fibers prepared, printed the poem on this paper, cut the paper into thin strips and spun it, and finally bound it into a book.

○ The result was the golden strands of a fairy tale. Not only does this book suggest the transformative act of language acquisition, but it also offers the reader new possibilities in the very act of reading. The designer chose the binding to work with the fragility of the cut & spun pages: sewing the pages onto book cloth that was then glued to the spine.

Designer: Weiqun Cai   Language: Chinese   Client: Committed to knitting culture   Page: 100

XIU-This Book Can Be Weaving

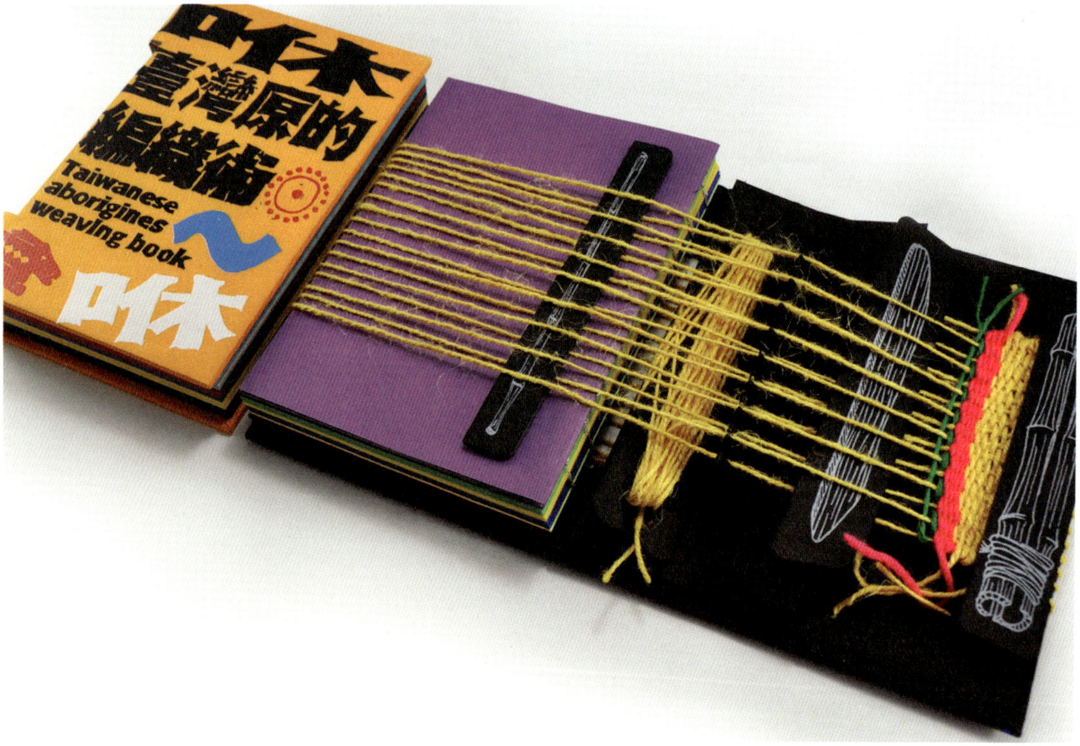

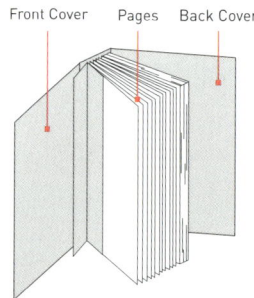
Front Cover   Pages   Back Cover

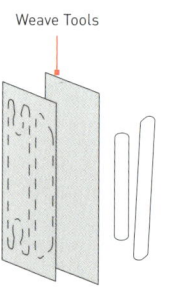
Weave Tools

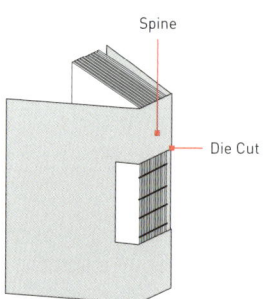
Spine

Die Cut

Print   Ultra-Violet Ray
Paper   Synthetic and Uncoated
          Colored Papers
Font   Source Han Serif
Binding   Coptic Binding

"XIU" is the sound made when weaving. The designers directly displays the weaving machine inside the book, by flipping through the book, and you can simply experience the process of weaving. Taiwan has a long history of aboriginal weaving culture, but the traditional weaving tools are too precious to obtain for the average person. And its complex process is too difficult to experience on ones own. So they hope, by experiencing simple weaving processes, one can initiate "interest" during the process, therefore, thoroughly understand the culture of weaving.

EXPERIENCE STEPS

Step.1

According to the steps on the book, carefully go along the dotted lines and gently take out the object (paper shuttle) on the paper.

Step.2

According to the signs on the book, open the book to the first page, wrap the thread onto the book.

Step.3

According to the signs on the book, use the thread and wrap it onto the paper shuttle.

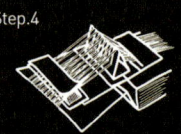

Step.4

Please make sure that the distance between the thread and the thread is correct, and finally clamp the thread clamp up and down, and fix the thread, then we can start weaving.

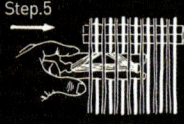

Step.5

Use the paper shuttle to go through the spaces between the threads.

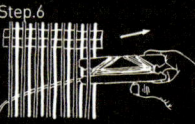

Step.6

Pull out the paper shuttle once it goes between all the threads.

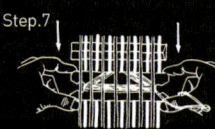

Step.7

Last of all, use the paper shuttle to compress down the threads, and then, one piece of cloth is completed.

Step.8

Once the position of the threads change up and down by flipping pages, use the paper shuttle to go back through in the opposite direction, and continue this movement repeatedly.

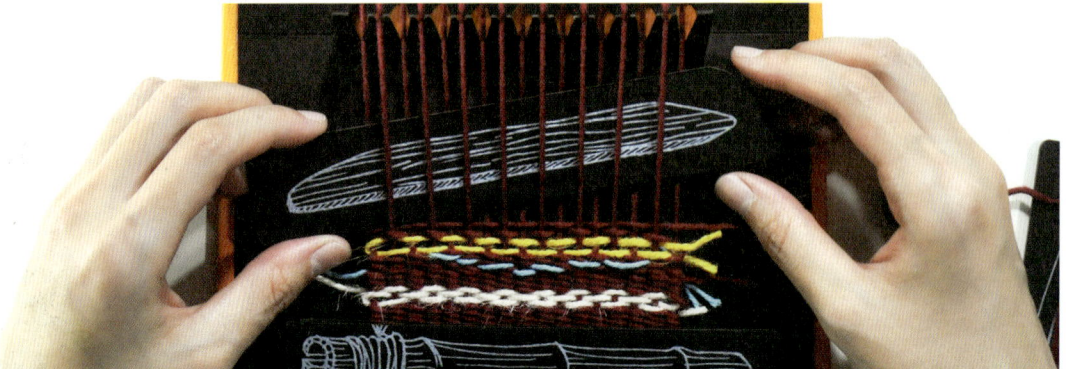

○ The designer simplified and reduced the traditional loom and put it into the book to create this weaving book. In order to pass on the precious weaving culture, he studied for a year to understand the principles and techniques of weaving and designed this book after integrating them. The book not only records the weaving culture and the meaning of aboriginal totems, but readers can also make use of the special mechanism in the book to experience weaving and even weave totems by themselves.

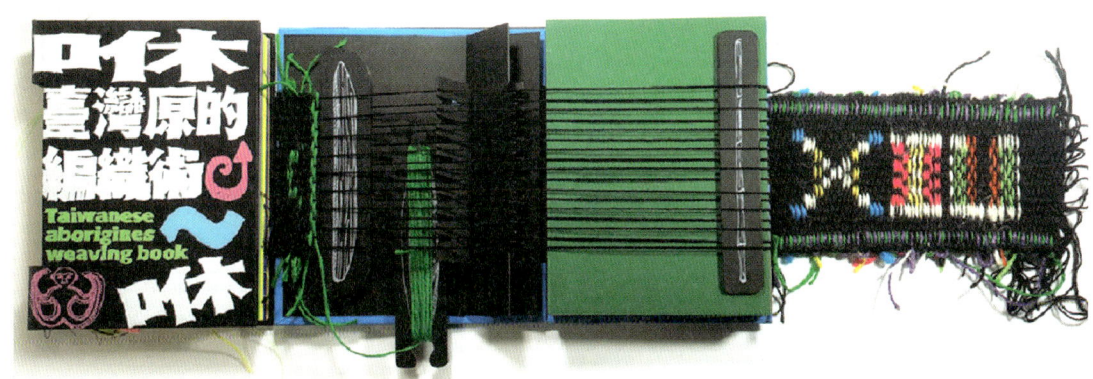

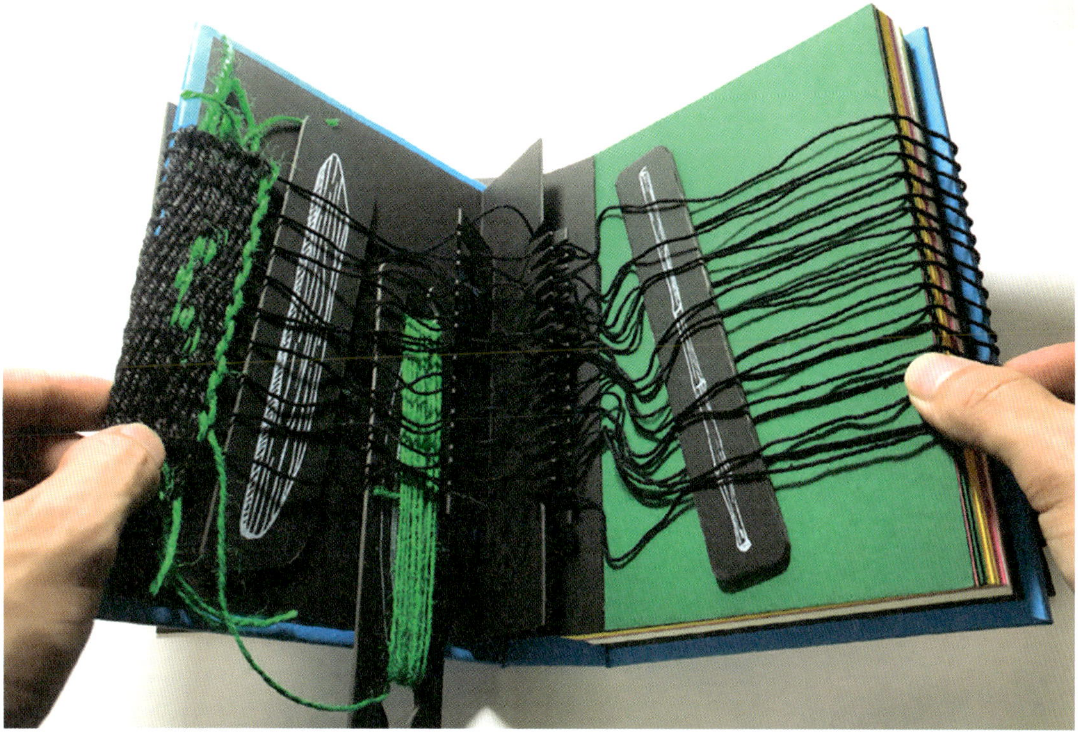

○ Using the structure design of the paper, everytime the pages are turned, there will be changes in the height between the threads. By putting in the weft, and flipping the pages repeatedly, the wrap and weft will criss-cross, in a result of the function of weaving.

Designer: Linlin Yin   Language: Chinese   Client: Chemical Industry Press   Page: 412

Stories Hidden in Chinese Characters

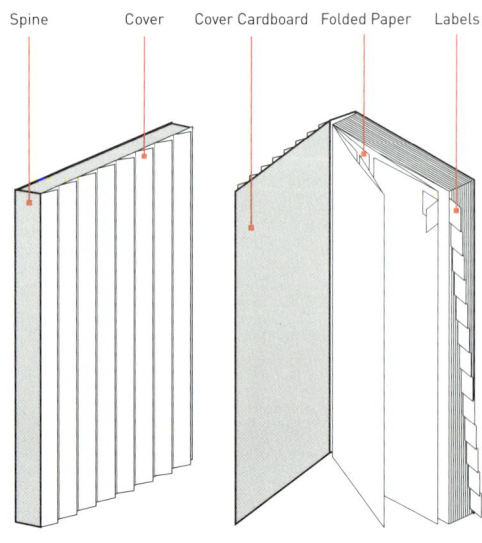

Format   178 × 297 mm
Paper   Eco-friendly Paper 120 gsm
         Mechine-made Chinese Art
         Paper (xuan paper) 80 gsm
Print   PMS-black, PMS-golden
Binding Perfect Binding

Spine   Cover   Cover Cardboard   Folded Paper   Labels

This book is a study of the etymology of Chinese characters from the point of view of their glyphs. This is the meaning of the word "original (previous)," which corresponds to the word "later". The spatial folding is to express the change of time. The cover is designed with 8 groups of folded pages, each arranged with 8 groups of Chinese characters, "revealed" and "hidden" correspondingly, and 100 simplified Chinese characters are arranged on the space of "revealed". When you turn over the hidden folds on the front cover, the 100 characters in hot-stamped seal script are revealed one-by-one, and when all 8 folds are turned over, the 100 gold-colored characters reversed time. The interior design is made of 100 sheets of machine-made rice paper closed and folded, and the order and rhythm of turning the short and long pages are used to adjust the design of the sequential reading order and the reading motion of the text.

○ The unique book form and the way of flipping constitute the overall design idea. The cover uses a variant form of Bamboo slips (an ancient Chinese binding), and the size, length and width ratio of the whole book recalls the origin of Chinese book forms. The paper simulation of the signature strip can be flipped to reveal the hidden golden text, which has a sense of ceremony. The narrative structure of the interior pages is rich in drama, with the opening of the folded pages presenting the glyphs of each character, the process of formation of the font, in an interesting and orderly arrangement. Each folded page has die-cut windows of standardized font characters that can be opened and interacted with, corresponding to interpretations ranging from oracle bone inscriptions, ancient style of calligraphy, and Chinese bronze inscriptions. It also forms an organized sequence on the mouth of the book for easy retrieval. The text printed in gold on a black background on the outside of each page is thick and introspective, contrasting strongly with the white background of the inner pages, and reading is filled with a sense of conversational magic.

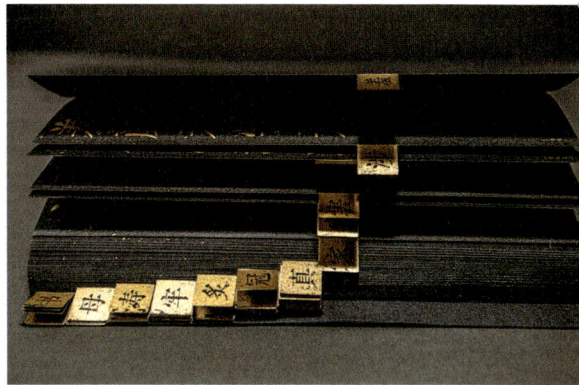

BREAK

Think out the box and beyond imagination

Format, shape,
and material, to be different,
to be brilliant. The design object of book design
not only is the explicit text information, but also includes the
format, material, shape, and so on. If the books are all the same,
fixed format, and uniform font, then the world of books will not
be as colorful as it is now. These designs are not only to make the
books stand out in the crowd but also to strike a breakthrough and
exploration of the conventional design by the designers and their new
thinking about the world.

Designer: AIKA   Language: Chinese   Client: ALINE STUDIO   Page: 260

What is Design? 7th Anniversary Handbook

 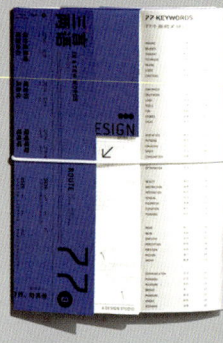 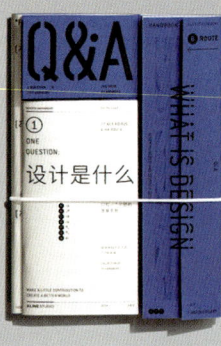 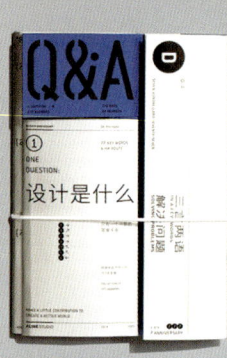
 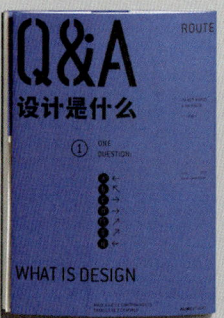 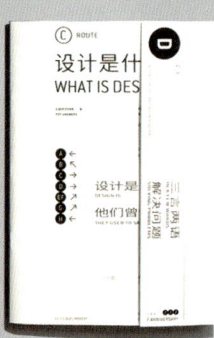 

Format	200 × 280 mm
Paper	Cover 1	Lumbini Uncoated- 280 gsm Newly Dyed Fairy Blue
	Cover 2	Rebel Uncoated - 180 gsm Flat Gold Silver, Asian Silver
	Outer	Lumbini Uncoated - 280 gsm Newly Dyed Sample Gray
	Text	Jingpin Uncoated - 70 gsm High Quality Super Smooth Milk White
Print	Single-Color Black Printing, Die-Cutting, Matte Film, UV Two-Color Black and White Printing
Font	Source Han Serif CN, ITC Conduit
Binding	Stitch Binding, Stringing

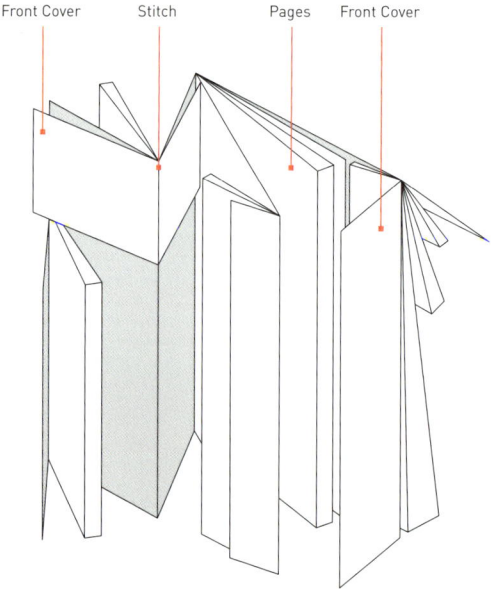

In honor of its seventh anniversary, ALINE STUDIO has launched an in-depth design exploration. The studio was inspired by a simple question, "What is design?" Answers were collected from people of all backgrounds through 777 questionnaires. These answers are skillfully divided into 7 main chapters and 24 sub-chapters, presenting readers with a multi-dimensional interpretation of design.

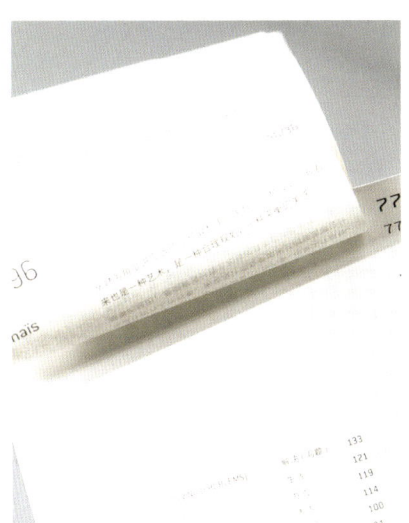

○ The key point of creation is how to integrate and present the answers logically. The design concept of the manual is centered around the core concept of "highway," which implies that everyone's path of design exploration is unique. This is not only reflected in the content, but also in the appearance, material and structure of the manual. The overall design starts from the content in order to avoid the fatigue of repetitive content, they structured it in a way that would soothe this fatigue. Inspired by the idea of the "highway," they chose saddle stitches. For added interest, they designed the book to open and close in a variety of ways, so that the reader can experience a randomized reading sequence and more ways to explore the answers.

○ It is hoped that in the world of design, everyone has his or her own unique path and concept, and that we should cherish and explore our own design paths to find the one that truly belongs to us.

● Designer: Gloria (Wenya Zhang)   Language: Chinese, English   Page: 36

Memory Lossing

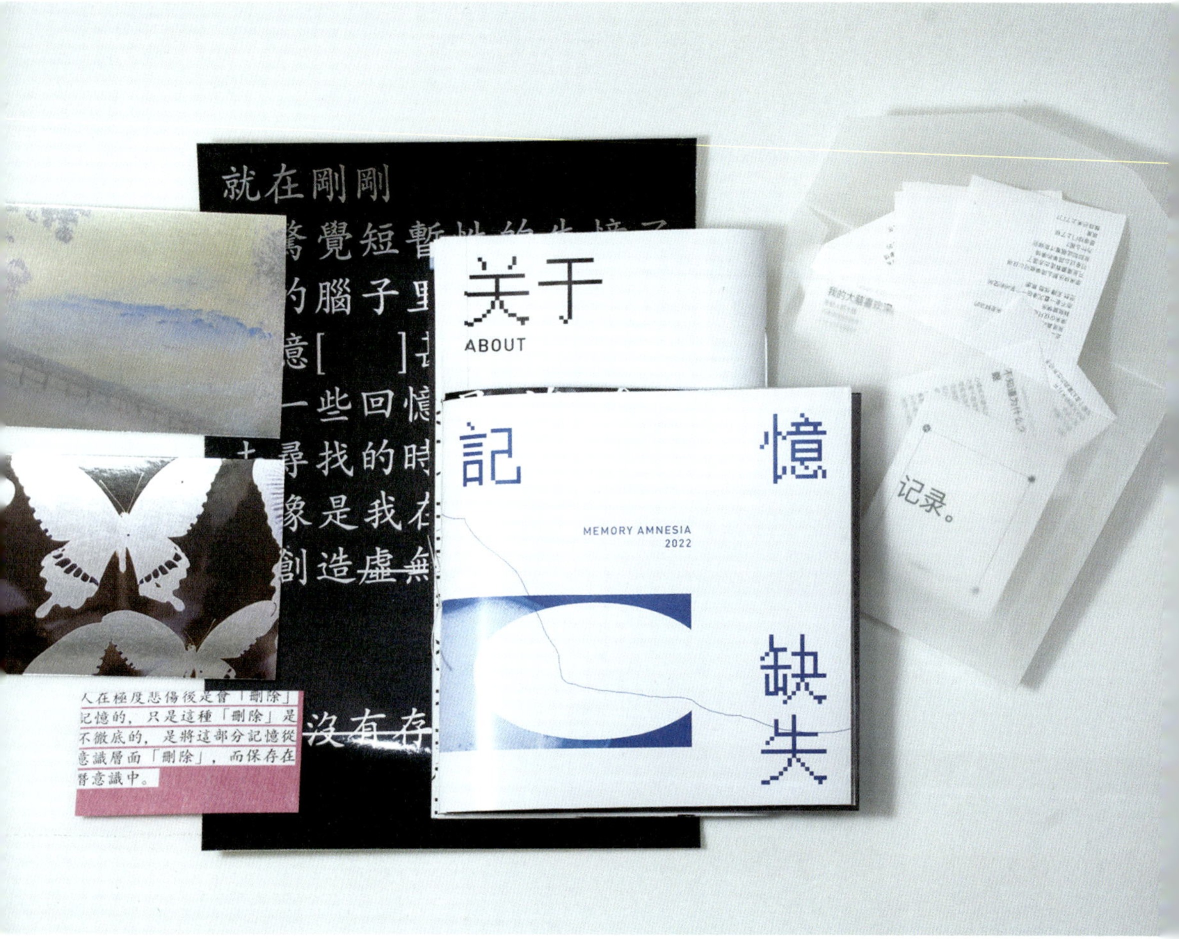

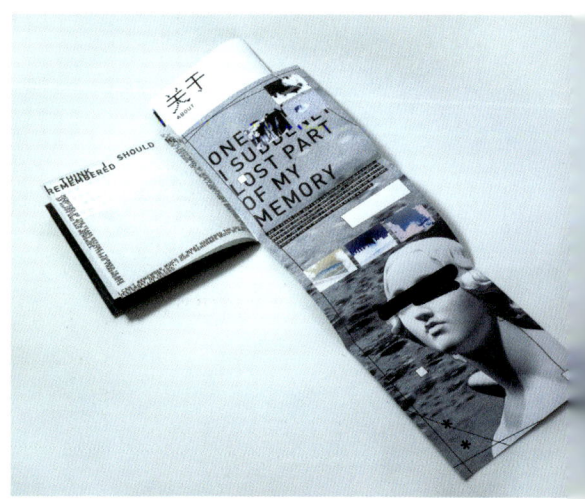

"The memories I am stockpiling are like a set of blind boxes that are always filling up the shelves, and someone often draws from them, not knowing whether they are happy or sad, and leaves with the memories, and I fill in the gaps, and the cycle repeats itself." As time is compressed, as if it were a single day, our memories of ourselves become uncertain and gradually blurred and forgotten. Based on the theme of "Memory Loss Disorder," this project explores the issue of transient memory loss in the context of the author's life records, using bubbles as the main vehicle for memory.

○ The design of the work attempts to present the discussion of memory loss in a question-and-answer format, and so the binding is divided into different sizes and openings on the front and back, with many different sizes of paper on the inside, to better represent the variations of "memory," which is intermittent and blurred.

Format	390 × 210 mm
Paper	Silk Paper, Transparent Pet, Tiger Paper, Mirror Silver Card
Font	Adobe Kaiti Std
Binding	Thread Sewing

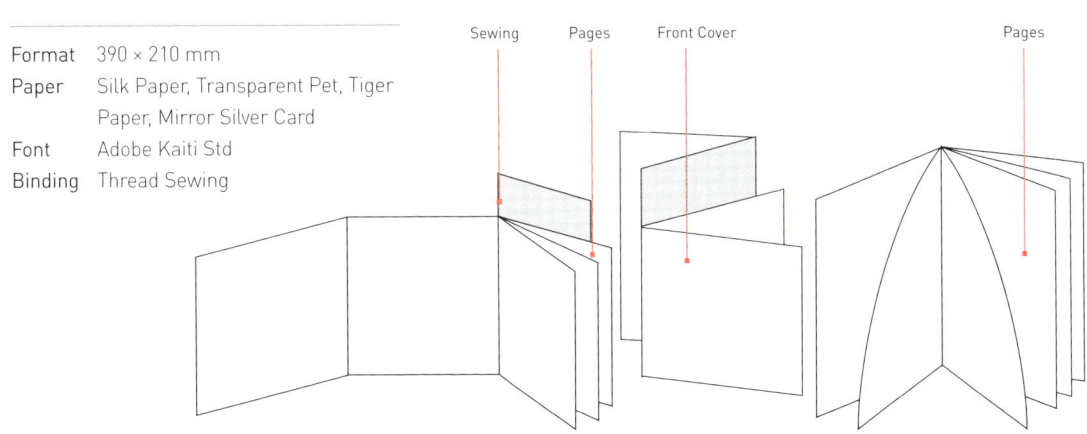

● Designer: Yiru Liao   Language: Chinese   Client: Shungkei Construction Company Limited   Page: 56

The Coast Street Diary

Format
Cover | 125 × 200 mm
Book A | 135 × 160 mm
Book B | 135 × 210 mm
Book C | 145 × 220 mm
Postcard | 140 × 90 mm

Paper
Cover | Glossy Paper 200 gsm
Inside | Bird Of Paradise 95 gsm
Postcard | Recycled Paper 205 gsm
Packaging | Aluminum Foil Pouch And Molded Sticker

Print
Four-color Printing, Sampling, Folding, Postcard / Stickers

Font
Genryu-font

Binding
Sewn Binding, Three Volumes Mounted, Bagged

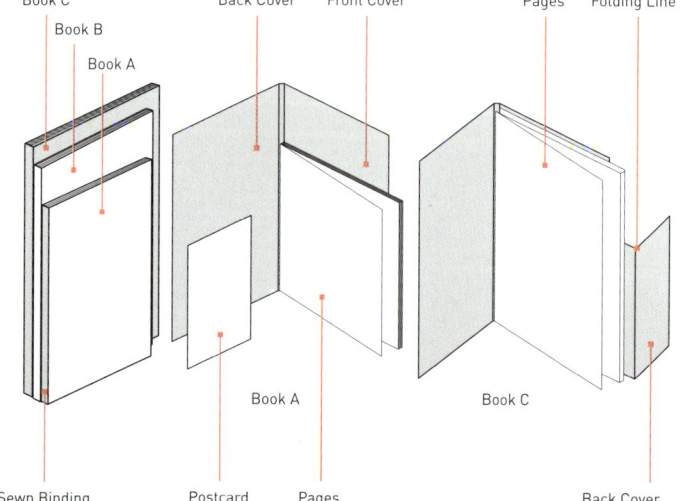

In the Nanliao Seaside's gentle, relaxed, and leisurely life, there is a sense of vitality in the *Coast Street Diary*, as well as in the street, the sea, the home, the peace, the warmth, the affection, and the growth. They have created a book in the form of a "diary," which is a collection of small stories for each day, responding to the name of the project and emphasizing the romance and enjoyment of Namliao's seaside life.

◯ The book consists of three series of 19 daily prose poems that describe the daily life of Nanliao's vitality in terms of scenery, human leisure, and food. In addition to the delicate and lyrical text, the visual style is also very original, with a saturated aquamarine color as the main theme, a gradation that alludes to the beauty of the flow and overlap of the sea water, and a light earthy gray and translucent color that is the embodiment of the land and the sandy islands. The handwritten text and illustrated maps in the details bring out the vitality of the diary, echoing the text and photographs in the booklet, and creating a scene of slow living with the sea breeze in the cool summer months.

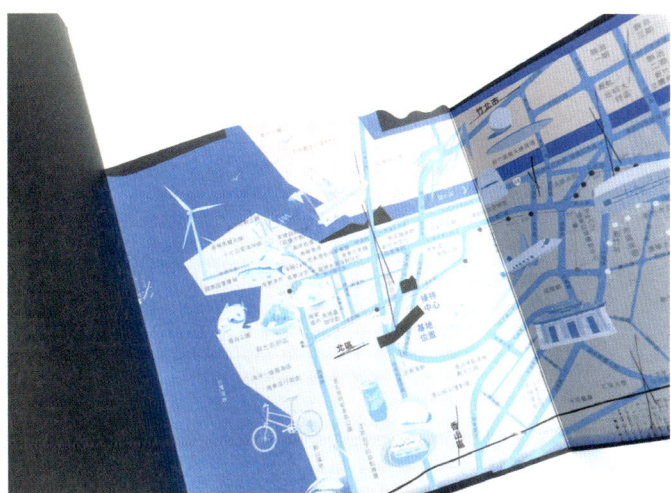

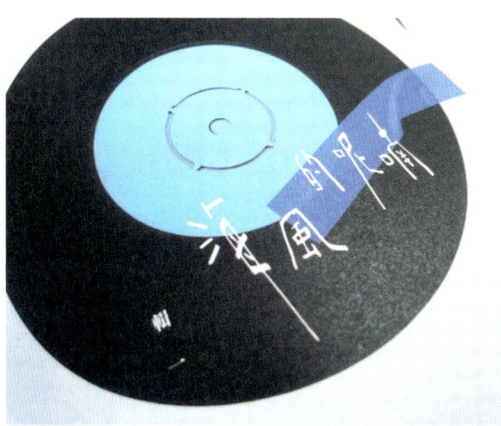

Designer: Yunqi Peng   Language: Chinese, English   Page: 93

Cyber Isolation

Format	210 × 297 mm
Paper	Tiger Paper, 80 gsm, Newsprint, 80 gsm
	Field Film Tablets PET 120 g
Print	Digital Printing
Font	Helvitica Neue
	Times New Roman
	Source Han Sans Sc
Binding	Loose-Leaf Iron Ring Binding

Pages

Cover

Book Profile

Cyber Isolation is a visual representation and narrative study of a sense of loneliness that is specific to virtual space in this era – because of the instability of virtual communication. The back-and-forth conversations of real life are replaced by the dilemma of "being ignored by an unknown number of people passing by," a subtle feeling that often arises while waiting on the screen for the time lag caused by the speed of the internet intersecting with countless other spaces. And as a particular era creeps into the world and begins to spread, individual feelings cascade and eventually become a collective memory.

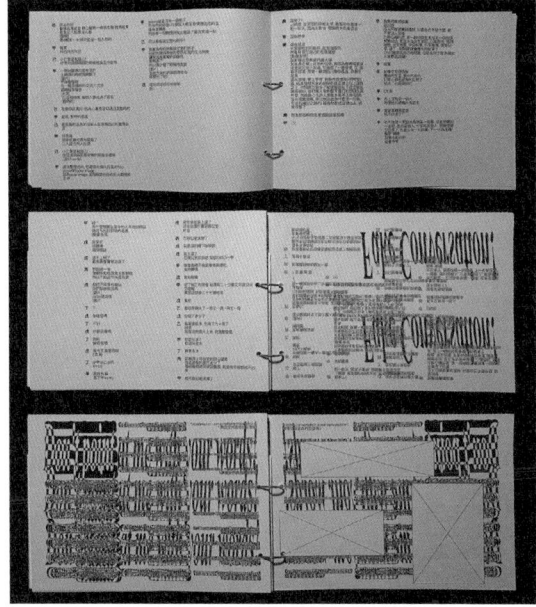

○ The book is made up of four sections, bound in a circular loose-leaf format, to allude to a state of infinite overlap and continuity.

○ The 1st section: printed on one side the square newsprint, the abstract line illustrations resemble static frames extracted from an animation, depicting the story of an imprisoned light bulb who thinks he is free but is overwhelmed by isolation, alluding to the double-sided nature of the virtual world.

○ The 2nd section: the keyword "Cyber Isolation" is printed on transparent PET material, the transparency of the material allows for a richer overlay effect when flipping through it, a black shadow of numerous stories referred to by numerous keywords, making it impossible to distinguish the content of each individual.

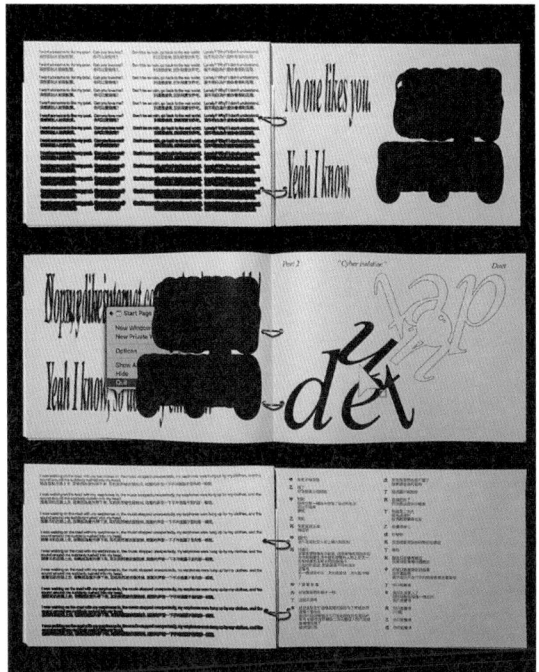

○ The 3rd section: printed on indelible translucent tiger paper, a visual representation of each of the keywords in the second section, with numerous fragmentary images and text boxes popping up on the paper, interacting and permeating each other due to their material.

○ The 4th section: composed of text and text-based visual content, profiling or writing directly about the loneliness of the cyber world, has a somewhat coherent narrative structure compared to the fragmented structure of the first three parts - even if the narrator remains less than objective.

○ This is a project-based, independent, and self-published publication in which the designer attempts to move the concept into the portable and disseminative realm of publication, using paper as a medium and exploiting the subtle differences between different papers metaphorically.

Designer: Camille Palandjian   Language: French   Client: Individual project   Page: 64

Fragments d'un voyage

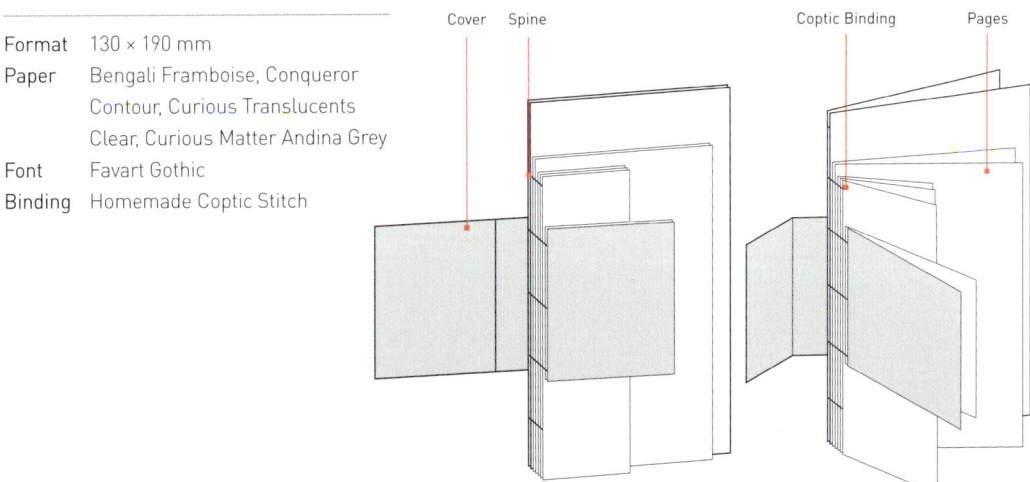

Format   130 × 190 mm
Paper   Bengali Framboise, Conqueror
         Contour, Curious Translucents
         Clear, Curious Matter Andina Grey
Font   Favart Gothic
Binding Homemade Coptic Stitch

This book comes from a reflection: we take a huge amount of photos nowadays but we barely look at them, and that's because they are locked into a hard disk, invisible, lost among thousands of others. By bringing those images back into the tangible world, in a beautiful object made of paper, the designer offered them a place to be seen easily. You just need to grab the book from the shelf when your eyes catch it and flip through these memories.

○ The main idea behind this project is to create a collection of books with pictures taken during her travels. One book for one destination. When the designer visited Berlin, she had four major feelings about the city: the importance of history, the size of spaces, the transparency (everything is made of glass), and the omnipresence of construction work. Dividing the book into four parts was the best way to show these different specificities. Signatures complete each other's and create some words that give the image a sense of reading. To show that the city is made of all those themes, you can read the name of Berlin only when the four of them are reunited.

● Designer: Ivy Chen   Language: English   Client: Individual Project   Page: 31

Telephone Game

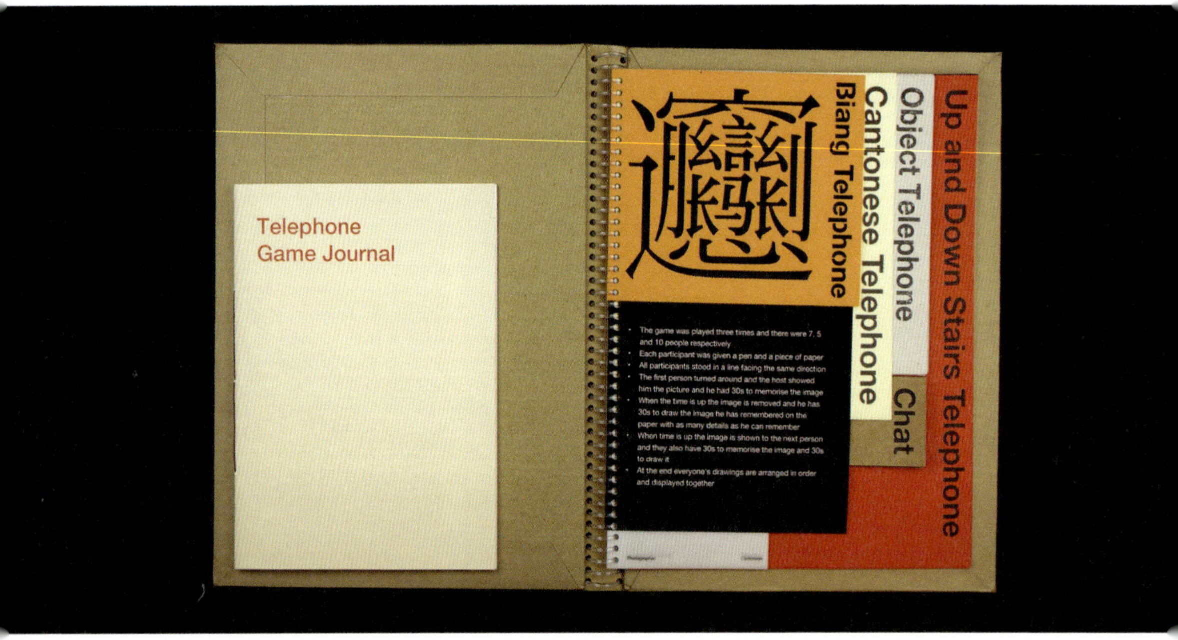

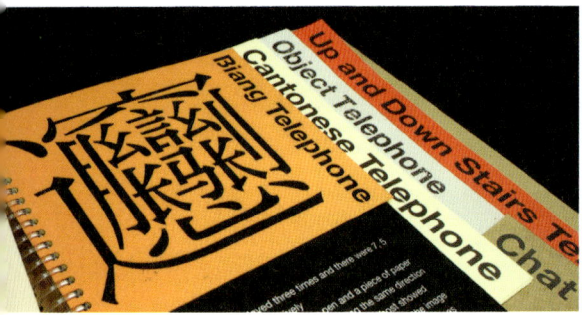

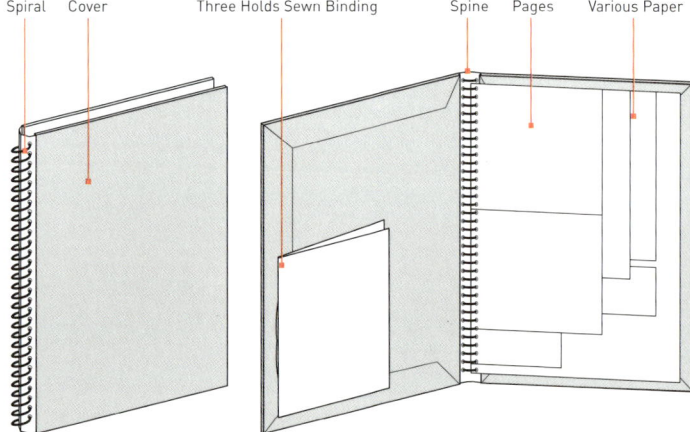

Format 210 × 297 mm
Print   Digital Printing
Paper   Kraft Paper, Gray Board
        Sugar Paper, Tracing Paper,
        Color Paper
Font   Helvetica

This project is based on the communication model proposed by Shannon Weaver in 1948. How does information change during the communication process? Does it affect the effectiveness of communication? The author designed a series of telephone games and invited her classmates to participate, thus visualizing the communication process. By organizing the collected data, she documented the game process into the publication, *Telephone Book*.

○ Refer to the idea of "The process is the project" in the *Conditional Design Workbook*, where the telephone game workshops, she organized were the content. She aimed to present the results of these workshops in an interesting way to the audience. So how can she use different materials and binding methods to present different workshops and combine them into one book? The author chose the flexible coil book binding, which is a pun on the title of the book, "Telephone Book," which is a punchline on words.

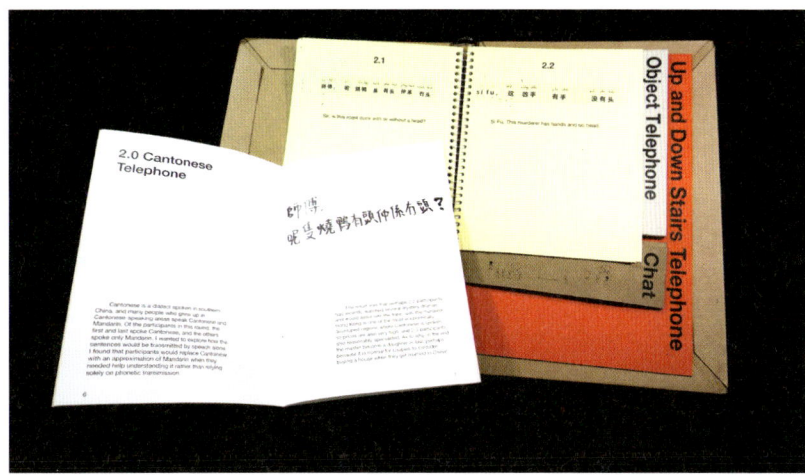

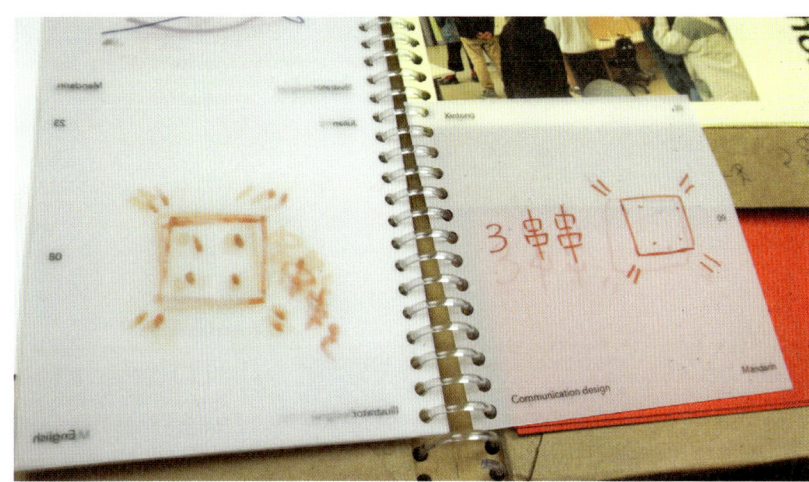

Now Lost

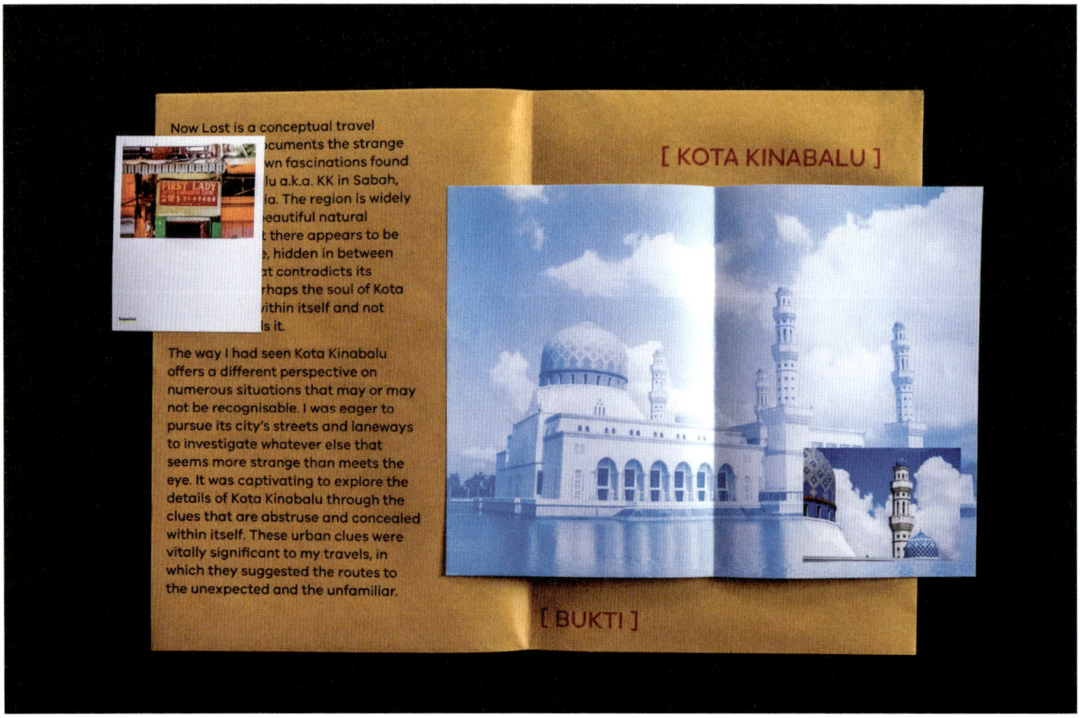

Now Lost is a conceptual travel journal that documents the strange and unknown fascinations found in Kota Kinabalu a.k.a. KK in Sabah, Malaysia. The region is widely recognised for beautiful natural landscapes, but there appears to be something unique, hidden in between its attractions that contradicts its perception. Perhaps the soul of Kota Kinabalu lies within itself and not how one perceives it.

The way I had seen Kota Kinabalu offers a different perspective on numerous situations that may or may not be recognisable. I was eager to pursue its city's streets and laneways to investigate whatever else that seems more strange than meets the eye. It was captivating to explore the details of Kota Kinabalu through the clues that are abstruse and concealed within itself. These urban clues were vitally significant to my travels, in which they suggested the routes to the unexpected and the unfamiliar.

Now Lost is a conceptual travel journal that documents the strange and lesser known fascinations found in Kota Kinabalu a.k.a. KK in Sabah, east of Malaysia. The region is widely known for its beautiful natural landscape, but there appears to be something else, hidden in between the streets, that contradicts its reputation. Perhaps the soul of Kota Kinabalu lies within itself and not what surrounds it.

Format	210 × 297 mm
Paper	Bond 100 gsm, Eco 80 gsm, White Card 120 gsm
Print	Digital Printing
Binding	Folder Assembling Format, Stapled and Clipped

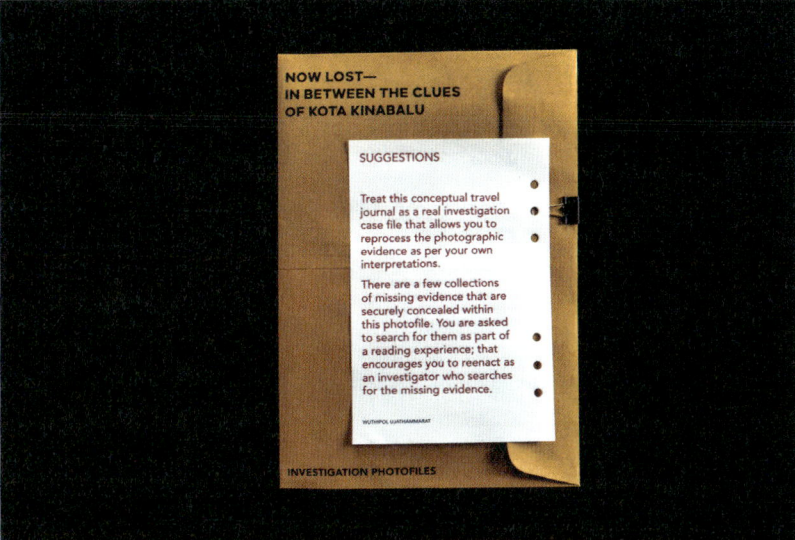

○ Within this case, the file is a collection of photographic evidence in an urban investigation that surveys a fascinating detail of Kota Kinabalu where its inner treasure is awaiting to be discovered. The way the author had seen Kota Kinabalu offers a different perspective on numerous situations that may or may not be recognizable. He was eager to pursue its city's streets and laneways to investigate whatever else that seems more strange than meets the eye. It was captivating to explore the details of Kota Kinabalu through the clues that are abstruse and concealed within itself. These urban clues were vitally significant to his travels, in which they suggested the routes to the unexpected and the unfamiliar.

Designer: I Like Birds Studio Language: German Client: BB Schöenfelderhof Page: 148

ICH LIEBE DICH WIE APFELMUß 2013

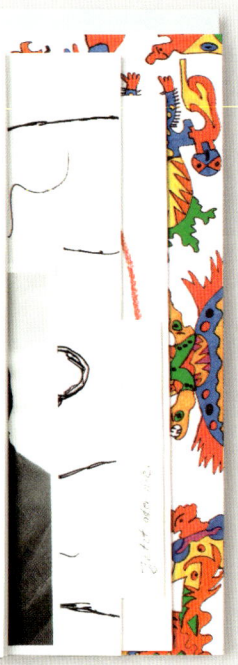

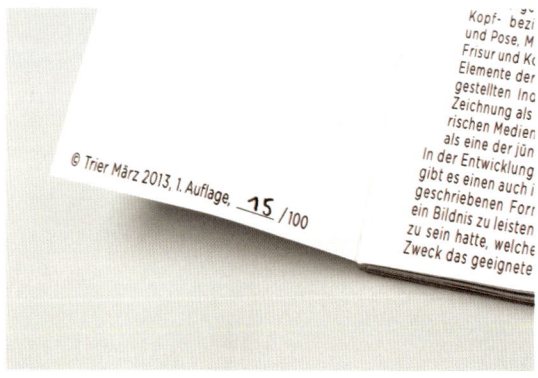
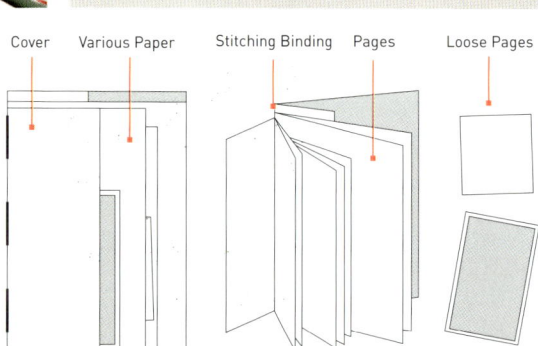

Format	Various, 175 × 245mm (Max)	
Paper	Coated, Uncoated	
Font	Beardshop Superslim (Custom Made)	
	Courier New	
Binding	Thread Stitching, Open Spine	

"I love you as I like applesauce" (Ich liebe dich wie Apfelmuß) is the title of an outsider art exhibition on poetry and illustration. The works presented in the catalog all come from artists from various psychiatric institutions.

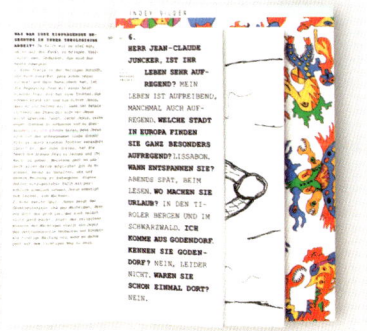

○ The design studio "I LIKE BIRDS" designed various media for the exhibition, such as an invitation card, poster and an accompanying artist catalogue, which stands out due to its unusual concept: on one hand, the works are available in different formats and on different papers, on the other hand, they were not bound, but are partly attached loosely, almost chaotically, which is more reminiscent of a portfolio than a catalogue.

Designer: MMWW Design   Language: Chinese   Page: 136

MMWW VI MANUAL

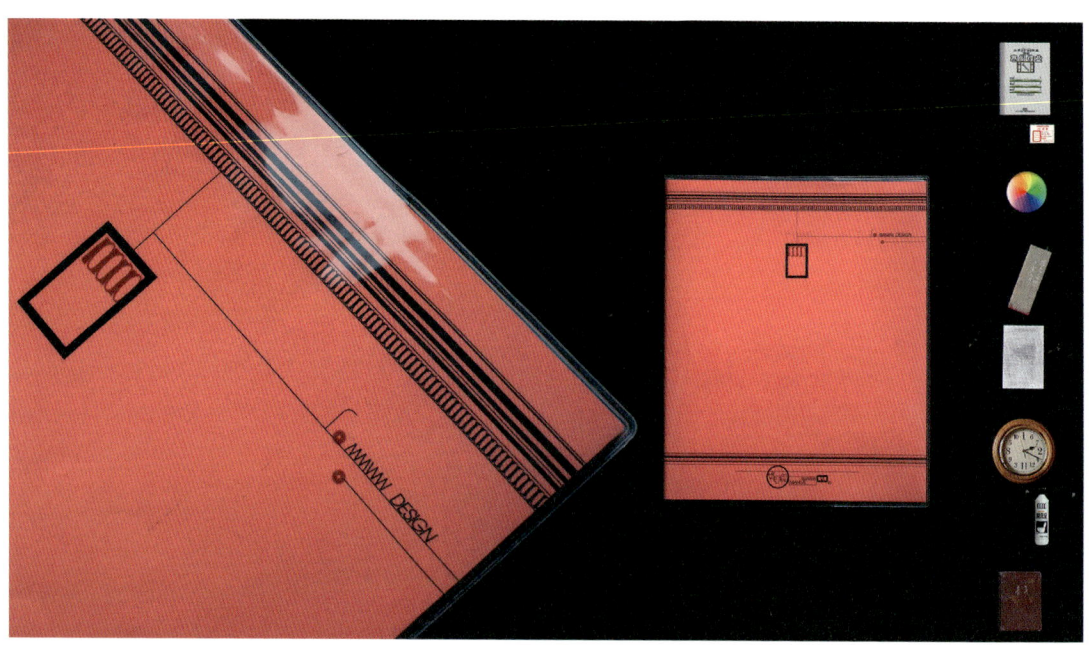

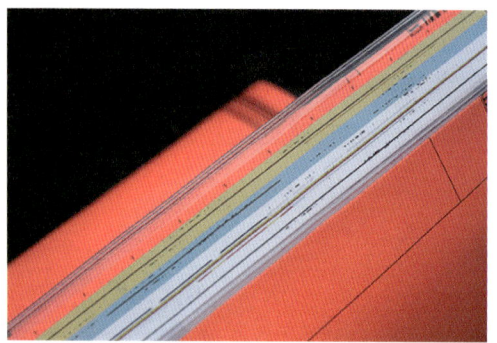

Format   225 × 270 mm
Paper   Colored-paper, Astrobrights-papers (rocket red, stardust white)
Print   Offset Print, Screen Printing
Binding Thread Sewing, PVC Cover

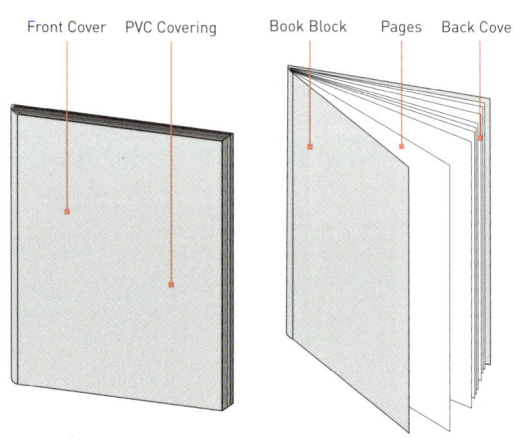

The design team produced a manual using the VI form carrier of "*MMWWdesign*." Alphabet for visual, MMWW is reversal and stable. Chinese for meaning, *MMWW* is an abbreviation to derive words, from the classification method to society, to spirit then re-endowed with content and forms, constituting MMWW VI's ever-changing scenery. Please read it. It's both a system and a game.

○ The structure of a book is produced for its content. The team uses the manual as a carrier and VI form to express the content, and the cover uses a PVC book cover with screen printing to present the feeling of a "manual". In addition, the biggest highlight in the book structure is the use of four kinds of color paper, corresponding to the classification of the content, in the last white paper called stardust white is covered with color debris, to express the importance of "noise" and "dust" in their design.

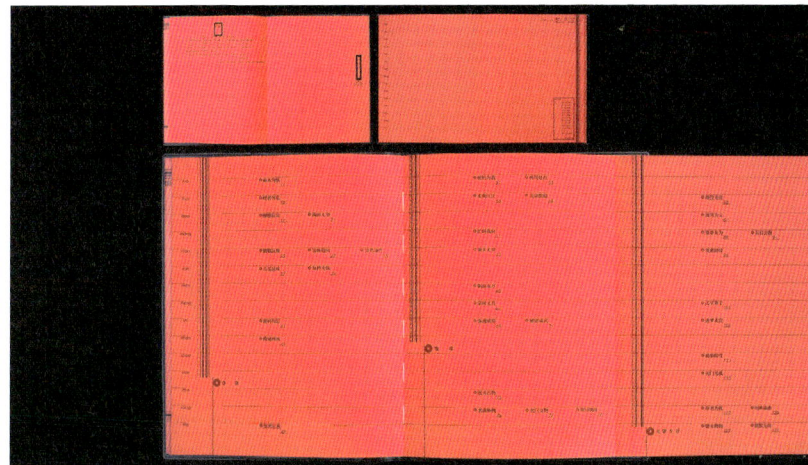

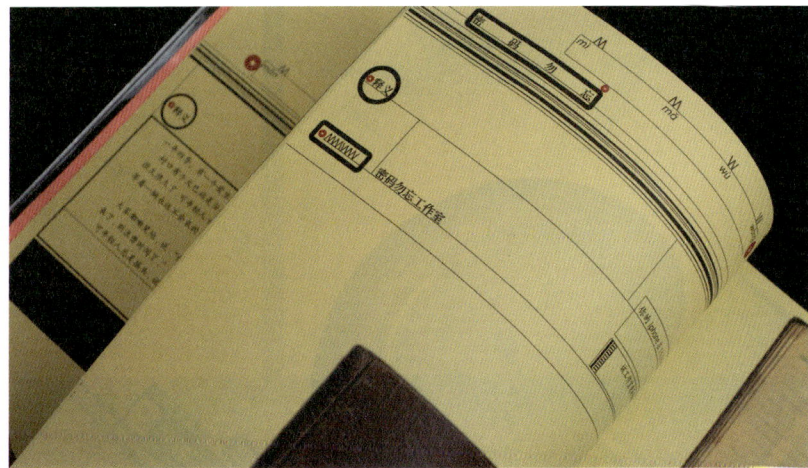

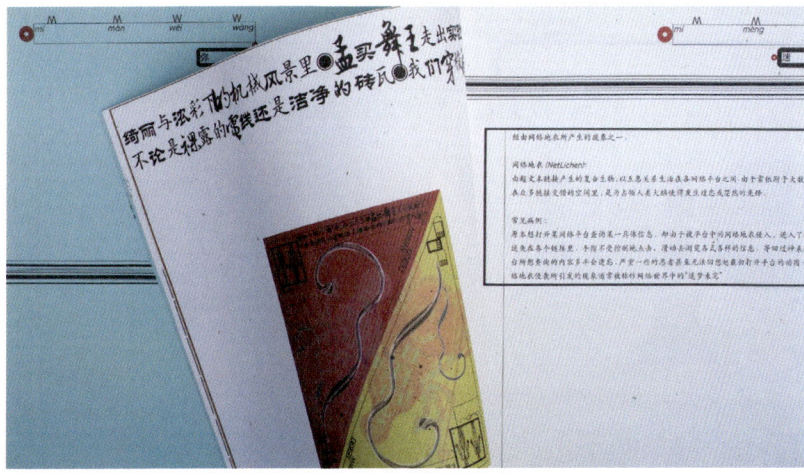

● Designer: Xing Guo   Language: English   Page: 60

Left Behind Children

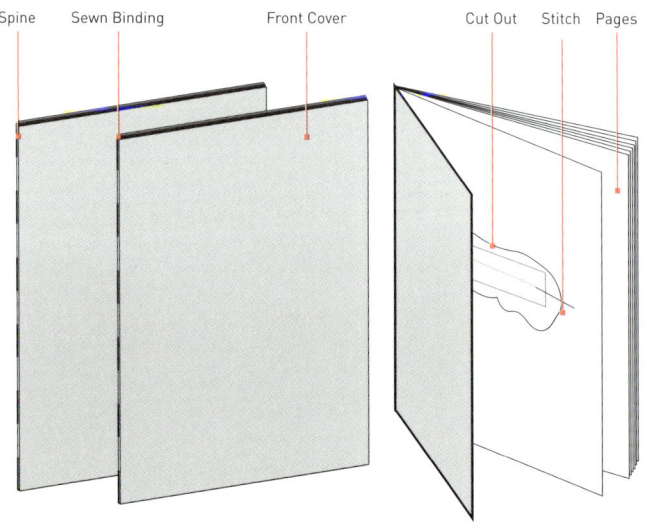

Format   210 × 297 mm
Paper   Translucent Paper
         Specialty Paper
Print   Laser Printing
Font   Avenir
Binding Handmade Sewn Binding

This work explores the phenomenon of left-behind children in book form. Recording individual children's stories as short textual fragments with the aim of engaging the reader and finding empathy within them, the designer has experimented differently with the text as a material by cutting, scanning, and sewing it into the pages during the production of the book. On the one hand, this enhances the appeal of the story, and on the other hand, it increases the reader's interest in the act of reading.

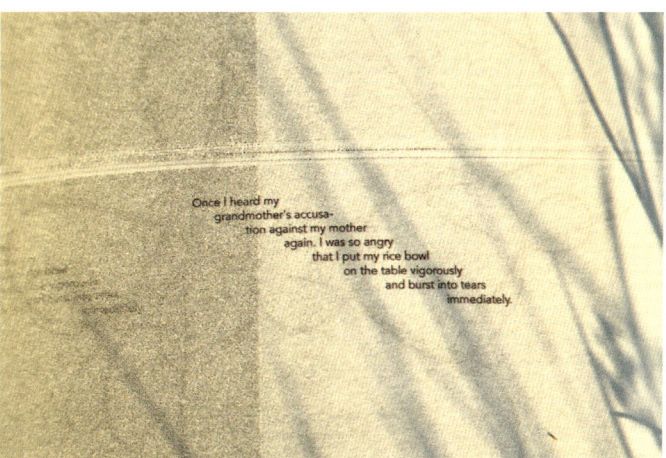

○ Through this project, the designer would like to call for more attention to the "left-behind children" and to understand their current situation. Let the parents of left-behind children realize that what their children need is their companionship, not just the satisfaction of material needs.

Designer: Gerald Wang   Language: Chinese, English   Page: 31

Dinner, Man and Woman

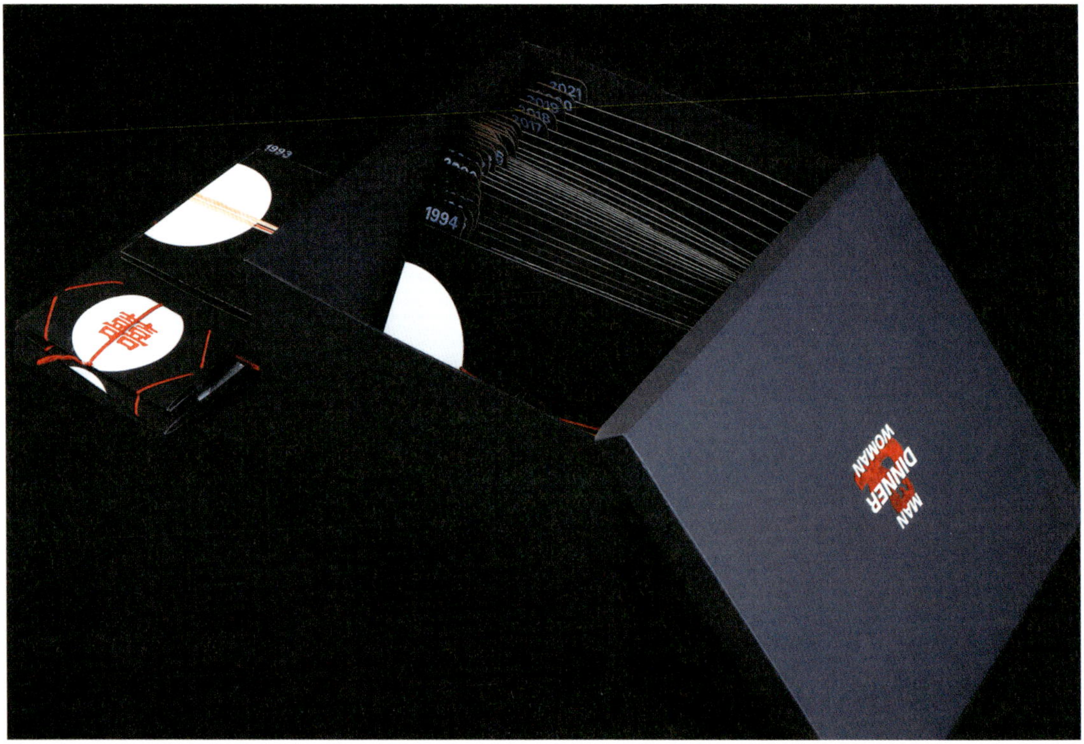

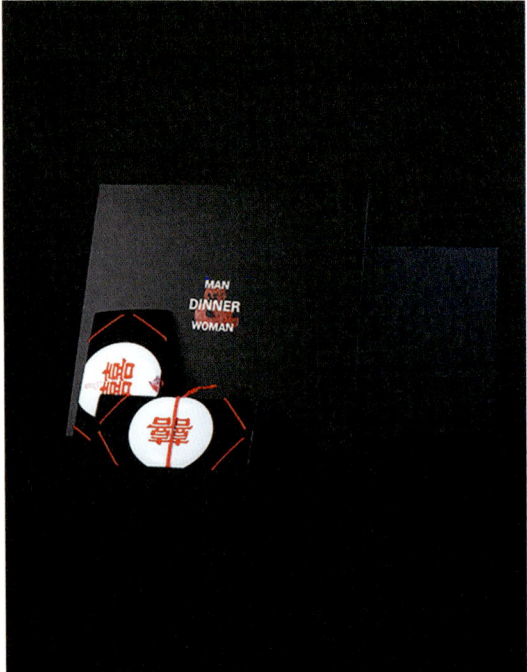

Format	Book	297 × 210 mm
	Box	240 × 310 × 340 mm
Paper	Black Cardboard
Print	Laser Cutting, Movable Type Printing, Thermal Transfer Printing, Wax Fluid, Stitching
Font	Univers Bold
Binding	One-Page Boxed

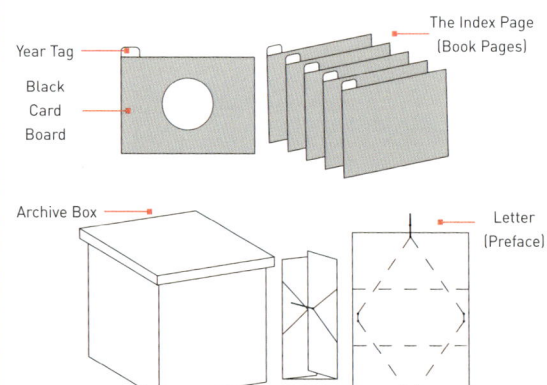

Thirty years of marriage is a long one, and each year's experience and subtle changes deserve emphasis, magnification, and attention. *Dinner, Man and Woman* gathers the symbols of traditional Chinese marriage red thread, red candle, bowl and chopsticks, and focuses the contradiction of lack of love in Chinese marriage on the scene of "dining".

○ The book consists of a "wedding invitations" as the preface and 30 black index pages in a "marriage file box". A 30-year marriage is presented in the form of a file, to show the emotions that have gradually drifted away and stagnated in the hearts of the couple. The bowls and chopsticks gradually move away from each other's, and the hollow in the center gradually expands; The red thread extends in between, increasing to thirty, symbolizing the increasing entanglement of the two. The red candle solidified between the red threads represents the emotions that no longer flow in their marriage.

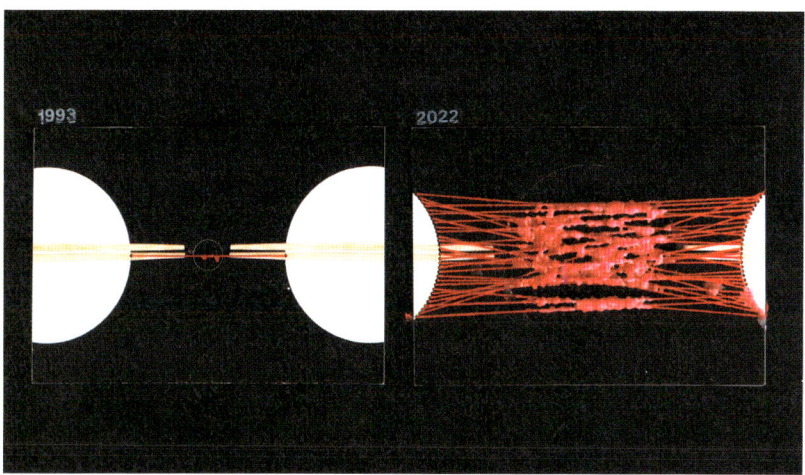

○ The complementarity of book structure and story concept is one of the core concepts of this book. The temporal and spatial attributes of the archive box bring a "sense of volume and weight" to the work. Different from the traditional form of flip-page reading, the presentation of independent pages not only takes into account the sense of volume of the medium of wax liquid, but also gives readers the right to extract, taste and scrutinze independent stories from the macroscopic "30-year marriage."

Designer: Da Cao　Language: Chinese, English, and Japanese　Page: 52

Tokyo TDC 1991-2023 Award Winning Book Design Exhibition

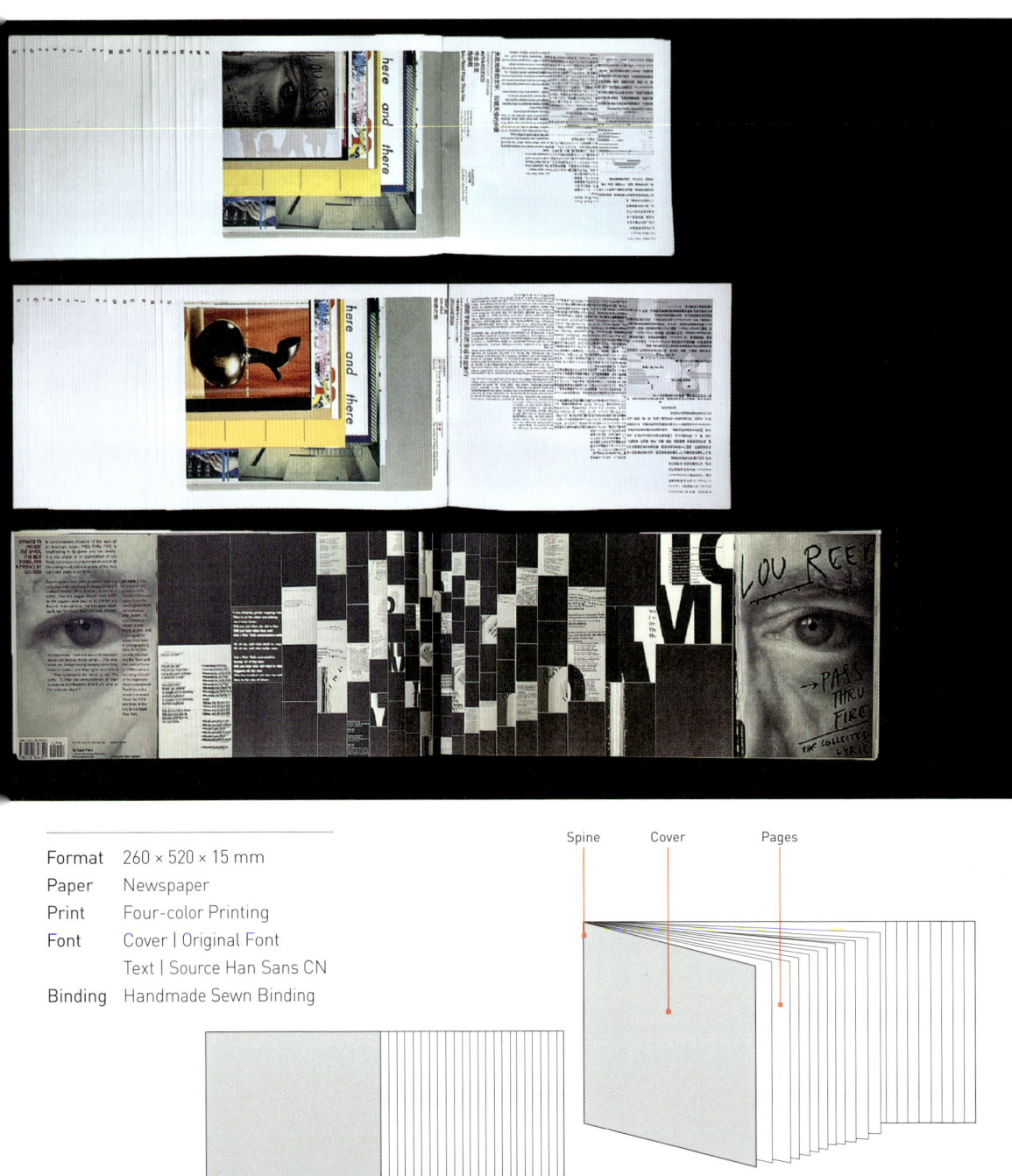

Format	260 × 520 × 15 mm
Paper	Newspaper
Print	Four-color Printing
Font	Cover | Original Font
	Text | Source Han Sans CN
Binding	Handmade Sewn Binding

Continuing Tokyo TDC's focus on typography, the design team designed 26 alphabets, produced 26 reading videos, and exhibited the book on 26 steps. The research for the Tokyo TDC award-winning books was a stepwise and sustainable process, and they integrated the concepts of laddering and recycling into the design of the exhibition and the booklet.

○ The editorial design of the booklet is divided into two units: the information unit of the award-winning books, and the cover and interior pages of the award-winning books. The text in the booklet continues the international character of Tokyo TDC and is organized in multilingual illustrations, with stepped text boxes to show the information of the winners and the winners' introduction of the works; fixed text combinations to show the information of the works and the researcher's one-sentence understanding of the award-winning books; and a corresponding book cover layout based on the habit of reading on the screen. The inner page unit fills the whole page with the proportion of the actual size of the book, and shows part of the inner pages of the book, or even a part of the book, in a sensual rhythm, so as to convey the visual language of each book to the readers in a fragmented way. Similar to the current public's habit of fragmented and fast reading, this reading habit is experimented in the book layout.

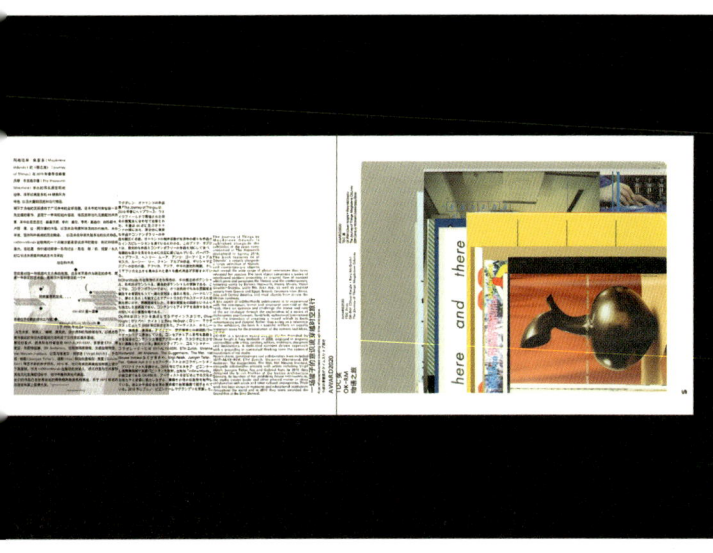

○ The structure of the book comes from the concept of the ladder in the exhibition space, where the pages are gradually lengthened by one centimeter to form the main structure of the book, and the content layout is also presented in the form of a ladder with text boxes in five languages including pictures, namely Chinese, English, Japanese, picture language, and explanatory text language. Experiments with multilingual layouts in different sizes were conducted. The second layout fills the page in proportion to the size of the book included, forming different graphic languages corresponding to the exhibits, filling the book's inner pages with wonderful moments. The use of the above two structures, the first based on the logic of proportions and dimensions is relatively rational, and the second based on the interception of moments of the book is relatively emotional, in a highly international context, breaking the language barrier, people from all countries can read the same book.

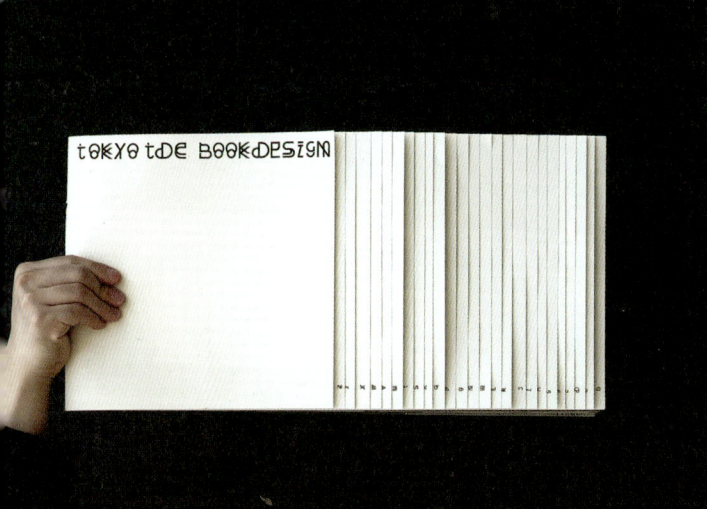

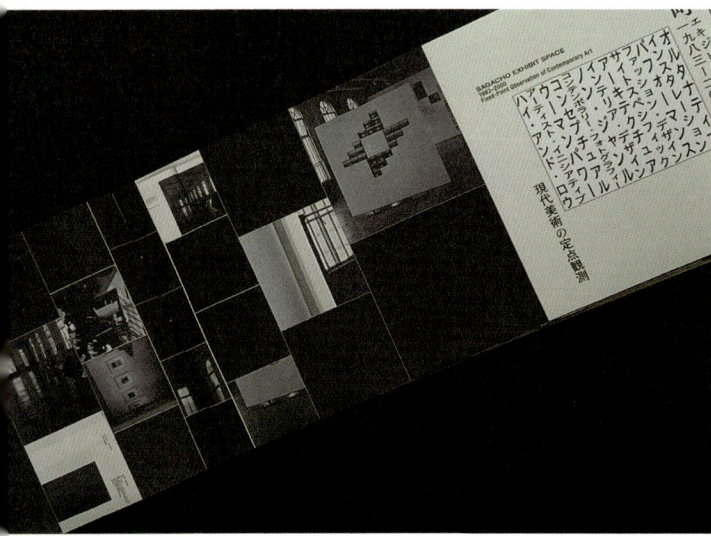

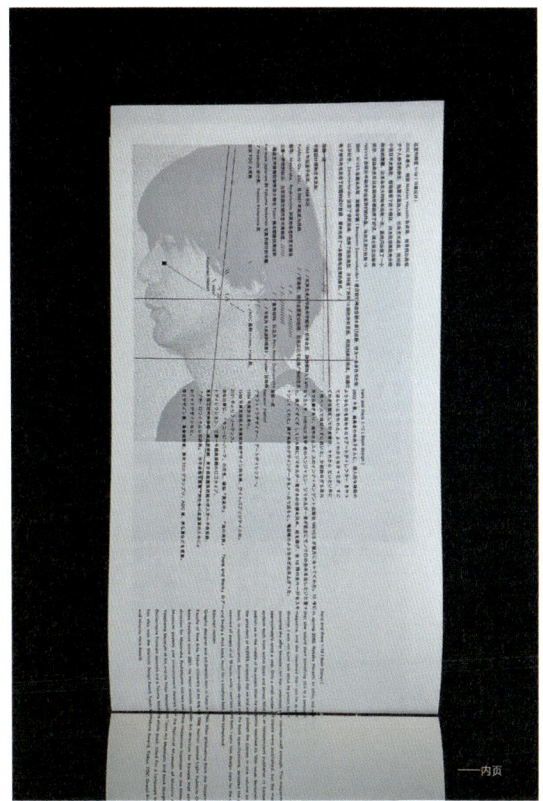
——内页

——封底

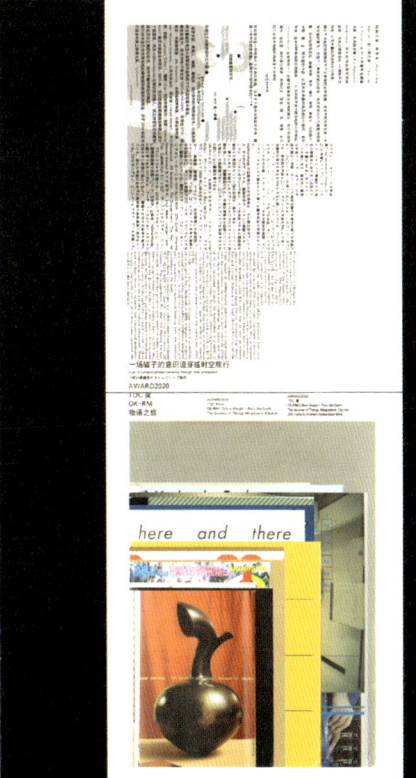
——内页

——内页

● Designer: Laura Hilbert   Page: 86,400

24 Stunden

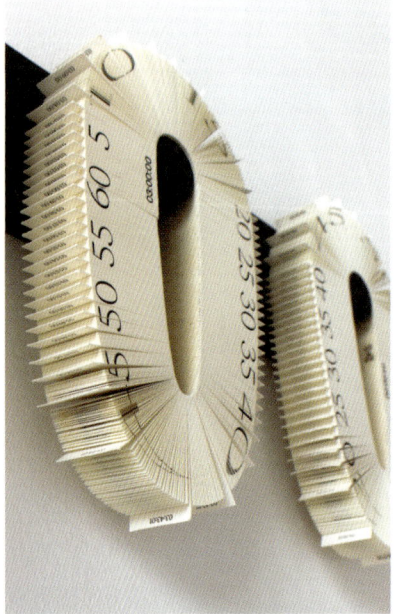

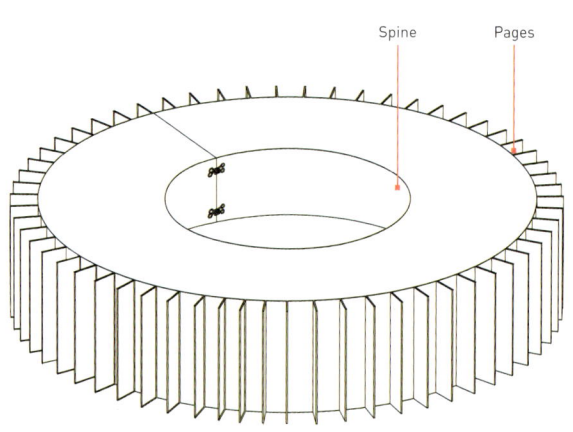

Format   37 × 52 mm
Paper   Munken Print Cream 115/300 gsm
Font   SangBleu Kingdom Light, SangBleu Sunrise
         Regular, Suiss Int'l Regular
Binding Adhesive Binding

24 Stunden is a book project that both visualizes time and allows you to physically count it. The structure of the book follows the initial idea of visualizing a clock and the ticking of the clock hands can be equated with flicking through the pages.

○ The designer's inspiration was a clock, bescause she wanted to design a book that looks and works like a clock. It includes a total of 24 books, each visualizing one hour of the day and each page representing one second of the day. At the intersection of each hour to the next, the book can be put together to form a circle, creating the image of a clock. While the books can function as a kind of calendar and offer the opportunity to record moments and experiences, tied to a very specific time, they can also be used as a stopwatch or timer. It takes about as long to turn the pages as the time indicated on the pages. The book spine with the ruler printed on it can be used as a tool for measuring objects. Additionally, the books can be used as tools to pass the time since they are very fun to play with and can be used as rearrangeable toys.

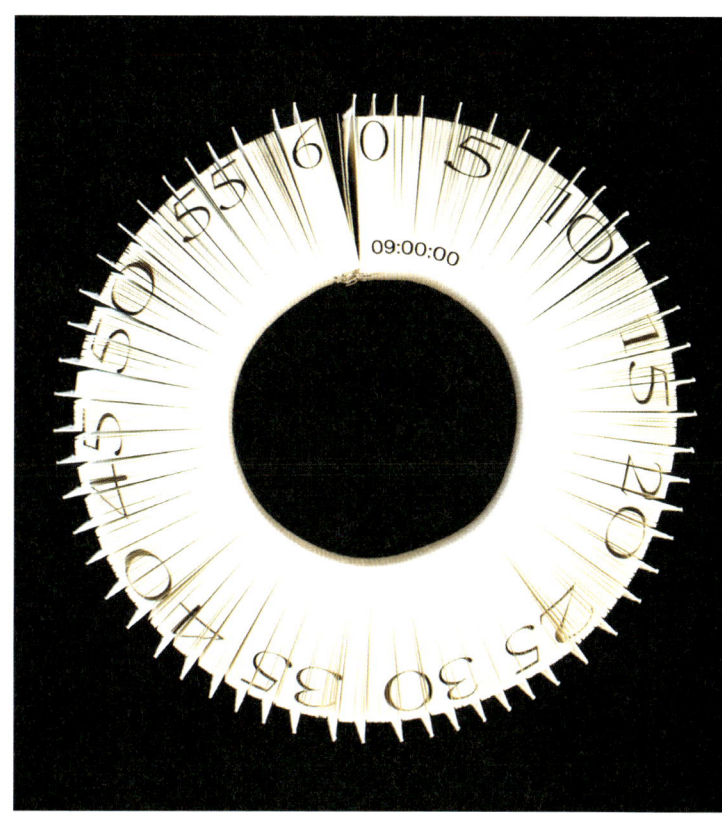

● Designer: Erin Egoh   Language: English   Page: 56

Sepasang Kaki Lima

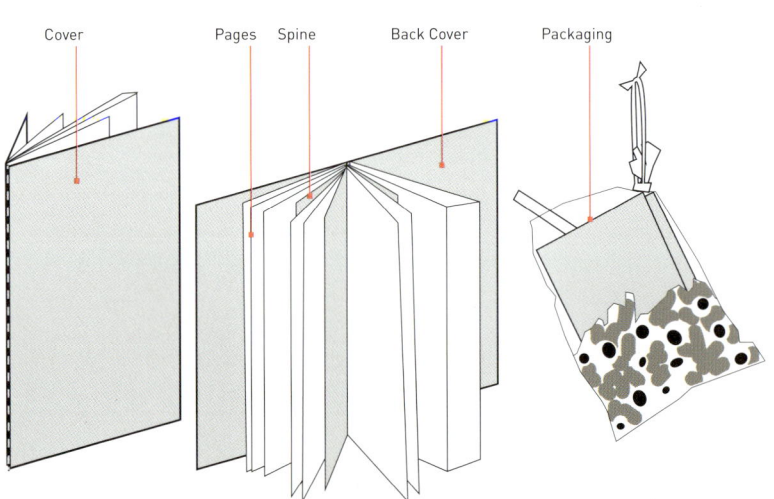

Paper	Mohwawk Superfine
Print	Laser Printing
Font	Big NoodleThing
	GTF Solina
Binding	Stitch Binding

Sepasang Kaki Lima is a zine that showcases stories and journal entries from the perspective of a stray cat who lives in the area. It is an abbreviation of "Sepasang Kaki di Kaki Lima," which translates to: "a pair of feet exploring the five-foot-way". The zine is concentrated around specific locations in Petaling Street - Air Mata Kuching, Rex KL, and Chef Ma Mee Tarik - while paying homage to Malaysian culture through its unique packaging, imitating the popular "ikat tepi" takeaway drink method. Drawing inspiration from real-life locations and events in Petaling Street, the zine immortalizes the unique experiences the street has to offer.

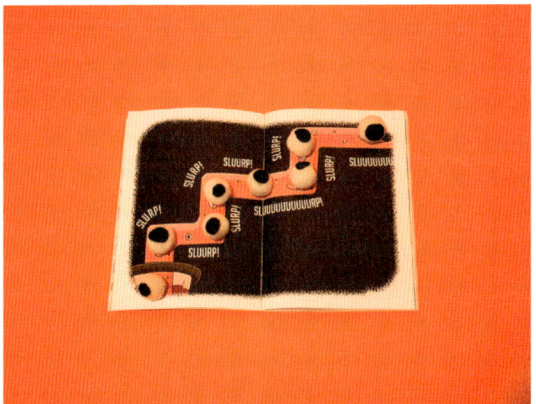

○ The zine's simple structure with Stitch Binding complements its visually impactful storytelling. Dividers between each story provide context for its visual counterpart, featuring journal entries based on real locations in Petaling Street. The zine also includes physical polaroid pictures of these locations, with color on one side and black and white on the other, representing the author's inspiration and the stray cat's perspective.

● Designer: CHAN HIU　　Language: Traditional Chinese　　Page: 196　　　　274

Made in Hong Kong vol.2 — The Knock-off Rebound

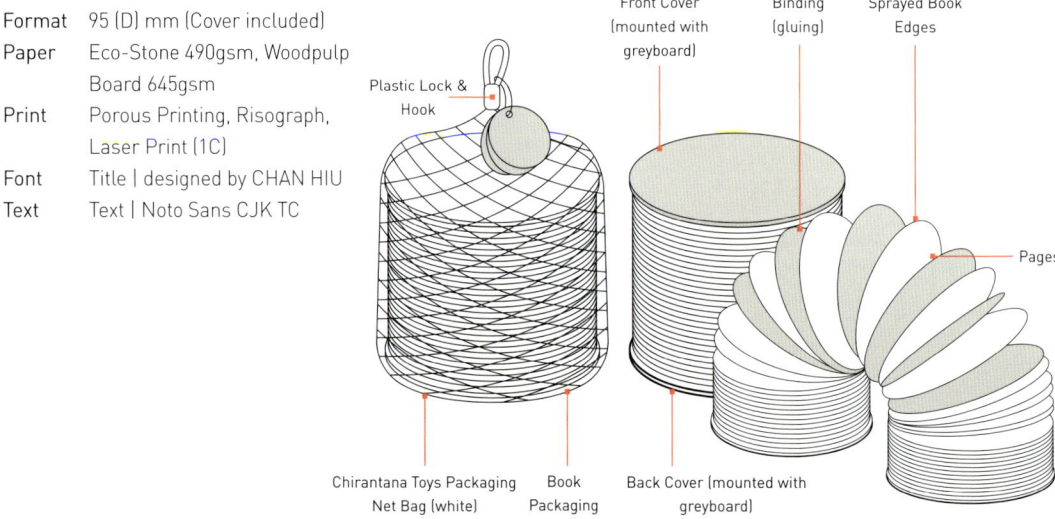

Format	95 (D) mm (Cover included)
Paper	Eco-Stone 490gsm, Woodpulp Board 645gsm
Print	Porous Printing, Risograph, Laser Print (1C)
Font	Title	designed by CHAN HIU
Text	Text	Noto Sans CJK TC

The Knock-off Rebound shows a timeline of the development of toys in Hong Kong. The book is modeled after a classic cottage toy, the slingshot. The slingshot was one of the most unique cottage toys in the 70s. It was simple in form but could be played with in a variety of ways, allowing players to choose freely. The whole series of books is structured around the idea of plastic cottage toys made in Hong Kong in the old days, which can not only arouse collective memories but also enhance the readers' interest in understanding the history of Hong Kong's cottage toys.

◯ The paper used for this series was made from gelatinized paper that is not easily torn, taking into account the wear and tear of books. *Made in Hong Kong* series is printed with perforated board, and the strong color contrast echoes the color scheme of the plastic cottage toys. It must be mentioned that people generally regard the decoloration and alignment problems of perforated printing as its bad side. However, the designer put this problem into her work. The loss of color when flipping through the book means the disappearance of the cottage toys, and the lack of accurate alignment sets off the roughness of the production of the cottage toys.

Designer: shuuhuahua   Language: English   Page: 32

WOODHOUSE SUNDAY

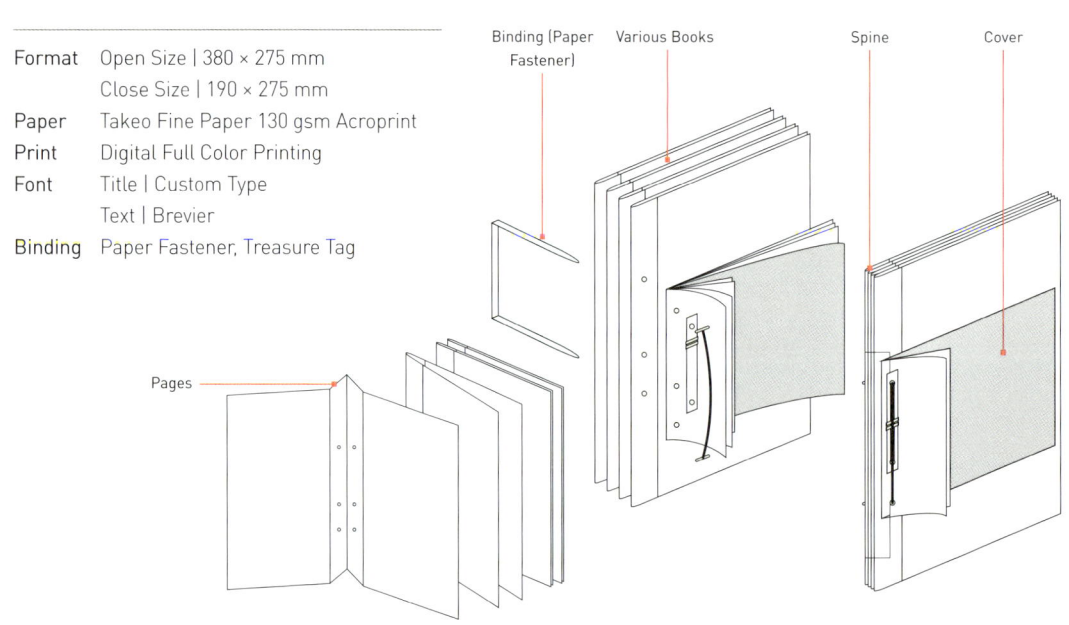

Format	Open Size	380 × 275 mm
	Close Size	190 × 275 mm
Paper	Takeo Fine Paper 130 gsm Acroprint
Print	Digital Full Color Printing
Font	Title	Custom Type
	Text	Brevier
Binding	Paper Fastener, Treasure Tag

The zine shares about families, woodworkers, and joiners, as well as the seemingly insignificant that happened in the woodhouse. The format takes its cue from old-school office documents. It is also the last item left standing after the wooden house was demolished, a never-spoken love act.

○ The structure was inspired by vintage office paperwork from a time when handwritten invoices and stamps were still often used. This gives readers a chance to experience the manual labour that was abandoned again through a unique image, similar to what a youngster might do while sketching on scrap paper or old invoices.

Designer: Thijs Verbeek, Yuri Veerman   Language: Dutch   Page: 24

Opon Up

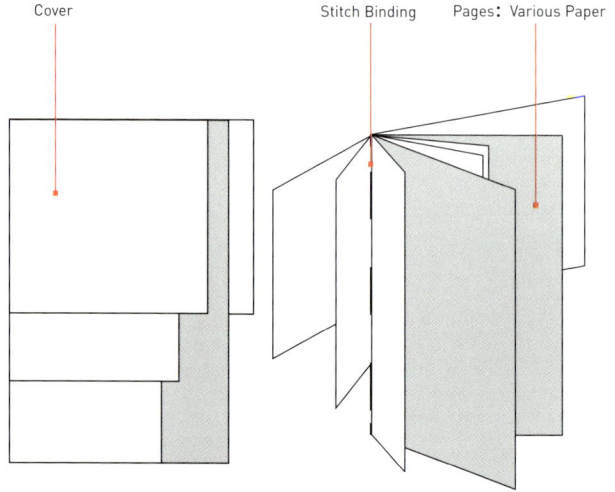

Format	160 × 215 mm (Various)
Font	Various
Binding	Stitch Binding

Mijndert Pon started his company in the late nineteenth century. What began as a small-scale and family-owned business selling soap, sewing machines, and bicycles, has grown into a global corporation. Today, almost 125 years later, PON is one of the largest companies in the Netherlands. From private and commercial vehicles to smart mobility solutions and from (electric) bicycles to heavy machinery. The brochure is intended both for former and new participants of "OPON UP" as well as a select group of employees at PON. It serves as inspiration and aims to open up further conversation about diversity within PON.

○ This brochure shows the first insights gained from a diversity project that PON initiated. They are presented in the form of short interviews with employees supplemented with illustrations. The brochure is printed in 7 pantone colors on 3 types of paper stock in 6 different sizes with 5 different fonts. The structure of the brochure is leading. Different paper formats create a colorful collection.

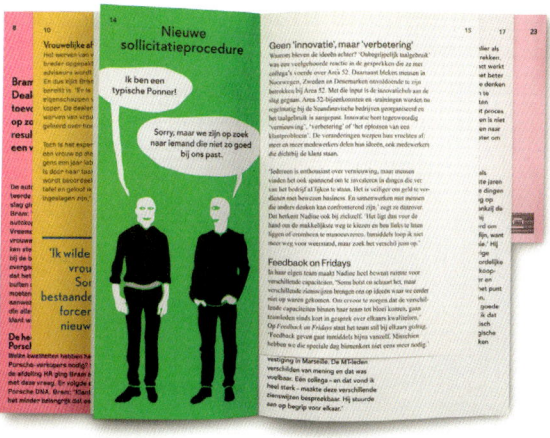

Designer: Pann Lim   Language: English   Client: Holycrap.sg   Page: 232

RUBBISH FAMZINE NO.7 Flash & Blood

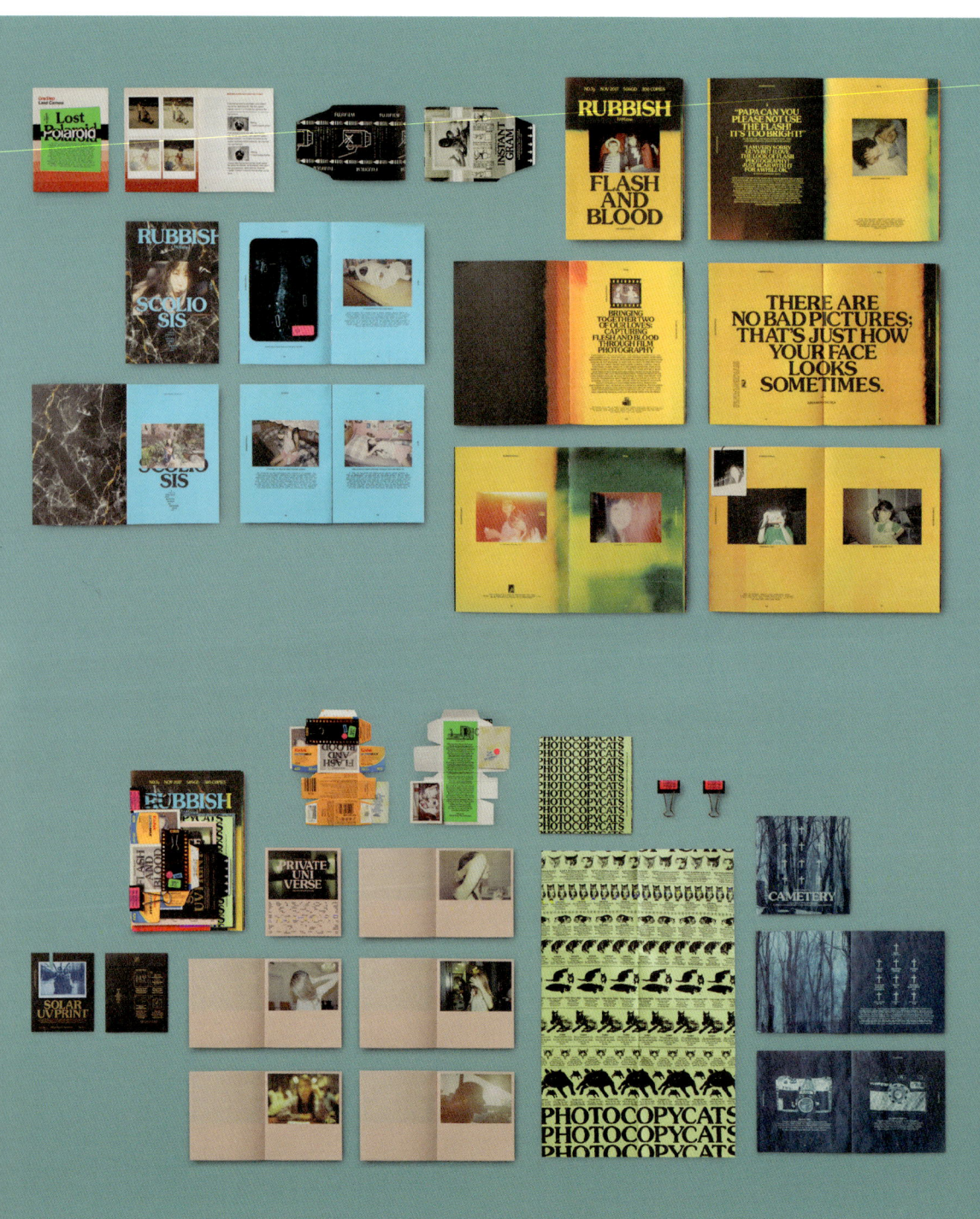

Flash and Blood is their affectionate play on the phrase "flesh and blood". It is a very personal interpretation that takes on the two things that the designers love dearly. The love for their kids, their passion and enjoyment of photography. All their zines have employed the use of the film camera to tell stories. Issue 7 simply takes it a step further. They highlighted the history of the camera and how photography came to be along side more personal anecdotes from their kids themselves through photos taken by them. Frankly, there is no better way to preserve precious memories than through photographs and printed pages.

Format   Multiple Formats
Paper   Various Paper
Font   ITC Souvenir, Courier
Binding Various Binding, Thread Sewn
         Stitch Binding

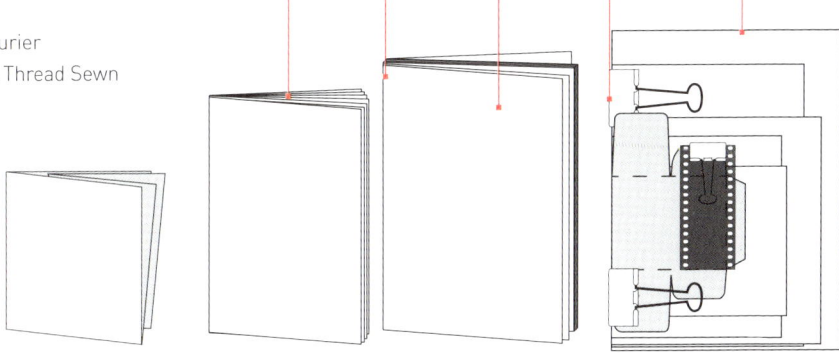

○ As this issue was focused solely on their love for photography and all things related to it, they felt that using a multi-formatted, multi-layered structure would further enhance the experience for the readers. An example of this would be having the photographs to be presented in various sizes within different booklets. There were also various textural design elements included such as the attachment of an actual Kodak Film box along with a strip of actual negative and a miniature photograph printed on archival paper.

Designer: NGvian   Language: Chinese   Page: 34

Cantonese Long Newspaper

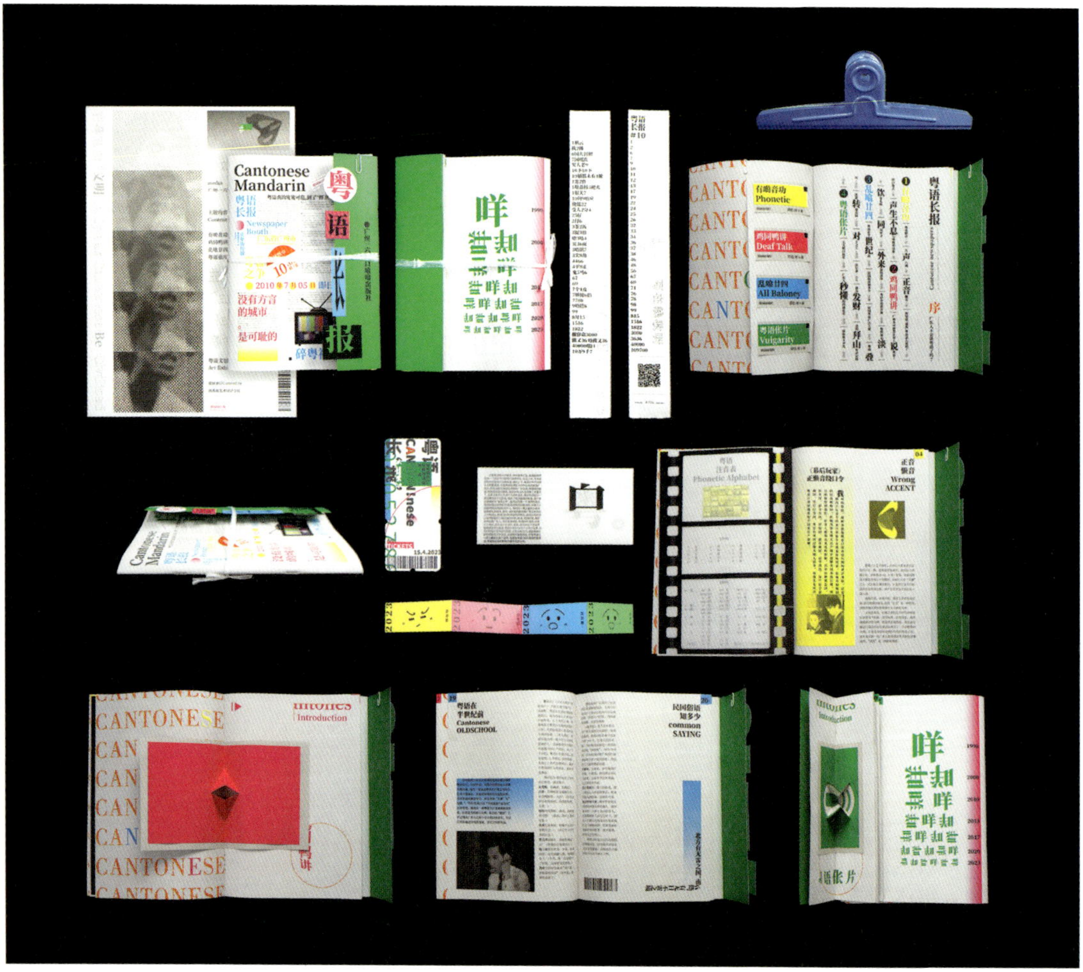

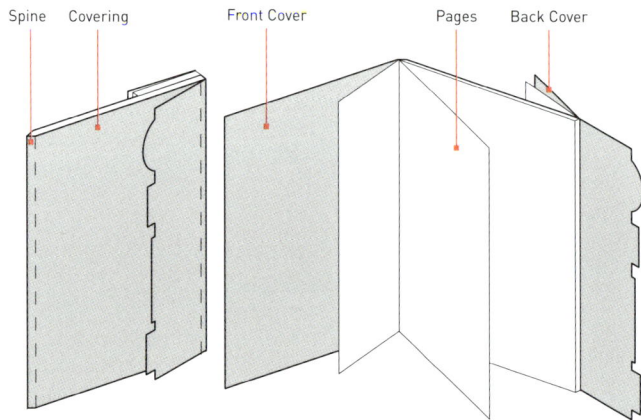

Format	225 × 297 mm
Print	Digital Printing
Paper	Kraft Paper, Gray Board, Sugar Paper, Tracing Paper, Color Paper
Font	Helvetica

Language is an important medium of communication for human beings, shaping and spreading our thoughts, as well as a projection of social culture and history. However, with the development of the times, the intermingling and fusion of various dialects and cultures with Mandarin has become an inevitable trend, and dialects, as representatives of regional cultures, have been gradually invaded and even assimilated.

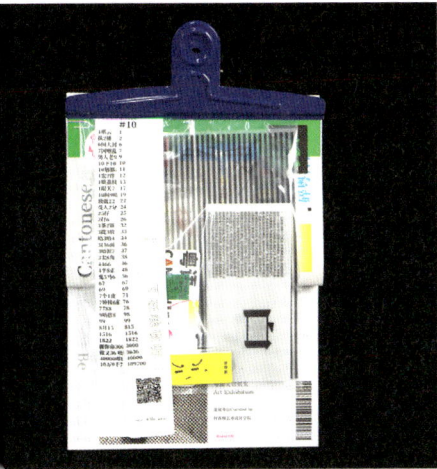

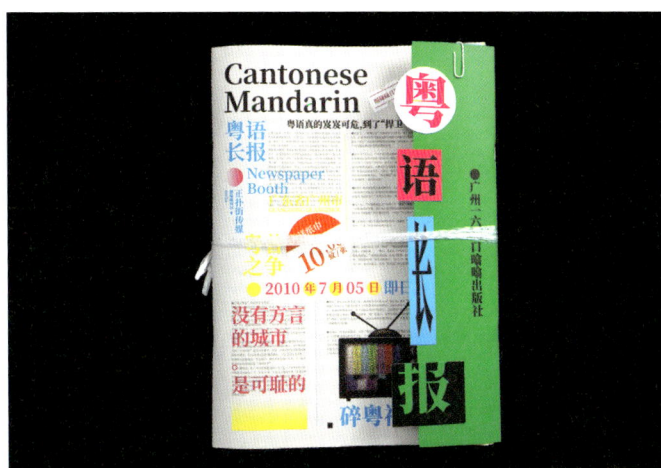

○ This book is designed for the popularization of Cantonese under the background of language assimilation. Starting from the perspective of the confusion and difference between Mandarin and Cantonese, it makes use of the stylistic elements of newspapers and street kiosks to add the concept of written expression to the traditional Cantonese culture, and through the carrier of the book design, it shows the cultural charm and historical heritage of the traditional Cantonese language, and calls for people's attention to and protection of the Cantonese dialect and culture, which is being gradually lost.

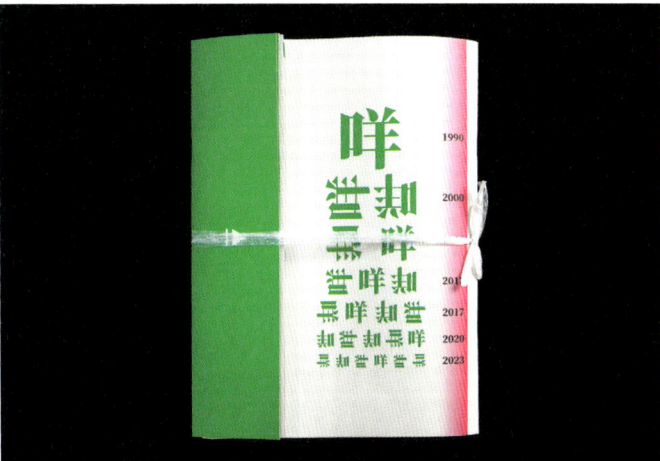

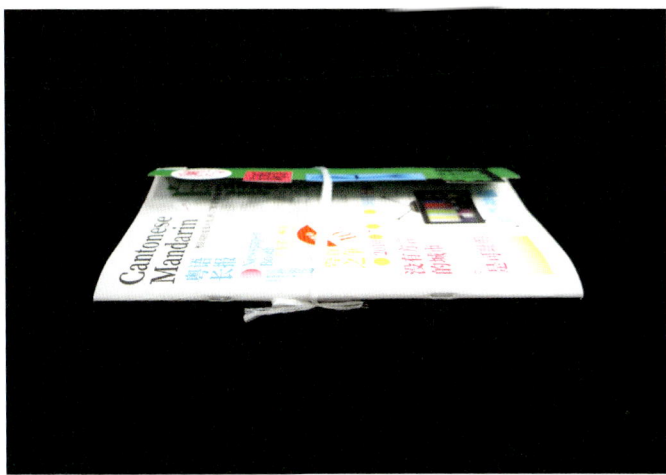

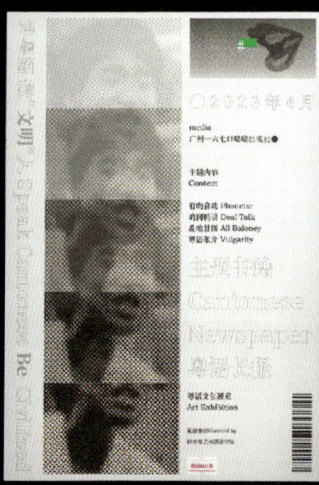
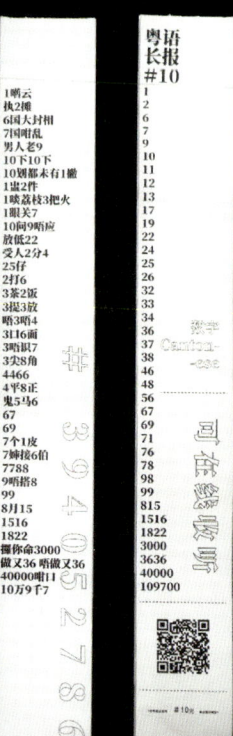

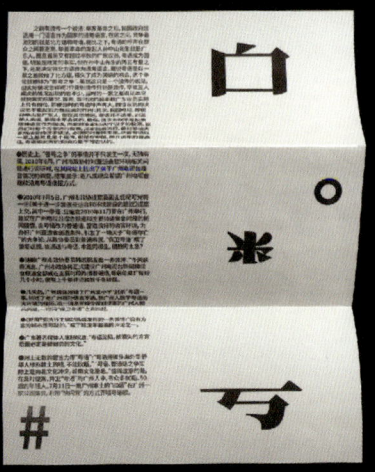

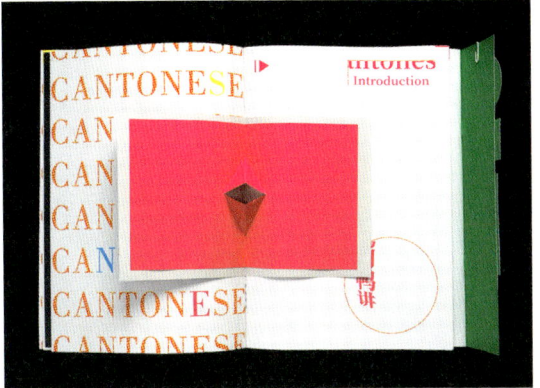
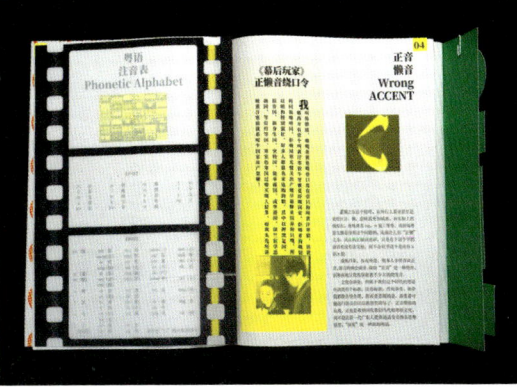
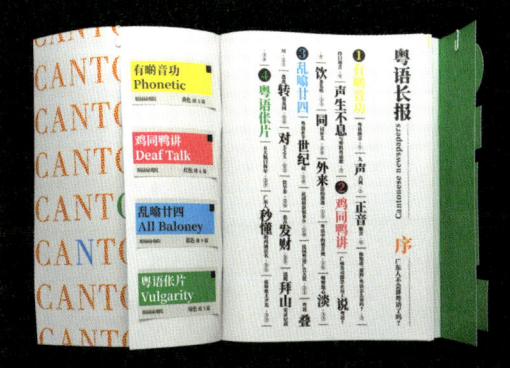

WRAP

Weave the pages from outside to inside

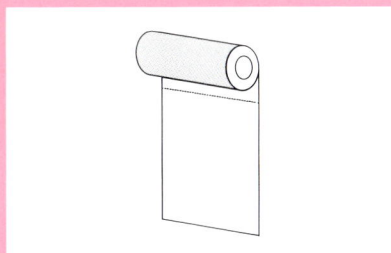

P78-79

P80-81

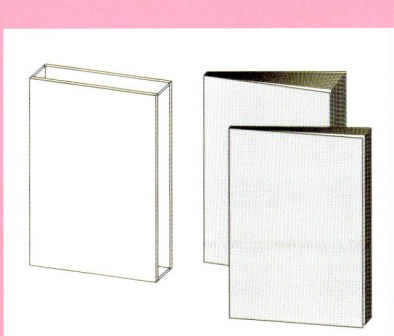

P82-83

P84-85

P86-87

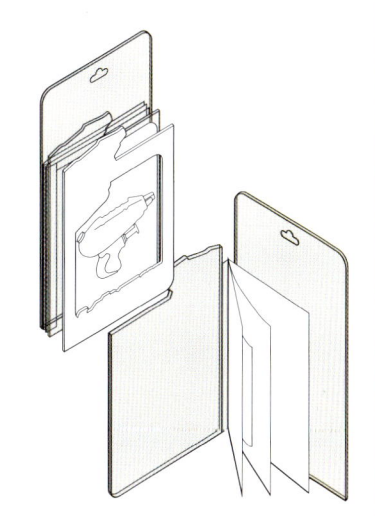

P88-89

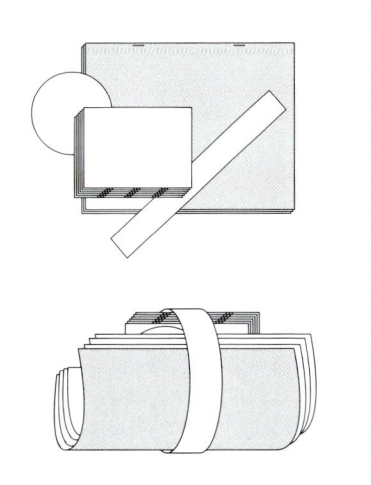

P90-93

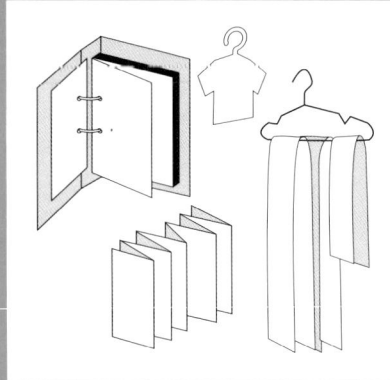
P94-97

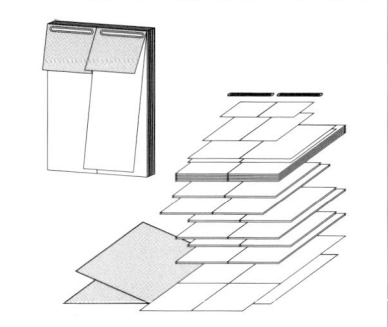
P104-105

P98-99

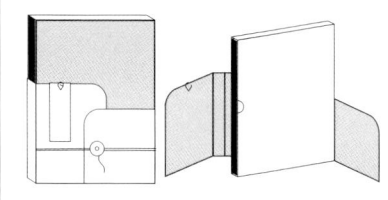
P106-107

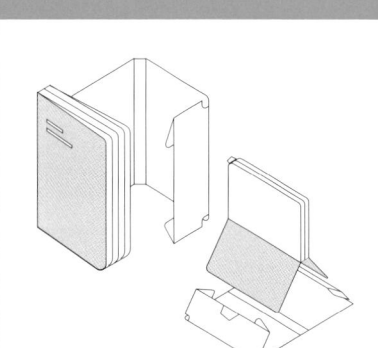
P100-101

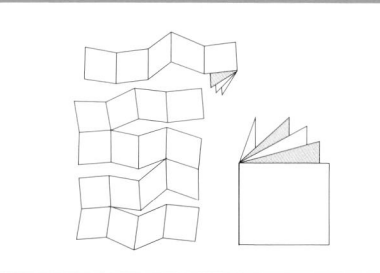
P108-109

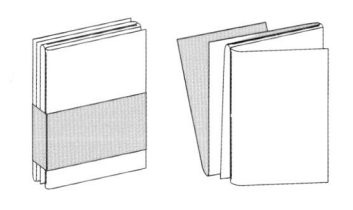
P110-111

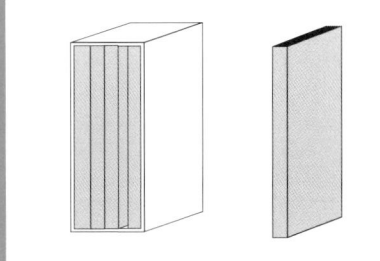
P102-103

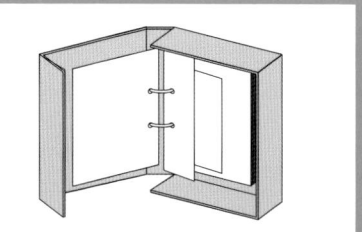
P112-113

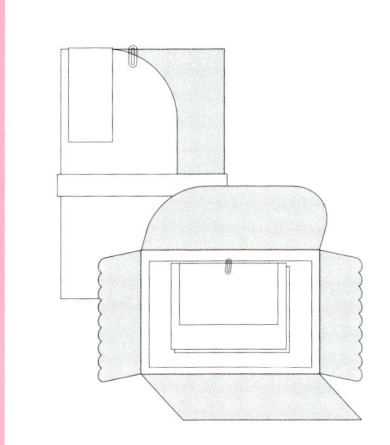

P114-117

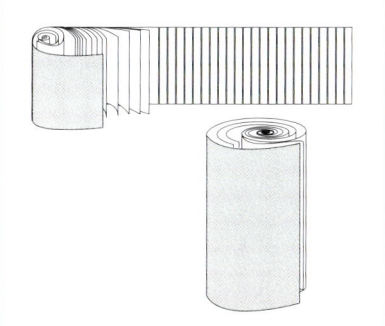

P124-127

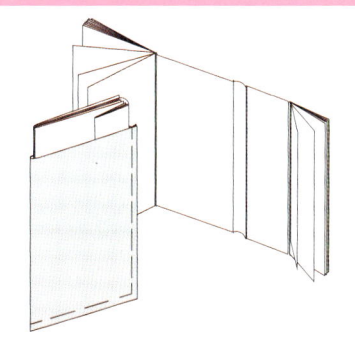

P128-131

HIDE

Find the hidden thoughts between pages

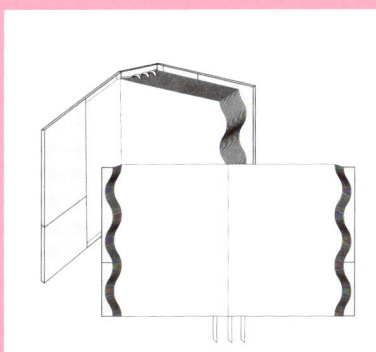

P120-121

P132-133

P122-123

P134-137

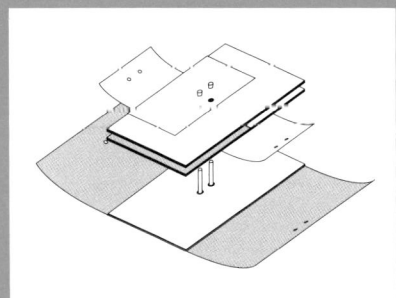
P138-139

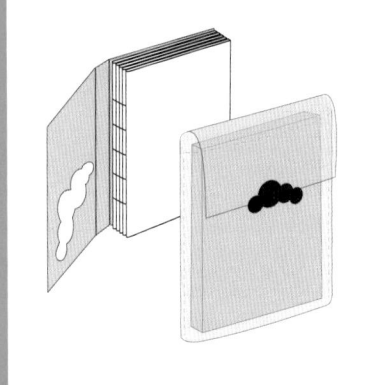
P140-141

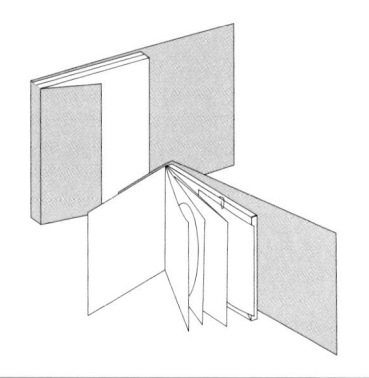
P150-151

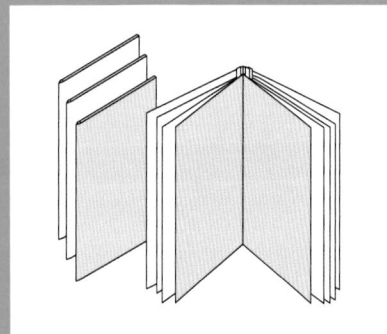
P142-145

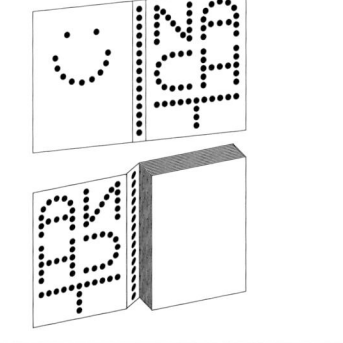
P152-153

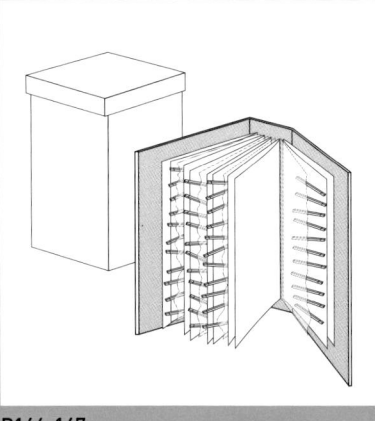
P146-147

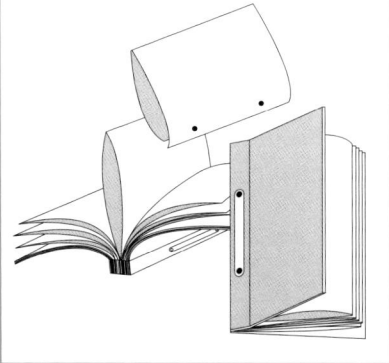
P154-155

FOLD

Present the unique folds on the paper

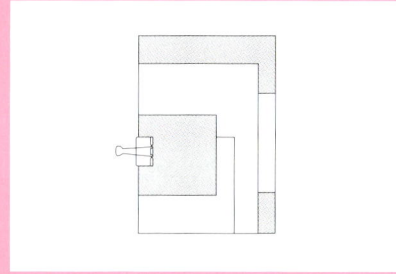

P156-157

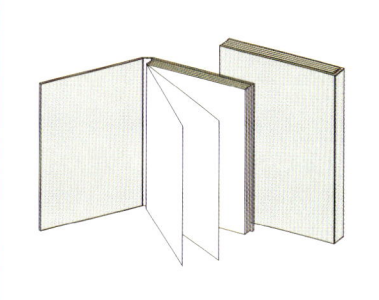

P164-165

P160-161

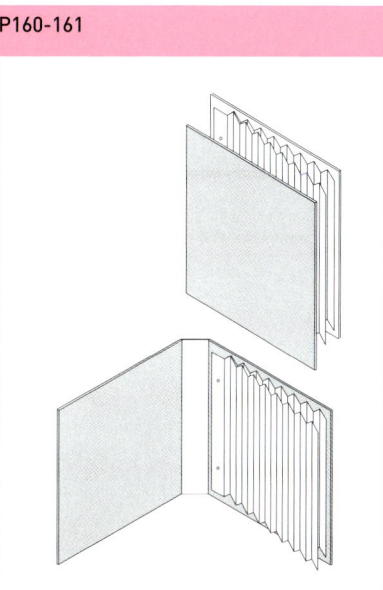

P162-163

P166-167

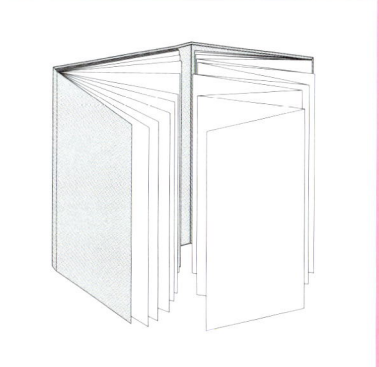

P168-171

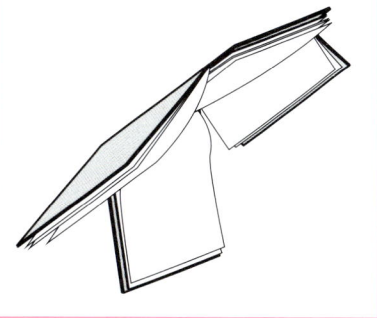

P172-173

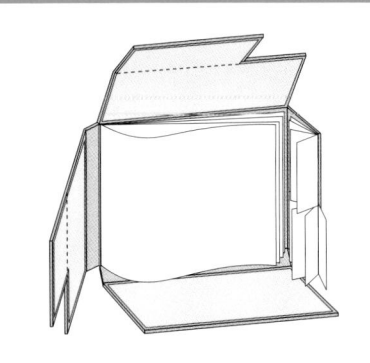
P174-175

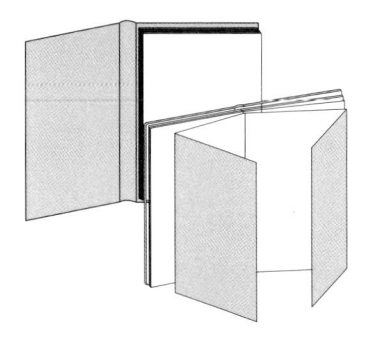
P182-183

P176-177

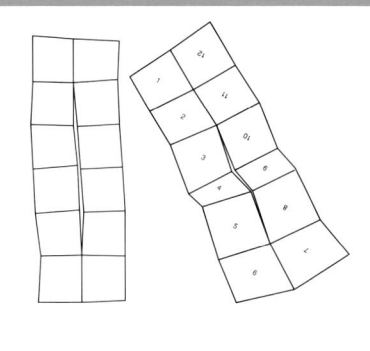
P184-185

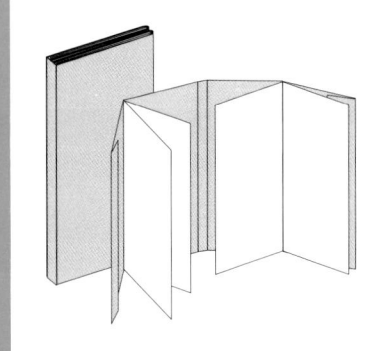
P178-179

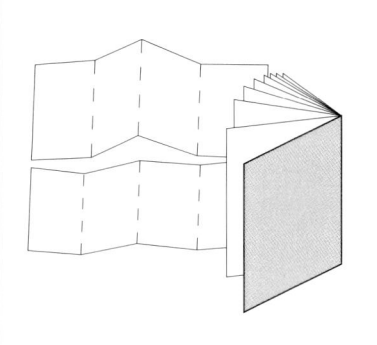
P186-187

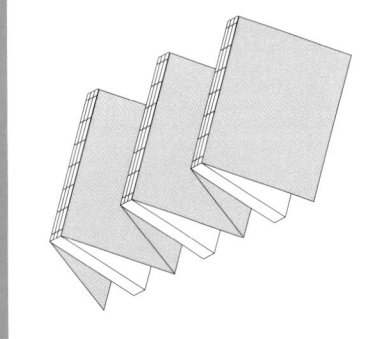
P180-181

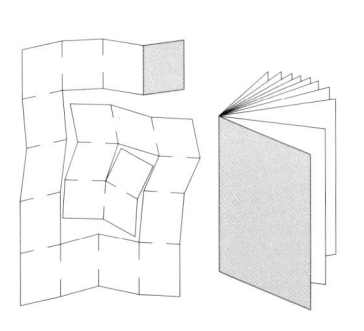
P188-189

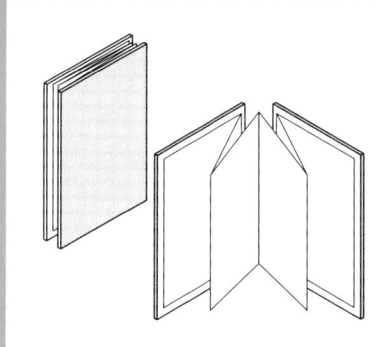
P190-191

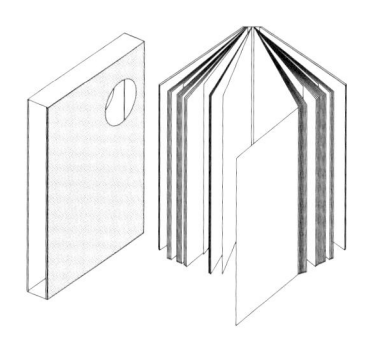
P200-201

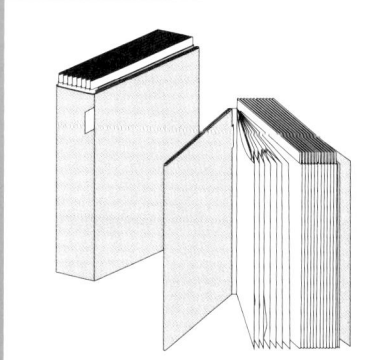
P192-193

CUT

Decode the secrets of arranging and deconstructing pages

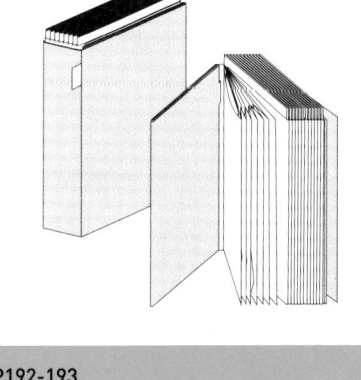
P194-195

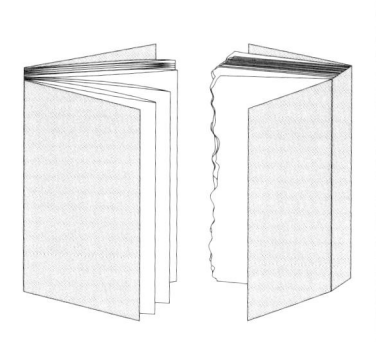
P204-205

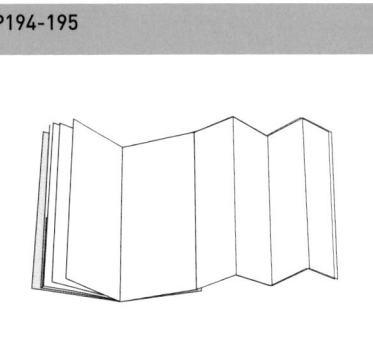
P196-199

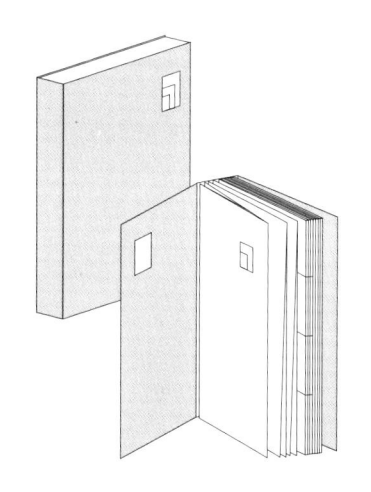
P206-207

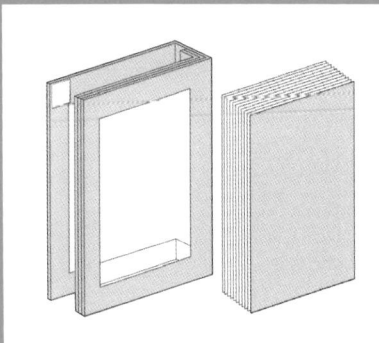
P208-211

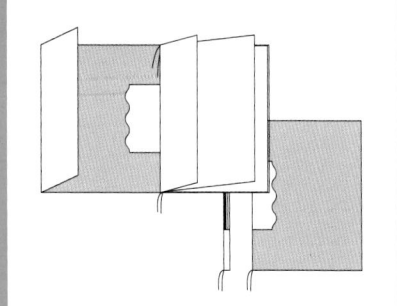
P218-221

P212-213

P222-223

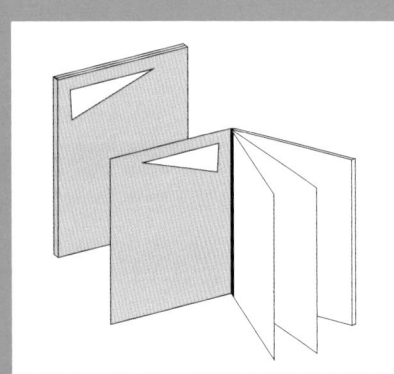
P214-215

P224-225

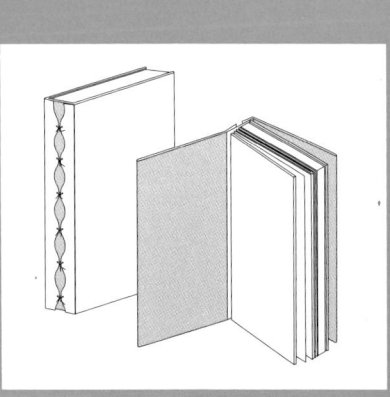
P216-217

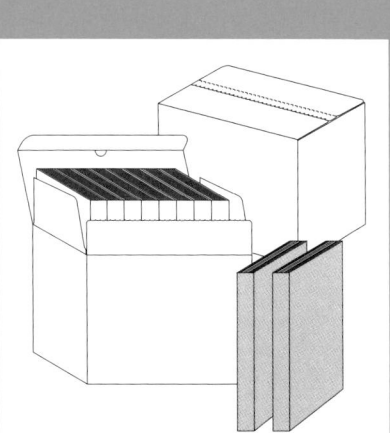
P226-227

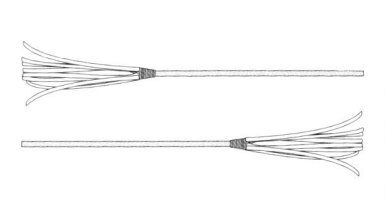

P228-229

BREAK
Think out the box and beyond imagination

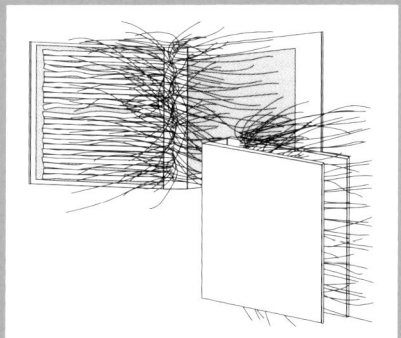

P230-231

P240-243

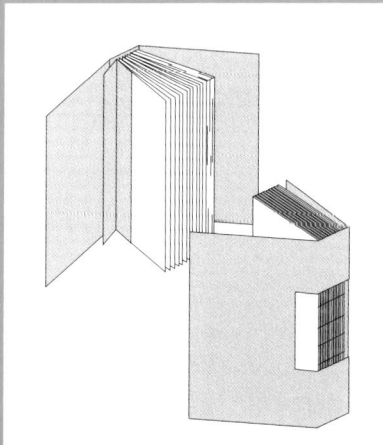

P232-235

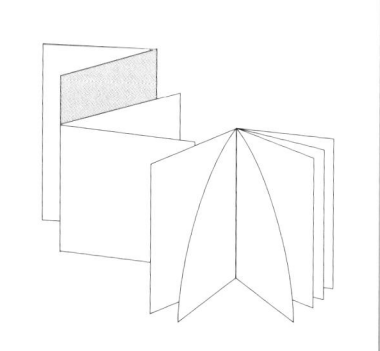

P244-245

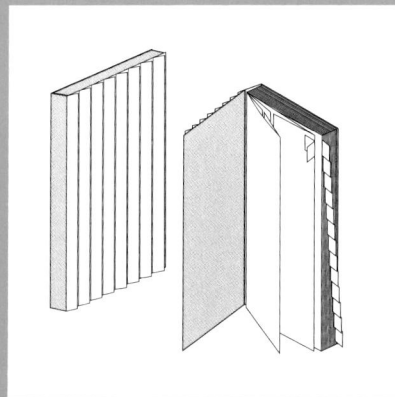

P236-237

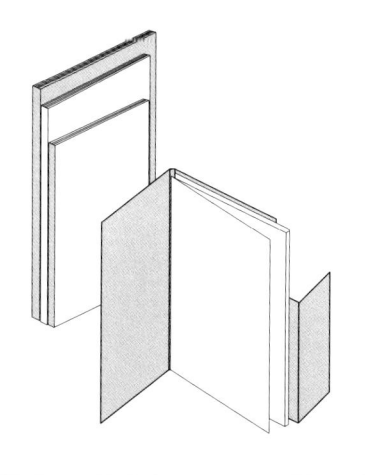

P246-247

P248-251

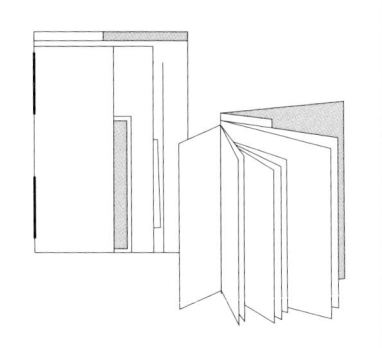

P258-259

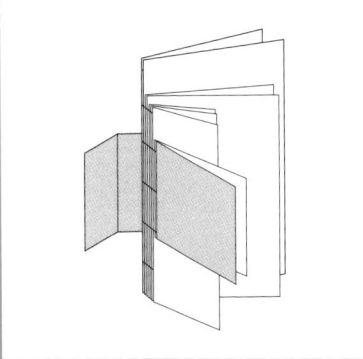

P252-253

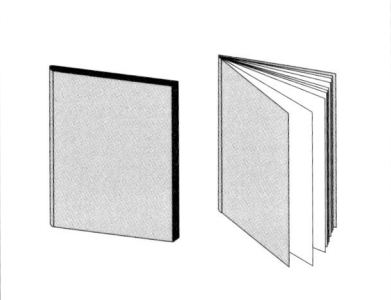

P260-261

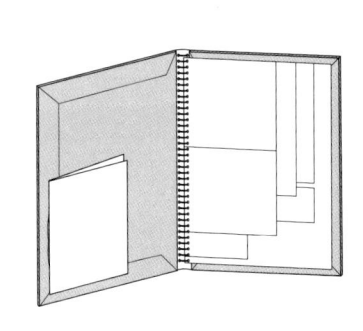

P254-255

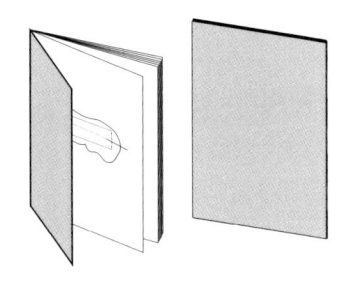

P262-263

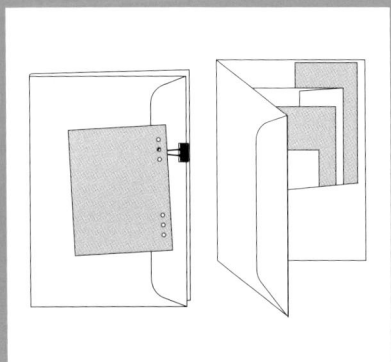

P256-257

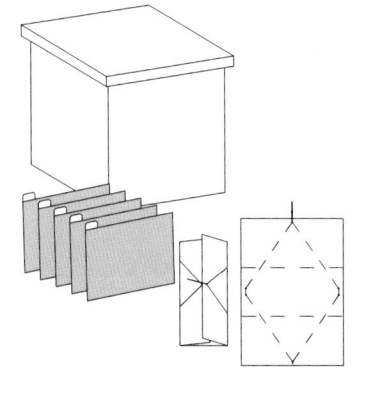

P264-265

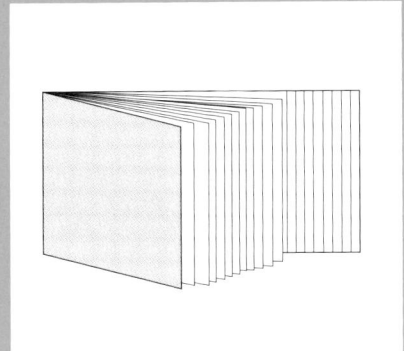

P266-269

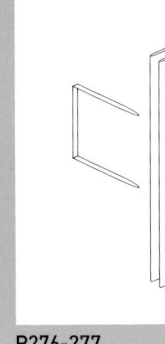

P276-277

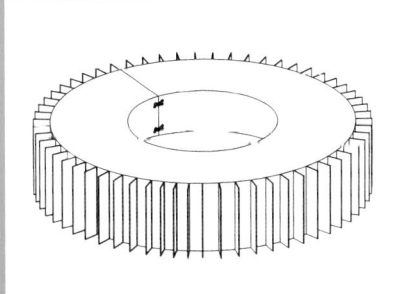

P270-271

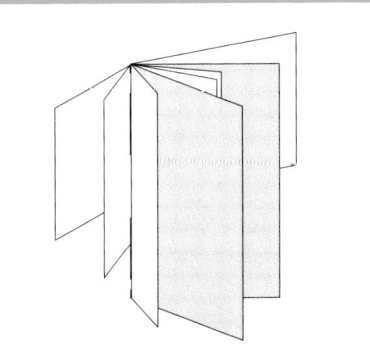

P278-279

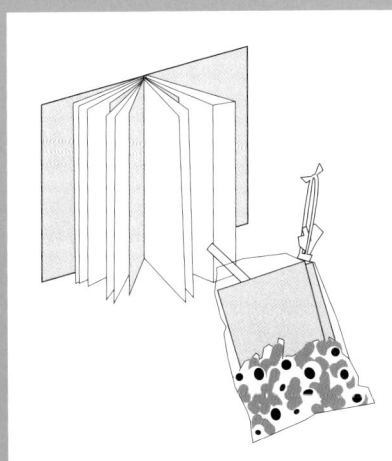

P272-273

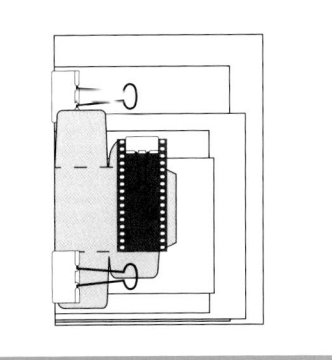

P280-281

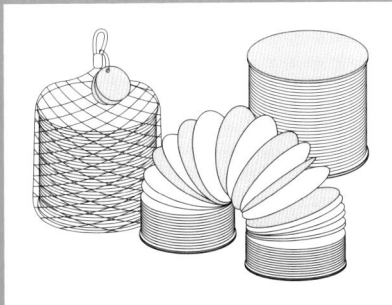

P274-275

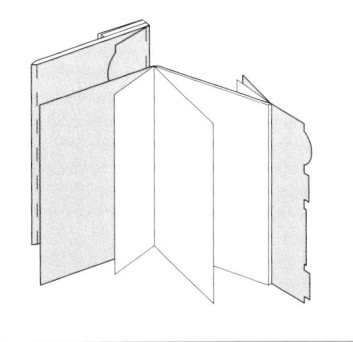

P282-285

A

Aniko Mezo
P82~P83
https://www.behance.net/anikomezo

Arithmetic Studio
P102~103
https://arithmeticcreative.com/

Atelier d'Alves
P168~171
https://atelierdalves.com/

Ana Leite, Eduarda Fernandes, Luana Barbosa, Thiago Liberdade
P180~181
https://www.behance.net/analeite_

ACRE Design
P212~213
www.acre.design

AIKA
P240~243
www.alinecreative.com

B

Belinda Ulrich, Louisa Kirchner, Alessia Oertel
P162~163
www.alessiaoertel.com

C

CHAN HIU
P88~89
P274~275
https://chanhiu.com/

Cheng Xin, Yuki
P94~97
https://chengxin-design.mysxl.cn/
https://einyvlates7.cargo.site/

Copyright Reserved Studio
P142~145
https://www.behance.net/copyrightreserved

Clip Zero
P190~191
https://zhuoyanhuportfolio.cargo.site/

Camille Palandjian
P252~253
https://camillepalandjian.com

D

Da Cao
P266~269

E

Explicit Design Studio
P100~101
https://explicitstudio.hu/

[e] De SIGN
P120~121
www.e-de-sign.com

Elizabeth Novianti Susanto
P132~133
www.matterofsomething.com

Esra Melody Butcher
P176~177
https://www.behance.net/esramelody9ef7

Emilie Terashi Boyer
P224~225
https://www.emilie.design/

Erin Egoh
P272~273
https://www.behance.net/erinegoh

F

for&st
P194~195
www.for-st.co

G

Gloria
P244~245

Gerald Wang
P264~265
www.instagram.com/24design_gerald/

H

Hannah Gebauer & Philipp Stöcklein
P86~87
https://www.hannahgebauer.com/
https://www.duckdicheinufo.com/

Happycentro
P98~99
http://www.alu.com/

Hybrid Design
P218~221
P222~223
https://hybrid-design.com/

I

Ivy Chen
P178~179
P184~185
P254~255
https://ivychendesign.uk/

Idealform Co.
P200~201
https://idf-office.com/

I Like Birds Studio
P258~259
https://ilikebirds.de/

J

Jiang Song
P122~123

Jieun Hahm
P226~227
https://jieunhahm.com/

L

Lim Zhi Yee
P150~151
https://www.behance.net/zhiyee

Linlin Yin
P192~193
P206~207
P216~217
P236~237
https://weibo.com/u/1374517232

Laura Hilbert
P270~271
http://www.laurahilbert.de/

M

Marta Guidotti
P148~149
https://be.linkedin.com/in/marta-guidotti-332649220

MMWW Design
P260~261
mm.net.ww@gmail.com

N

Ng Kai Wei
P140~141
https://www.behance.net/ngkaiwei

NGvian
P282~285

O

out.o studio
P128~131
www.outostudio.com

P

Pann Lim
P280~281
https://www.instagram.com/holycrap.sg/?g=5

R

Robbin Ami Silverberg
P146~147
P172~173
P174~175
P228~229
P230~231
https://www.robbinamisilverberg.com/

S

Sangwon Haman Jo
P138~139
https://josangwon.com/

Sandra Teschow
P152~153
https://sandrateschow.de/

shuuhuahua
P276~277
https://shuuhuahua.myportfolio.com/

T

Toby Ng Design
P110~111
P112~113
P164~165
P214~215
www.toby-ng.com/

The Third Studio
P182~183
https://thethird.com.mx/

Thijs Verbeek Graphic Design
P204~205
P278~279
www.thijsverbeek.nl

U

United Design Lab.
P80~81
P160~161
https://u-d-l.com

V

Vanissa Foo
P106~107
P114~117
https://www.instagram.com/humana_art/

W

Wuthipol Ujathammarat
P108~109
P154~155
P156~157
P186~187
P188~189
P256~257
https://www.wuthipoldesigns.com/about

Weiqun Cai
P232~235
https://www.instagram.com/group_cai/

X

Xinyi Liu, Xuemin Song
P104~105

Xing Guo
P262~263
https://www.behance.net/GUOXING

Y

Ye Pang, Ling Peng, Bingzi Xiang, Guojian Liang
P78~79

Yeh Chung-yi
P84~85
https://www.instagram.com/yehchungyi/

Yunqi Peng
P90~93
P248~251
https://pengyunqicheapball.myportfolio.com

Yujian Huang
P208~211
https://www.behance.net/Yujian97

Yiru Liao
P246~247
https://www.behance.net/q1231231346

Z

Zhipeng Xie, Jiangping Liu, Xiaoman Chen
P124~127

Zephtang Design
P134~137
P166~167
P196~199
https://zephtangstudio.com/